PREFACE

This book comes from a large research endeavour of the European Union's 6th Framework Programme, called 'Microcon', standing for the micro-foundations of violent conflict. In its entirety, Microcon consists of 28 component projects undertaken by 22 research centres across Europe, under the coordination of Sussex University. The Microcon website (www.microconflict.eu) gives a full account of participants, objectives and results. The project runs from 2007 to 2011.

The present collection of papers represents the first half of one component project, under the title 'Ethno-Religious Conflict', directed by Michael Emerson and Amel Boubekeur. Its second half will address issues of 'Changing Models of Multiculturalism', and will be initiated in 2009 with approximately the same team of researchers who contributed to the present book.

This sequence of working stages is deliberate, in that the present book analyses ethno-religious conflict in Europe as a problem, whereas the second will address the search for constructive solutions.

The book also forms part of a wider set of studies on Islam-related issues undertaken by CEPS. Most relevant to the present work was a volume published in 2007, *European Islam – The Challenge to Society and Public Policy*, edited by Samir Amghar, Amel Boubekeur and Michael Emerson, which dealt with the social, economic, cultural and political conditions affecting the new Muslim minorities within the EU. Another CEPS book published in 2007, *Political Islam and EU Foreign Policy*, edited by Michael Emerson and Richard Youngs, analysed the role and ideologies of democratic Islamist parties in the south Mediterranean states, followed by a further work, *Travels among Europe's Muslim Neighbours,* on the same theme by two Members of the European Parliament, Joost Lagendyk and Jan Wiersma.

Brussels, 16 February 2009

ETHNO-RELIGIOUS CONFLICT IN EUROPE

TYPOLOGIES OF RADICALISATION IN EUROPE'S MUSLIM COMMUNITIES

EDITED BY
MICHAEL EMERSON

AUTHORS
OLIVIER ROY
SAMIR AMGHAR
THEODOROS KOUTROUBAS, WARD VLOEBERGHS & ZEYNEP YANASMAYAN
TINKA VELDHUIS & EDWIN BAKKER
RACHEL BRIGGS & JONATHAN BIRDWELL
PATRICIA BEZUNARTEA, JOSÉ MANUEL LÓPEZ & LAURA TEDESCO
ALEKSEI MALASHENKO & AKHMET YARLYKAPOV

CENTRE FOR EUROPEAN POLICY STUDIES
BRUSSELS

The Centre for European Policy Studies (CEPS) is an independent policy research institute based in Brussels. Its mission is to produce sound analytical research leading to constructive solutions to the challenges facing Europe today. CEPS Paperbacks present analysis and views by leading experts on important questions in the arena of European public policy, written in a style geared to an informed but generalist readership.

The views expressed in this report are those of the authors writing in a personal capacity and do not necessarily reflect those of CEPS or any other institution with which they are associated. This project has been funded by the European Union's 6th Framework Programme. CEPS's broader work programme on Islam-related issues is supported by grants from the Compagnia di San Paolo and the Open Society Institute, which are gratefully acknowledged.

With grateful thanks to François Schnell for allowing us to use his photo on the cover, showing a burning car in Strasbourg torched during the 2005 riots.

ISBN 978-92-9079-822-4

© Copyright 2009, Centre for European Policy Studies.

All rights reserved. No part of this publication may be reproduced, stored in a retrieval system or transmitted in any form or by any means – electronic, mechanical, photocopying, recording or otherwise – without the prior permission of the Centre for European Policy Studies.

Centre for European Policy Studies
Place du Congrès 1, B-1000 Brussels
Tel: 32 (0) 2 229.39.11 Fax: 32 (0) 2 219.41.51
e-mail: info@ceps.eu
internet: http://www.ceps.eu

Contents

Preface i

1. Introduction and Summary
   Michael Emerson 1

2. Al-Qaeda in the West as a Youth Movement: The Power of a Narrative
   Olivier Roy 11

Case Studies

3. Ideological and Theological Foundations of Muslim Radicalism in France
   Samir Amghar 27

4. Political, Religious and Ethnic Radicalisation among Muslims in Belgium
   Theodoros Koutroubas, Ward Vloeberghs & Zeynep Yanasmayan ... 51

5. Muslims in the Netherlands: Tensions and Violent Conflict
   Tinka Veldhuis & Edwin Bakker 81

6. Radicalisation among Muslims in the UK
   Rachel Briggs & Jonathan Birdwell 109

7. Muslims in Spain and Islamic Religious Radicalism
   Patricia Bezunartea, José Manuel López & Laura Tedesco 136

8. Radicalisation of Russia's Muslim Community
   Aleksei Malashenko & Akhmet Yarlykapov 159

About the Authors 193

1. INTRODUCTION AND SUMMARY
MICHAEL EMERSON

This book addresses what is perhaps the greatest source of societal tensions and violent conflict in contemporary Europe: tensions and violence involving people from minority groups of Muslim culture. Six country studies are presented: on Belgium, France, the Netherlands, Spain, Russia and the United Kingdom. The societal tensions are flowing typically from two quite different sources: on the one hand, the broad and relatively soft issues of social and economic disadvantage and discrimination affecting Mulsim groups on an extensive scale, and, on the other hand, the narrowly concentrated but very hard issues of terrorist violence inspired by radical ideas. Both types are seen in the countries under study to some degree. The justification for addressing both together is that, while categorically different, they are nonetheless dynamically inter-connected, feeding on each other and leading, in some cases, to escalation.

The selection of case studies is not comprehensive, but it does encompass a range of essential variables, notably as regards the length of time the Muslim minorities have been established in Europe and their countries of origin. A core West European group in the sample – Belgium, France, the Netherlands and the UK – all have immigrant Muslim communities that started coming in large numbers early in the second half of the 20th century. Thus the Maghrebians in Belgium, France and the Netherlands, and the Turks in Belgium and the Netherlands, and the South Asians in the UK are often now families with second or even third generations born in their new homelands. Spain, however, has a shorter experience of immigration, which became important only towards the end of the 20th century. At the other extreme one finds Russia's Muslim minorities, who are mainly not immigrants at all, such as the Volga Tartars and the inhabitants of the Northern Caucasus, representing centuries of history from the early expansion of Islam and then of the Russia empire.

All these communities have been affected in some degree by the waves of radical Islamic influence building up in recent decades, intensified by the after-shocks of the iconic global terrorist act of September 11th, 2001, and other subsequent acts that have been at least mentally filed under the same category by much of the population, irrespective of whether or not the terrorists had al-Qaeda connections. Five of the countries studied have experienced their own iconic events, which had massive media and political impact. Three countries witnessed horrific terrorist acts: the Madrid bombings of 11 March 2004, the London bombings of 7 July 2005, and in Russia all too many events on an even bigger scale including the Beslan hostage-taking of 1 September 2004. In the Netherlands, it was the successive assassinations of Pim Fortuyn on 6 May 2002 and Theo Van Gogh on 2 November 2004 and in France the categorically different riots of the Paris suburbs and other urban centres in November-December 2005.

The incidence of terrorist violence has been highly variable from one country to another. Russia has seen the most numerous and deadly terrorist acts, but there the development of Islamic radicalisation has been grafted on top of the war of attempted secession by Chechnya in the 1990s. In Western Europe the UK has seen the most extensive series of terrorist acts; in Spain there has been just one major case; in France mostly foiled attempts; and in the Netherlands some individualised assassinations. Belgium, for reasons we shall explore later, has an immigrant community of the same order and origins as neighbouring France and the Netherlands, but it has so far escaped major violence.

Irrespective of the frequency, or absence of terrorist acts, this book is concerned with the full range of tensions and trends towards violence involving the minorities of Muslim culture or faith. While the acts of terror are highly individualised, societal tensions between the Muslim communities and the majority populations are highly diffuse. In some cases, broader societal grievances and tensions have spilled over into collective violence, the most notable examples being the race riots that afflicted some northern English cities in the 1990s and the even more destructive riots in the Parisian suburbs in 2005. Here the ethnic aspect has been conspicuous while the religious aspect was largely absent.

1. Typologies

This variety in the nature of violent conflict led the team to adopt a formal analytical matrix on the typology of violence, formulated by Samir Amghar, and presented in Table 1.

Table 1. Matrix-typology of radicalisation generating tensions through to violent conflict

	Muslims to non-Muslims	Non-Muslims to Muslims	Muslims to Muslims
Politico-religious Jihad, Islamist terrorism			
Religious, non-political Apolitical, neo-fundamentalists (Salafism, Ahbashs, Tabligh…) Customary, pseudo-religious (honour killings, female mutilation)			
Political, non-religious Banlieues riots/violence, rap, extreme left, and extreme right movements of native populations			

Three broad categories of tension and violence are distinguished. The first is what might be called politico-religious radicalisation, where the inspiration is grounded in Islamic texts or interpretations that can range from the scholarly to simplistic fantasies. This justifies the jihad, which employs terrorist violence with a view to overthrowing the secular or non-radical Islamic political regimes of Muslim states, or even in the most fantastic visions of installing Islam in non-Muslim states.

The second category concerns religious but non-political movements. These are fundamentalist in theology and doctrine, but abstain from politics or societal integration. While these groups may themselves abstain from violence, it is sometimes argued that they serve as the breeding ground and stepping stone for individuals to pass in due course into violent action of the jihadist type.

A very different sub-category are 'customary' or 'pseudo-religious' traditions that involve violence, including so-called 'honour killings' and female mutilation, and which might be called 'family terrorism'. While their incidence in Europe may be quite limited, this category is significant for its impact on the climate of relations between Muslim minorities and the majority populations, since these practises are widely mediatised, and create negative prejudices on a wider scale.

Finally, the third category concerns radicalisation of attitudes and behaviour leading to collective violence of the types seen in recent years in some northern English cities, and the French suburbs. We here observe violent conflict that is not terrorism, nor does it have religious motivation. These are largely spontaneous movements that amount to political statements of grievance by loose collections of people with some ethnic identity in common. The grievances may concern housing and employment prospects, or perceptions of discrimination.

In the other dimensions to the matrix there is place to register the violence that may be detonated or provoked not only by Muslims towards non-Muslims, but also by non-Muslims towards Muslims and between Muslims. The provocation of violence by non-Muslims towards Muslims concerns the actions of some extreme right political parties or groups. Instances of conflict between Muslims in Europe are also reported, for example between Kurds and Turks.

In the next chapter, Olivier Roy presents hypotheses of interpretation of al-Qaeda-inspired terrorism as a deterritorialised and globalised phenomenon. He presents two main theses on the roots of terrorism, the first being a top-down 'vertical' approach where al-Qaeda acts as a revolutionary organisation indoctrinating its militants with the political objective of toppling corrupted regimes in the Middle East and replacing them with a caliphate based on sharia law. The strategy also includes attacks on the West itself in order to undermine the support it gives to current Arab regimes. The second line of analysis, termed 'horizontal', focuses on the role of individuals who perpetrate terrorist acts in Europe, and who are not so interested in either the Middle East or Islam as a faith, but rather in the struggle against the US global hegemon or more broadly radical anti-imperialist struggles of the types seen already several decades ago (for example Che Guevara, the Baader Meinhof gang, etc., which had nothing to do with Islam). This leads the author to reject the idea of a general theory of terrorism, because the very terminology confuses

Muslims fighting for local political causes such as Palestine and Chechnya with those who have no concrete political agenda beyond the statement of protest and quest for heroic glory and matyrdom. The distinction is of strategic policy significance for Western Europe, whose experiences of terrorist acts at home best fit into the second category. Al-Qaeda in Western Europe is best understood as a youth movement, in which "young guys jump into violence", after a short and thin period of radicalisation. The degree of success achieved by Bin Laden has been not so much to have spread theology or ideology, but to have "invented a narrative that could allow rebels without a cause to connect with a cause".

Roy's major recommendation that follows from this logic is the need to destroy precisely this 'narrative' in the minds of the young populace, by integrating Islam as a normal religion, by de-Islamising perceptions of al-Qaeda rather than branding it as 'bad Islam', and by portraying the radicalised terrorists as unsuccessful delinquents and 'losers' rather than heroes.

The present project is about analysing the 'micro' foundations of conflict, hence its abbreviated name of 'Microcon'. The thesis that emerges is that Europe's experience with globalised terrorism turns out, perhaps paradoxically, to be indeed much more 'micro' than might have been supposed. Illustrating this 'micro' aspect of the globalised terrorism through the story of an individual, Roy cites the case of a Hindu from East Africa, who after settling in Great Britain went on to Kasmir where he married a Malay woman from Thailand, and then became involved in terrorist plots in London and New York.

2. Six case studies

The ideological and theological foundations of the major Islamic groups in France serve as the major focus of the chapter by Samir Amghar, distinguishing in particular between radicalised religious movements that have no political agenda or involvement in violence, and those that combine religious inspiration with politically motivated violence. In the first category, the 1990s saw the arrival in France of militant Salafists, fleeing from the repression of the Algerian regime, whose original purpose was the violent overthrow of that regime. After some years this group has been changing its approach, and espouses a pious non-political Salfism with withdrawal from and rejection of French society. Further movements sharing these characteristics are the Ahbash, led originally by Lebanese students in France, and the Tabligh which spread to the continent from its Indo-Pakistani base in the UK. Notwithstanding the peaceful ideology of these groups, the French authorities have viewed them as breeding grounds for individuals who may pass on to violent radicalisation. Of the jihadist groups devoted to politically motivated violence, the author traces the evolution of three tendencies. First are those aiming at the revolutionary overthrow of repressive regimes in their countries of origin, notably the Algerian *Groupes Islamiques Armées* (GIA), who turned to terrorist acts in France itself (the St Michel metro bombing in 1995) with the intention to dissuade the French government from supporting the Algerian and other Arab regimes. Its actions in France also involves small-scale criminal operations to collect funds and weapons to support operations in the home country. Second, and reflecting the failure of these first strategies, support develops for actions of al-Qaeda inspiration aimed at the US hegemon and Jewish state. The nature of their combat changes not only by its de-territorialisation, but also by its technique and ideological foundation – from guerilla warfare to suicidal martyrdom. Third, there develops a tendency for radicalized individuals to go and fight in support of fellow Muslims under attack elsewhere in the world, for example in Bosnia, Iraq, Afghanistan, etc. All these tendencies have been manifest in France, but without any major terrorist attack on French territory, attributable in part to the vigilance of the French security services. However France did have its own iconic event in 2005, with the massive riots in the suburbs of Paris and other French cities over a period of some weeks. These riots involved disillusioned youths of Muslim backgrounds, but without religious motivation, or precise political agenda; rather, they represented protest movements against social and employment conditions and perceived discrimination.

Tinka Veldhuis and Edwin Bakker review the tensions and violent conflicts involving Muslims in the Netherlands. The first signs of Islamic radicalisation in the Netherlands are traced back to the 1980s, although it was only in 1996 that its security services spoke of possible terrorist attacks. There has developed a rich collection of Islamic movements or groups, many of which are Dutch branches of Islamic multinational organisations. The Netherlands has not experienced either major terrorist acts as in the UK, or violent confrontations in urban or suburban settings as in France. On the other hand, inter-ethnic tensions have been mounting in recent years, undermining the country's image as a liberal, tolerant and pluralistic society. Two assassinations highlight this. In May 2002 came the murder of

Pim Fortuyn, head of a populist party and outspoken critic of Islam and Muslims in the Netherlands. Even though the murderer was a native Dutch left-wing activist, it provoked deepening inter-ethnic tensions, and mounting racist and anti-Islam sentiments among right-wing youth groups. In spring 2004, the security services issued warnings of growing radicalisation among certain Muslim groups alongside growing anti-Muslim sentiment in Dutch society. And then in November 2004, a young Dutch-born man of Moroccan descent, member of the Hofstadgroep, murdered the film-maker Theo van Gogh, whose works were blatantly provocative towards Muslims. This further inflamed inter-ethnic tensions, to the point that the spectre of escalating conflict was conceivable. But then a surprise occurred when Gerd Wilders, a Member of Parliament who is notorious for his anti-Muslim statements, released a film that many feared would trigger a replay of the Danish cartoon affair of 2005 and provoke violent reactions on a global scale. Contrary to expectations, this did not happen. The reactions of the Muslim community in the Netherlands were mild. In their conclusions, the authors wonder whether the tide may have turned; or more precisely whether the idea of a breakdown of traditional Dutch values has been exaggerated, and that its society has begun to rediscover its traditional values of tolerance and mutual respect.

The least violent of the six cases studied is that of Belgium, analysed by Theo Koutroubas, Ward Vloeberghs and Zeynep Yanasmayan. In Belgium there have been no terrorist acts, no major riots, no assassinations. This must make the researcher ask why, since the Muslim ethno-religious minorities in Belgium are in their scale, origins and history typical of Western Europe, and most similar to neighbouring France and the Netherlands. Belgium, however, has not been without its tensions. Its Arab-European League movement has been adamant in pushing for equal rights for Muslim people, in criticising Islamophobia in Europe, and in its support of the Palestinian cause. This has both provoked, and been provoked by, the extreme-right wing Vlaams Blok party (which after being banned in 2004 reconfigure itself as Vlaams Belang), with clashes in Antwerp verging on the violent, involving patrols of quasi-militia Arab groups. In Brussels there have been serious tensions within the Turkish community, with rowdy demonstrations seeing nationalist Turks in verbal and physical conflict with Turkish Kurds, mixed up with protests at the heavy-handiness of the Belgian police. There have been reports of one or two terrorist attacks on the EU institutions being planned in Morocco, which were foiled at the preparatory stage. But there has been no real act of terrorism. Why? The comparison with the Netherlands is particularly striking. One hypothesis is that Belgium's linguistic-cultural-political divisions become an asset in the present context. If the nation's divisions seem at times to make it ungovernable at the federal level, the corollary is that the immigrant groups face less of a monolithic 'other' in the shape of the domestic national identity, from which they may perceive exclusion. Living in a complex multi-cultural society, the Muslim immigrants may perceive discriminatory attitudes and practices less intensely than elsewhere in neighbouring countries, and this means a less fertile ground for radicalisation. This has to be a speculative interpretation, but not one to be dismissed.

By contrast the United Kingdom has seen the most terrorist acts of West European countries, and perhaps the most pervasive set of radical Islamic networks, as analysed in the chapter by Rachel Briggs and Jonathan Birdwell. The British security service, MI5, believes there are 2,000 individuals in the UK who pose a direct threat to national security, and since 2001 there have been more than 200 terrorist convictions. The London bombings of 7 July 2005, with multiple and simultaneous attacks on public transport, manifestly drew inspiration from New York's 9/11, and became similarly engraved in public awareness as London's 7/7. The authors wrestle with the question of 'causes' of these dreadful acts. They identify 'radicalising agents', and in an interesting table place numerous terrorist acts into several such categories, including 'key places', 'charismatic leaders', 'relationships', 'experiences' and 'grievances'. But it remains difficult to know which factors have been instrumental, rather than just present. The authors go on to discuss the huge number of Islamic groups or movements in the UK within the three categories set out in the matrix above – the religious and political, the religious and non-political and the non-religious but political. They confirm that these analytical categories have to be seen as a rough approximation, with many groups moving across these boundaries in practice. While the authors consider that the threat from radicalisation and violence will remain for a long time yet, they see nonetheless a positive side to the rich mosaic of political mobilisation of Muslims in the UK. This mosaic has to be better understood, for it may contain elements of solutions through offering alternative venues other than violent radicalisation for those who feel disillusioned and voiceless.

Unlike the situation in all the other countries studied, the majority of Muslims over the age of 16 in Spain are first-generation immigrants, with 57% of them coming from Morocco. Jose Manuel Lopez, Patricia

Bezunartea and Laura Tedesco in their chapter show that on the whole this immigrant population retains relatively favourable views of their new home country, compared to the conditions in their countries of origin. The authors see this as an opportunity for Spain to avoid the mistakes made by other European countries as its immigrant communities become more deeply entrenched. However any complacency over this relatively benign situation was shattered by the multiple and coordinated bombings in Madrid of 11 March 2004, in which 191 people were killed and 1,755 injured. The perpetrators of the Madrid bombings were found to be youths of Moroccan origin, some of whom were childhood friends from Tetouan. In the course of their trial it became evident that al-Qaeda certainly inspired them, but did not organise or control them. They were part of the virtual Jihad space fed by the Internet, where cells decide individually on their operations. Subsequently there have been several arrests of individuals forming part of international terrorist groups, such as the Algerian and Moroccan al-Qaeda in the Islamic Maghreb. The Madrid bombings have created a new state of public awareness and opinions, in which the community of people earlier characterised by Spanish society as just 'immigrants' are now seen as 'Muslims', and this focuses attention on the quest for adequate methods of political representation and models of societal integration.

The Muslim population of Russia is around 20 million, considerably more than in the EU as a whole, and the incidence of terrorist violence over the last decade has caused incomparably more fatalities than in the whole of Western Europe. Aleksei Malashenko and Akhmet Yarlykapov provide a detailed survey of radicalisation within the Muslim community in Russia, citing 24 terrorist acts over the last decade causing 1,566 deaths (this excludes the wars within Chechnya). While the large majority of Russian Muslims come from communities in the Northern Caucasus and the Volga basin, which were Muslim well before their incorporation into the Russian empire, there is also a sizeable new immigrant community of around 3.5 to 4 million. Radical Islam is most strongly present in the Northern Caucasus, with elements from Chechnya moving into neighbouring districts. Radical elements have been detected in the Volga area on a much thinner scale. Radical tendencies developed seriously from the 1990s, especially among youth 'jamaats' in the Northern Caucasus, with Dagestan as the main breeding ground. In the second half of the 1990s, the leadership elements gradually changed, as young imams returned from studies in the Middle East, with the profile of young intellectuals. An apparently stable set of young, radical Islamic leaders seems established, with support for them boosted in reaction to the growing Islamophobia in mainstream Russian society. In the view of the authors, violence inevitably follows from the ideology of radicalisation. The chapter records the long list of terrorist bombings in Russia in the decade from 1996 to 2006, with many minor acts in addition to major hostage-taking tragedies such as occurred at Beslan in 2004. Looking ahead, however, the authors judge it unlikely that there will be a repetition of acts on this scale, quoting one North Caucasian separatist leader as saying that the 'big terror' acts were a tactical failure achieving nothing, since the Kremlin refused to negotiate at any cost. In addition no charismatic leader is likely to emerge since the killing of Shamil Basaev. On the other hand the Russian state policy has been too crudely repressive, and the authors plead for a more flexible and selective policy, combining contacts with relatively moderate elements with the suppression of extremists. The authors see a continuing Islamisation among Russia's Muslim communities, with an increasing expansion of sharia law to be just a matter of time.

So where does this leave Europe? The decade of the 2000s was indisputedly the decade of global terrorism, starting with the attacks of 9/11 of 2001, amplified by President Bush's 'war against terror', and sustained in the rapid succession in 2004 and 2005 of the Madrid bombings, the London bombings, the Van Gogh murder and Beslan. Since those events, has the tide turned? This might be suggested by the absence of further spectacular terrorist events, and for example by the low-key response in 2008 to the Gerd Wilders film in the Netherlands. The turning–of-the-tide thesis might be based on the view that European civil society is trying to work harder at integrating its immigrant minorities, while the great majority of the Muslim communities have other preoccupations than the jihad, with the al-Qaeda 'narrative' maybe indeed on the wane. Several of the country studies cautiously hint at this. To be sure the advent of the second decade of the 21th century is now being marked by a different crisis, that of the global economy suffering a financial crash and recession on a scale not seen since the 1930s. Does this mean that this other story is taking over? There should be no betting on this. The truly remarkable failings of the Western economic model now on display may perhaps come just in time to give a renewed boost to Islamic radicalisation.

2. AL-QAEDA IN THE WEST AS A YOUTH MOVEMENT: THE POWER OF A NARRATIVE
OLIVIER ROY

Why do we bother, in Europe, about 'Islamic radicalisation'? The answer seems obvious. There are at least two good reasons: one is terrorism, with its security implications; the other is the issue of integrating second-generation migrants in Europe, apparently the most fertile ground for recruiting terrorists. For most observers, the link between terrorism and integration is a given fact. Al-Qaeda-type terrorist activities carried out either in Europe, or by European residents and citizens abroad, are seen as the extreme form, and hence as a logical consequence, of Islam-related radicalisation. There is a teleological approach consisting of looking in retrospect at every form of radicalisation and violence associated with the Muslim population in Europe as a harbinger of terrorism.

This approach is problematic, not so much because it casts a shadow of suspicion and opprobrium on Islam as a religion and on Muslims in general, but because it fails to understand the 'roots of violence' and it arbitrarily isolates 'Muslim' violence from the other levels of violence among European youth. This, in turn, has two negative consequences: it does not allow us to understand the motivations for violence among people joining al-Qaeda (who are far from being, as we shall see, devoted Muslims fighting for their Middle Eastern brothers), and it unduly concentrates on "what is the problem with Islam", precisely playing on al-Qaeda's own terms, and spawning a debate that will have little or no impact among the segments of the population who are susceptible to joining al-Qaeda. As we shall see, comparing *good Islam* to *bad Islam* does not make sense, not because Islam is all bad or all good, but because the process of violent radicalisation has little to do with religious practice, while radical theology, as salafisme, does not necessarily lead to violence.

Any counter-terrorist policy has to be based on an analysis of the roots of terrorism. If not, such a policy could not only be ineffective, but also counter-productive, by inducing some of the phenomena it claims to combat.

Roughly speaking, there are two approaches: one vertical, one horizontal. The vertical approach involves establishing a genealogy of radicalisation from the Koran and the first Islamic community to the present Islamist radicals, going through radical theology (Ibn Taymiyya), ideologisation (Hassan al Banna and the Muslim brothers) and the history of Middle Eastern conflicts, from Bonaparte's campaign in Egypt to the present conflicts in Palestine, Iraq and Afghanistan. This approach tends to lump together all kind of violence linked with Muslim populations, for example ethno-cultural tensions affecting migrants (crimes of honour), petty delinquency and terrorism. The horizontal approach, by contrast, consists of putting the 'leap into terrorism' into the context of the contemporary phenomena of violence affecting our societies in general, and specifically youth. The two approaches are not exclusive of course, but I will argue that the link between them is to be understood less in sociological and political terms than in terms of a narrative. The success of Osama Bin Laden is not to have established a modern and efficient Islamist political organisation, but to have invented a narrative that could allow rebels without a cause to connect with a cause.

We examine the two views below.

1. The debate on the roots of terrorism

1.1 The vertical approach

Al-Qaeda is a revolutionary organisation in the continuation of the Middle Eastern Islamist movements (Muslim Brothers, Said Qotb, Ayman al Zawahiri). Its strategy is defined by a precise ideology: to topple the existing regimes in the Middle East and replace them with a caliphate based on sharia law. Hence the political radicalisation is part of a process of theological radicalisation, known as salafisme. Islam is at the core of al-Qaeda legitimacy and thinking. It plays on the nostalgia of the Muslim community for a Golden Age.

Ideology is the key: people join al-Qaeda because they share its ideology and political goals. Indoctrination is the basis of recruitment: militants do read books and leaflets, even if they use the internet more than the street corner bookshop. Conflicts in the Middle East are at the core of the 'Muslim wrath'; Muslims living in Europe do identify with their oppressed brothers of the greater Middle East.

To counter al-Qaeda, one should address the political grievances of the sympathisers. Whatever different conceptions exist about a settlement of conflicts in the Middle East, there will be no de-radicalisation without improving the situation in the Middle East. A global war on terrorism makes sense because similar trends and ideas are at work among most of the Muslims involved in local as well as global conflicts.

This vertical approach is at present largely dominant among politicians, journalists and experts of the Middle East. It can lead to two different conceptions, both based on the premises of the clash of civilisations theory. The first assumes that there is a definitive gap between Islam and the West, and the only policy is 'authoritarian integration' (banning the burqas and even the veil, enforcing acculturation, limiting religious freedom). Personalities as different as Daniel Pipes, Fadela Amara, Fritz Bolkenstein and far rightists are on this line. The second approach is to promote 'good Islam', through the so-called 'dialogue of civilisation', bringing together Western thinkers and Middle East religious authorities, as well as European authorities and Muslim community leaders, and promoting some sort of multi-culturalism or 'reasonable accommodation', in order to try to establish a common ground between East and West. The 'Alliance of civilisations' project and the interfaith conferences recently promoted by the Saudi government are along these lines.

1.2 The horizontal approach

This approach is based on the analysis of the individual biographies and trajectories of people who have been actually involved in terrorist activities in the West or who left the West to perpetrate terrorist activities in the Middle East. It concludes that the vertical approach does not help to understand the process of radicalisation, and considers it more productive to establish a transversal comparison between the different forms of violence existing among the various milieus that could support terrorists. It tends to downplay the impact of Middle Eastern conflicts and Islamic religious radicalisation. The arguments run as follows:

- There is a break between al-Qaeda and the traditional Islamists movement: al-Qaeda has no real political programme of establishing a territorial Islamic state based on sharia. There is a clear gap between islamo-nationalism (Hamas, Hezbollah, Iran) and the global de-territorialised jihad of al-Qaeda. AQ's references to Islam are for the sake of creating a narrative, not of establishing a genuine political agenda. Ayman Zawahiri, Bin Laden's deputy, is an exception (the only AQ member coming from the elite of the Muslim Brothers) and is unduly seen as the ideologist of al-Qaeda.

- Instead of promoting a territorial caliphate in the Middle East, al-Qaeda is committed to a global struggle against the world power (the US) in the continuation of the radical anti-imperialist struggles of the 1960s and 1970s (Che Guevara, the Baader-Meinhof gang). It stresses political activism and addresses a wider audience than just the Muslim community (hence the converts).
- Al Qaeda does not play a vanguard or a leading role in the conflicts of the Middle East, but is trying to impose its own agenda even against the local Islamists (Hamas). There are continuous tensions between internationalist fighters and local insurgents in Iraq, Afghanistan and even Lebanon.
- The West should address the different Middle Eastern conflicts from a political perspective (a struggle for territorial control from different actors) and not by ascribing to them an ideological perspective (caliphate and sharia).
- Ideology plays little role in the radicalisation of the jihadist internationalist youth: they are attracted by a narrative not an ideology.
- The process of radicalisation is to be understood by putting it into perspective with the other forms of violence among European youth.
- Any process of de-radicalisation should address youth populations, and not an elusive Muslim community, which is more constructed (particularly by government policies and by self-appointed community leaders) than real.

This perspective is undoubtedly a minority view. But it is finding more ground among police and intelligence practitioners, who now have an important database of radicals coming from or acting in Europe, and see the discrepancy between the individual profiles of the radicals and the motivations that are attributed to them from outside.

If we adopt the first version, the Middle East is at the centre of the process of radicalisation and hence should be at the centre of the de-radicalisation policy. There is no real difference between islamo-nationalists and territorialised movements such as Hamas on the one hand and internationalist jihadists of al-Qaeda on the other. We should study radicalisation essentially from the top down: How do ideas and propaganda spread from AQ headquarters to would-be radicals? What is AQ's strategy of recruiting? In this sense the young radicals are picked and manipulated by the organisation.

If we adopt the other view, we should, as a necessary first step, delink territorialised and nationalist conflicts from supra-national jihadism, both in the Middle East (such a policy has been the basis of the *surge* strategy initiated by General Petraeus in Iraq) and in Europe (by stopping the mixing-up of radicalisation and the Middle East). We should also acknowledge that ideology has little to do with radicalisation. We should study radicalisation essentially at the individual level, addressing the reasons why young people who are not linked with a given conflict would join AQ. The main de-radicalisation objective is to destroy al-Qaeda's narrative, not to provide an ideological or theological alternative, because both dimensions (ideology and theology) are simply not relevant.

1.3   Is there a general concept of terrorism?

The general category of 'terrorists' or 'suicide bombers' is not very helpful. We should put terrorist actions into their political and strategic contexts.

If we consider terrorist activities in the Muslim world, there is clearly a difference between territorialised violence (Palestine, Chechnya) and de-territorialised violence (al-Qaeda). The first is linked with a struggle for national liberation and is part of a broader use of politically motivated violent means with a precise objective: to free a territory from what is perceived as a foreign occupation. This violence does not spill over in other countries except occasionally into the territory of the occupying country. It goes along with other forms of violence (from intifada to guerilla warfare) and is hinged on a precise political agenda; the violence thus could be suspended or triggered according to the circumstances and the expected results.

By contrast, global terrorism is defined by the following criteria:
- The terrorist action is not part of a broader spectrum of political and military actions; it is relatively isolated from the local political context.

- There is no concrete political agenda (although there might be, as we shall discuss, a strategy of confrontation with the dominant power).
- Terrorists are not rooted in a given society (even if they are integrated): they don't fight in their country of origin (with the possible exception of Saudi Arabia), and they have no or little background of militancy or participation in communal works. They are often circulating between three countries: country of origin of their family, country of residence and radicalisation and country of action, although the last two could coincide (the London bombings in 2005).

2. Al-Qaeda as a global de-territorialised movement

The first and probably more common explanation of radicalisation, as we saw, is to understand it as a consequence of the conflicts in the Middle East, and of the sense of humiliation they create among Muslims. But, if we refer to the bios of terrorists from Europe, it is clear that the motivating factor for violence is not based on personal humiliation or oppression experienced by the terrorists. There is an almost radical discrepancy between the map of the actual conflicts in the Middle East and the map of recruitment. Terrorists operating in the West are home-grown terrorists. When they have a foreign familial or personal background, it is North Africa, Pakistan, East Africa, the Caribbean islands or just … Europe. There is also a significant proportion of converts. Al-Qaeda is not only the sole 'Islamic' political organisation to have a very high level of converts (estimates range from 9 to 20%), but it is the only one to give them positions of responsibility (both Muslim Brothers and the Islamic revolution of Iran attracted some converts, but none of them was ever to be found in a position of responsibility; Hizb ut-Tahrir has many converts but, until now, none is in the leadership). Let's mention the French Christophe Caze, Jean-Marc Grandvisir, Jérôme Courtailler and the German Christian Ganczarski (Djerba attack in 2002), and more recently the Frenchman Willie Brigitte (tried in 2007 in Paris), the British Yeshi Girma (born in Ethiopia), wife of a man convicted for the 21 July 2005 failed attempt in London, the British Andrew Rowe (arrested in 2005) and Dhiren Barot, the Dutch (and former policewoman) Martine van der Oeven, member of the Hofstadt group, Abdallah Andersen sentenced in Copenhagen (2008), Fritz Gelowicz, arrested in Germany in 2007, Anthony Garcia (also known as Rahman Benouis), sentenced in 2007 in London, and Pascal Cruypeninck, sentenced in 2008 in Brussels. Many converts are of Caribbean origin (French and British): they find in the Islamist milieus a fraternity free from racism and may recast the anti-racist and anti-colonial struggle in 'Islamic' terms; within al-Qaeda they achieve positions of responsibility that they would not have access to elsewhere. We may mention Grandvisir, Brigitte, Jermaine Lindsay (London 2005) or Abu Izzadeen (born Trevor Brooks) (sentenced in April 2008 by a British court). Here traditional anti-imperialism merges with Islamism.

The Europeans in al-Qaeda tend to take one of two routes to conversion: there are those who have pursued a personal path and joined AQ after having converted in a mosque, and those who followed their Muslim 'buddies', when, often after a story of petty crimes, they decide to 'go for action', usually under the influence of a group leader, seen as a guru. The 'group effect', as Marc Sageman[1] calls it, is far more effective in terms of triggering radicalisation than reading propaganda books. Dhiren Barot, born a Hindu from parents who left East Africa to settle in Great Britain, and who went to Kashmir, married a Malay woman from Thailand and was involved in different plots both in London and New York, embodies the perfect example of the de-territorialised jihadist. A remarkable case is that of the Belgian Muriel Degauque (who carried out a suicide bombing in Iraq with her husband in 2005), for it signals a recent development: the arrival of a generation of women in al-Qaeda, which until now has tended to be misogynistic (which shows that the converts also bring another form of deculturation).

Interestingly enough, very few Western Muslims from Iraqi or Palestinian origin are involved, not only in terrorist actions perpetrated in Europe, but also in their countries of origin (the argument that it is because they are fighting in their own country does not make sense: during the 1970s, Palestinians were heavily involved in international terrorism). By the same token the jihadists who travelled inside the Middle East to fight in Iraq are presently mostly Saudis and North Africans (including Libyans), and not people who have experienced a direct Western form of aggression. Furthermore al-Qaeda has seldom attacked Israeli or Jewish targets (contrary to more 'secular' Palestinian movements like Abu Nidal), with of

---

[1] Marc Sageman, *Understanding Terror Networks*, Philadelphia, PA: Philadelphia University Press, 2004.

course some exceptions (Istanbul and Casablanca). And finally, with the exception of some Pakistanis, no second-generation radicalised Muslim has gone back to the country of origin of his or her family to fight a local jihad.

To sum up, the process of radicalisation in Europe is not a direct consequence of the conflicts in Middle East, although these conflicts are re-interpreted through the 'narrative' of al-Qaeda.

I consider that a dominant characteristic of al-Qaeda's type of violence is de-territorialisation: specific conflicts play a role only as narratives and not as geo-strategic factors; the radicals are not involved in actual conflicts, but in an imaginary perception of the conflicts. The de-territorialisation factor might also explain new forms of radicalisation among Middle Eastern Muslims. The third generation of Palestinian refugees in Lebanon for instance (insurgents of the Nahr al Barid camp in Northern Lebanon) have experienced a process of de-Palestinisation; they are no more geared towards Palestinian politics, have no hope of ever coming back, but did not receive a new identity or citizenship in exchange. They may jump from a desperate national struggle into identification with the global *ummah*. The phenomena may happen in Palestine itself because the hope to achieve a viable statehood is receding (as illustrated by the unexpected breakthrough of the Hizb ul-Tahrir party in the West Bank in 2007-08, for which the caliphate is more important than the nation-state).

Al Qaeda's senior figures, grassroots cells, transnational networks and chain of command are thus rooted in personal bonds, forged either in Afghanistan or at the local level in the West, and which are then transposed to a transnational, 'de-territorialised' dimension (trips, moving to other countries, multiple nationalities, etc.). The West is the key place of radicalisation. Interestingly enough, many of the North Africans involved in radical violence in North Africa had at a time a project of migration to Europe. An FBI team sent to Kabul in 2001 to fingerprint all arrested insurgents made a surprising discovery: hundreds of arrested people in Afghanistan who were supposed to be local fighters (1% of the total) were already in the FBI's database for arrests ... in the US. Many arrests were for drunken driving, passing bad checks and traffic violations. That means that there were probably a far higher percentage of arrested 'insurgents' who went through the US without being arrested, and that the already arrested guys had 'normal' delinquency, not related to Islam.[2]

A second factor supposed to explain international terrorism (after the reaction against the conflicts in the Middle East) is al-Qaeda's strategy and ideology, embodied in the 'far enemy/near enemy theory'. It defines al-Qaeda as the ultimate stage of an ongoing Islamist revolutionary movement that strived to create Islamic states in Muslim countries, and then to establish a caliphate based on sharia. The subsequent failure to establish an Islamic state in a given country (whatever the reason: pressure of imperialism, lack of support among the population, strength of the ruling regimes or acknowledgement that utopia does not work) is supposed to have pushed the Islamists to go 'global', leading to the prevalence of the ummah on the nation, and putting jihad against the West on the forefront, because there was no way to defeat the near enemy (the Arab regimes) as long as the distant enemy was not checked or destroyed. Jihad is defined as a personal compulsory duty.

But in fact few of the present radicals have been involved in domestic Islamic radical activities in their country of origin (with the notable exception of Ayman al Zawahiri). Bin Laden himself turned against the Saudi monarchy *after* joining the global jihad. Meanwhile the strategy of AQ is to entrap US troops in protracted local conflicts and to parasite these local conflicts, without defining a coherent political strategy to attract the local population. There is no political blueprint from al-Qaeda on what to do the day after. They just don't care. The testimonies of the volunteers who joined al-Qaeda show that they go for jihad and martyrdom, not to create an Islamic State or impose sharia.

We tend to over-ideologise al-Qaeda in order to understand its attractiveness.

Although a study of the takfiri and jihadi thought certainly has its interest, it does not explain the personal radicalisation phenomena (even if it might provide an aftermath rationalisation),

To my knowledge, none of the arrested terrorists or suspects had Zawahiri or other books in their house, while they often have handbooks

---

[2] Ellen Nakashima, "Post-9/11 Dragnet Turns Up Surprises: Biometrics Link Foreign Detainees to Arrests in U.S.", *Washington Post*, 6 July 2008.

on how to make bombs or videos about 'atrocities' perpetrated against Muslims. Contrary for instance to the Hizb ut-Tahrir members, who always formulate their positions in elaborate ideological terms, al-Qaeda's members do not articulate before or after having been caught a political or an ideological stand (most of AQ suspects keep silent or deny any involvement during their trial, a very unusual attitude for political militants, who traditionally transform their trial into a political tribune). We should certainly not discard entirely the fact that some quarters in al-Qaeda are writing or thinking in terms of ideology, but this does not seem to be the main motivation for joining al-Qaeda.

A third explanation puts alienation at the core of the radicalisation process. There is certainly some truth in that, but the problem is how to define alienation. The socio-economic definition (deprivation, poverty, racism, social exclusion) is not supported by data. We find people from all backgrounds in al-Qaeda: engineers, former drug-addicts, social workers ... The fringes from where the radicals come are not socio-economic. Another definition of alienation is based on the clash of cultures: the radicals become violent because they are torn between two cultures.

This ethno-cultural approach is reflected in the association of terrorism and crimes of honour under the label of 'Islam-related violence'. Notwithstanding the fact that 'crimes of honour' are a paradoxical proof of integration (they show that young Muslim girls no longer abide by traditional rules), there is no correlation between them and political radicalisation. Crimes of honour are always strictly connected with the ethnic (and often tribal) background: perpetrators are mainly Anatolian Turks (mostly Kurds) and rural Pakistanis, and involve very few North Africans, urban Turks, or Arabs from the Near East. Except for Pakistanis, there is no connection between the map of honour crimes and the map of political radicalisation. Moreover honour crimes are an endeavour to restore the 'integrity' of the family or of the clan; they usually involve a tight-knit family, where sons obey their parents. On the contrary, joining al-Qaeda is usually a posture of defiance towards parents and traditional family. Matrimonial patterns among al-Qaeda members are relatively modern: there is little difference in age between spouses, spouses choose each other, one often marrying a convert or the sister of comrades in arms, but never a cousin chosen by the family. In the group responsible for the Madrid attack, Serhane Fakhet married his friend Mustapha Maymouni's sister in 2002. In France, Jamel Beghal married Johan Bonte's half-sister. Malika al Aroud, widow of Abdessatar Dahmane, the murderer of commandant Masud in Afghanistan, is a good example: she previously bore a daughter out of wedlock, married a Tunisian, while she was a Moroccan-born Belgian; after the death of her husband, she married Moez Garsalloui, a man younger than her, whom she met through the internet; they live in Switzerland. While perfectly westernised (she writes and speaks in French and does not know Arabic), she behaves as a modern militant of a cause, but more as a dissident from inside the Western society than as a representative of a traditional Muslim culture.

Clearly, pro-Al Qaeda's radicalisation process is not linked with the outspoken condemnation of Western sexual liberalisation that is pervasive among conservative Muslim circles: homosexuality, co-education, sexual promiscuity (swimming pools), specific teachings (sexual education, biology) are never part of the agenda of al-Qaeda. Not to mention the fact that this rejection of loose morality is also on the agenda of many non-Muslim religious communities. AQ recruits are not specifically puritanical and often live or have lived the usual life of western teenagers.

3. Al-Qaeda as a violent youth movement

In fact it is more productive to understand al-Qaeda in Europe as a youth movement, which shares many factors with other forms of dissent, either political (the ultra-left), or behavioural: the fascination for sudden suicidal violence as illustrated by the paradigm of random shootings in schools (the 'Columbine syndrome').

The generational dimension is obvious: most of the radicals have broken with their families or become estranged. They define for themselves what should be the principles of their lives. They never refer to traditions or to traditional Islam, they don't mention fatwas from established clerics. They act on an individual basis and outside the usual community bonds (family, mosques and Islamic associations). They usually remain aloof from the communal group. The group effect concerns the 'small group': the process of radicalisation takes place in the framework of a small group of friends (they knew each other before, used to have a common place of meeting: campus, local neighbourhood, networks of petty delinquency, etc...). Many travelled together to Afghanistan. It is a movement of age peers, not based on hierarchy.

A 'transversal' approach (comparing youth violence among non-Muslims with al-Qaeda recruitment) sheds much light on the present process of radicalisation among youth, and seems more fruitful than a vertical approach in terms of Islamic intellectual legacy (from the Koran to Sayyid Qotb, through Ibn Taymiyya). Instead of looking vertically through Muslim history and theology to explain al-Qaeda's violence, one should connect it to the general phenomena of radical violence among youth.

The leap to violence is not the result of a long process of indoctrination and maturation. We have already noted the predominance of activism on ideological and intellectual formation: there is a very short time between religious re-conversion and passage to violent action. Violence is at the core of the fascination for al-Qaeda.

We underline below three aspects of this transversal fascination for violence.

i) The recasting of a traditional leftist anti-imperialism into Islamic terms

AQ is an avatar of the ultra-leftist radicalism. Its targets are the same as the traditional targets of the ultra-left: US imperialism, symbols of globalisation. When Bin Laden referred to Vietnam in his video speech of September 2007, instead of quoting the Koran, he was in fact addressing an audience more sensitive to the political dimension than to the religious one. When AQ executed western hostages in Iraq, it staged the execution by using the same *mise en scène* invented by the Red Brigades when they killed Aldo Moro.

The continuity is indicated by the map of recruitment of radicals in France. The map of radicalisation does not really fit with that of the Muslim population. As expected, there are many radicals coming from the Parisian suburbs, Lille/Roubaix/Tourcoing and Lyon, where there is a huge Muslim population. But why are there so few radicals coming from Grenoble and Marseille, where there is also a huge Muslim population? There has been a tradition of leftist radicalism in the first three places mentioned, which did not really exist in Marseille. Nevertheless Grenoble was also a centre of the ultra-left (Maoists and Action Directe). Why are there so few young Muslim radicals coming from Grenoble? In fact there is a lot of violence related to second-generation Muslims in Grenoble, but it is linked with organised crimes, not with the usual petty delinquency. The issue of the link between Islamic radicalisation and youth delinquency, although far from being systematic, should nevertheless be approached a bit more in depth.

ii) A delinquent generation?

There is a clear connection between radicalisation and petty delinquency, but not with 'high' organised crime. Many radicals have a background of drug addiction and delinquency. Jamal Ahmidan, a mastermind of the Madrid bombings, was a drug dealer (and a womaniser); many of his accomplices from Morocco were also delinquents. It is also a common pattern for many converts, who have ambivalent feelings towards conversion or a return to religious practice. On one hand, it is a way to redeem oneself, but on the other hand, ties are not severed with the less religious-minded former gang members, who are used to find money and logistical support. It is well known that in European jails, second-generation Muslims are overrepresented and may constitute the absolute majority of the inmates, which explains why jails are probably the best recruiting field, including for converts. But on the other hand, it should be kept in mind that Muslims are not responsible for the worst crimes: serial killings, mafia-related murders and armed robberies are more often perpetrated by whites than by Muslims. The generational phenomenon is obvious in these differential patterns of delinquency. But the more second-generation Muslims are aging, the more they tend to integrate 'hard' delinquency, but this time at the expense of their political engagement.

This may have unexpected consequences. Paradoxically, the formation of ethnic mafias used to be associated with integration, as illustrated in the US during the first half of the 20th century. When second-generation migrants join organised crime, they are less tempted by political radicalisation. If we go back to the example of Grenoble and Marseille, the lack of political radicalisation may be linked with the rise of an ethnic organised crime, where young (well, less and less!) North Africans are involved: they are superseding the traditional Corsican and Italian gangs. Grenoble is presently (2007-08) the scene of a high-level and bloody mafia war involving second-generation North Africans: the field of potential violence is taken by non-political forms of radicalisation. By contrast, elsewhere in France, second-generation Muslims are more involved in petty delinquency and thus remain in the floating margins of society. But we should add a caveat: in all these sorts of deviant violence (organised crimes, petty delinquency, terrorism), the involved groups are never entirely 'ethnic': mixed ethnicity is a general pattern, although there is usually a dominant ethnic pattern.

iii) Individual suicidal violence

A third category of transversal violence is the sudden leap into suicidal violence, as illustrated by the Columbine syndrome, i.e. the random killing by a student of schoolmates and teachers in his school, before shooting himself or being shot. There are many patterns in common with radical terrorists: a possible history of drug addiction, a lack of social life, the fabrication of a narrative through the internet, the recording of a video before taking action, search for fame, use of the internet, the attribution of a collective responsibility to the targeted random victims. In fact, the stress put on al-Qaeda by politicians, media and public opinion is probably concealing the increase of a more diluted phenomenon of youth terrorism (as illustrated by radical animal defence groups). The figure of the lone terrorist is more and more pervasive (as illustrated by the Frenchman who almost killed himself while making bombs to blow up road radars in June 2008).

4. Al-Qaeda and recruitment: The power of a narrative

But there remains a question: if there are common roots and patterns to explain a phenomenon of generational violence that is pervasive in the West, why do many youngsters choose jihad and not the other forms? More precisely, why do some who choose political violence, instead of re-creating ultra-leftist movements, join precisely al-Qaeda? It is because AQ provides a powerful narrative.

Al Qaeda provides not so much an ideology as a narrative. The first part of the narrative is the suffering of the "ummah". But this ummah is a virtual one: all crimes (depicted through gruesome videos) committed against Muslims anywhere in the world are put on the same level. These stories are not contextualised: the picture of a tortured man could come from Bosnia, Chechnya or Kashmir. The ummah is presented as an undifferentiated whole.

The second part of the narrative is centred on the individual who is suddenly put in the situation of becoming a hero who would avenge the sufferings of the community. It addresses an individual by combining different elements:

- Self-image: all personal humiliations or shortcomings are redeemed by the act of terrorism. The death is staged as is the self itself (hence the video, declaration, will, etc.).

- Salvation and death: there could be only one definite action that will turn the suicide bombers into a permanent icon; death is the definite seal on the story, it is part of the story.

The third part of the narrative is the religious 'qotbist' dimension, which also plays its role here: jihad is a personal compulsory duty, the vanguard of the ummah is made of a few outstanding and devoted heroes; salvation is through sacrifice and death. Sources and authors who were seen by the 'vertical view' as of utmost importance make a comeback here: occasional references to Ibn Taymiyya, Said Qotb or Palestine may be called to illustrate the narrative. The narrative allows the would-be terrorist to connect with history and religious genealogy.

But a fourth part of the narrative is less religious: it is the enactment of the fight against the global order. To people not specifically motivated by religion, al-Qaeda is the only organisation present on the market that seems to be effective in confronting the 'evil' that is the West. The fact that AQ is constantly presented by Western leaders as the biggest threat gives more value to the decision to join it. The narrative is substantiated by the Western reaction to it.

Al Qaeda gives a meaning to the flow of information that comes from the media, describing a world of violence, explosions, blood and wars. Al-Qaeda presents its action as some sort of a video game, where youngsters can easily identify themselves as actors. al-Qaeda also makes use of the dominant discourse on the clash of civilisation by inversing the values. It fits with the division of the world into two competing principles, good and evil. AQ plays on the mirror effect: we are what you say we are, that is your worst enemy, and the proof is not what we do, but what you say.

With respect to these four dimensions of the narrative, it is clear that al-Qaeda would not have such an impact without the amplification effect of the media and without its constant assimilation with THE evil alternative to civilisation.

De-radicalisation

The most effective way to combat terrorism is a combination of two levels: one level employs traditional intelligence and legal techniques to trace and neutralise cells and networks. But it is very difficult to prevent young guys from suddenly leaping into violence who have previously shown no inclination to do so. The very nature of AQ-related violence makes it difficult to pre-empt radical action. The second level would hence be to destroy AQ's narrative, that is, to de-legitimise it.

We should stop endorsing the mirror effect that is playing alongside AQ's words. As mentioned earlier, AQ's main assertions are:

1) AQ is the vanguard and the paroxysm of the 'Muslim wrath'.
2) Terrorists are heroes.
3) AQ embodies radical Islam, or more precisely "radically" embodies Islam.

To nullify the first statement, we should stop speaking of Muslims through the lens of terrorism, and should establish a coherent long-term process of integration of Islam as simply a religion in a Western context. To destroy the second assertion, we should stress the real nature of the radicals: not powerful devils, but petty and often unsuccessful delinquents, in a word, losers, who have no future. And by the way, this image already seems to be emerging: the repetitive dimension of AQ's actions diminishes their power of fascination and attraction; the fact that there are more attempts that failed miserably (the attack on Glasgow airport, for example) stresses the growing vacuity of terrorism. For the third element, we should stop promoting 'good' versus 'bad' Islam, because it supports the idea that AQ is a religious organisation. AQ is not a religious organisation; it is not the armed branch of salafisme. And by the way, to promote 'good Islam' through governmental means is to give the kiss of death to 'liberal' Muslim thinkers. If AQ is a modern phenomenon and not the expression of fundamentalist Islam, there is no point in promoting modern liberal Islam against AQ. The process of secularisation or accommodation of Islam in the West may take place, but to be successful it should be undertaken outside the anti-terrorism framework.

We should address the other issues related to second-generation Muslims (crimes of honour, salafisme) as they are, i.e. a socio-cultural transition, and not as harbingers of terrorism. We should de-Islamise AQ – not demonise it as 'bad Islam'. That is what secularism means.

3. Ideological and Theological Foundations of Muslim Radicalism in France
Samir Amghar

With nearly 5 million Muslims, France is home to more people of Islamic faith than any other European country. The French territory is regularly shaken by events relating to its Muslim population. While the French public authorities worry about the risk of terrorist attacks inspired by Islam, it appears that 'Islamic crises' are multiplying – from the 'Muslim riots' in 2005 and the development of the re-Islamisation phenomena, to the threats made by al-Qaeda against France. In the French public arena the 'Islamic threat', widely mediatised at the time of the attacks on the World Trade Centre in New York, has taken on a connotation of combat and revolution and become a synonym of violence and terrorism. Yet, far from constituting a homogenous movement, the Islamic threat is polymorphous. Islamic radicalism is neither incarnated in, nor limited to, al-Qaeda. It is a composite, heterogeneous movement based on the diverse projects (not always coordinated) of autonomous organisations or individuals acting alone or in small groups. As a circle of influence, it is both complex and continually evolving. It covers a wide range of political sensibilities stretching from religious radicalism, which is socially conservative and politically weak, and of which the sphere of action is based on religious training, to jihadism, which defends direct action, often with third-worldist overtones. Despite their divergences, these different veins of the Islamic threat have something in common: they have a direct impact on Muslim populations. In this chapter, we document the different forms of radicalism in France, with a view to understanding its permutations over the last 20 years, along with the various motivations of the members and sympathisers of these diverse forms.

1. Religious radicalism and sectarian groups

1.1 *Three religious groups convey religious radicalism*

Salafists

This movement was established in France at the beginning of the 1990s through ex-militants of the Salafist wing of the Islamic Salvation Front (Front islamique du salut, FIS) who were refugees in France, fleeing the repression of the Algerian regime.[1] In its initial phases, Salafism in France was very strongly impregnated with the political issues and situation of Algerian Islamism, particularly through the FIS. At the Tariq Ibn Ziyad Mosque on Rue Myrrha in the 18th district of Paris, Abdelbaki Sahraoui, the imam and vice president of the FIS, was strongly critical of the repressive policies of the Algerian regime in his sermons at the Friday prayer services. He was assassinated in 1995 by members of the Armed Islamic Group (Groupes islamiques armies, GIA).

This 'first-generation' Salafism, combining a spiritual mission with political vision and revolutionary objectives was also represented by Abdel-Hâdî Doudi, the current imam at the al-Sunna al-Kebira Mosque, on the so-called 'international boulevard' in Marseille. Graduating from the University of al-Azhar at the beginning of the 1980s, Abdel-Hâdî Doudi was also the brother-in-law of Moustapha Bouyali (the founder of the first Algerian resistance movement in 1983) and the teacher of Ali Benhadj. He belonged to the Algerian Salafist movement, which later became part of the FIS at the beginning of the 1990s. He was sentenced to death by the Algerian regime, and then to life imprisonment for his support of the attacks led by his brother-in-law. But his sentence was later commuted to life in prison. He arrived in France in 1987 with the consent of the Algerian services, and was responsible for the introduction of the movement in the region around Marseille and in the Parisian suburbs, especially in Nanterre.

Revolutionary vision, political perspective and religious rigour were the characteristics of the Salafism of the 1990s. But, owing to the emergence of the second generation of Muslims born in Europe and the international evolutions of political Islam, it was progressively to become an actor in re-Islamisation.

---

[1] See S. Amghar, "Les salafistes français : une nouvelle aristocratie religieuse", *Maghreb-Machrek*, No. 185, printemps-été 2005.

While in its initial stages, Salafism incarnated a form of religiosity that was linked to a political and revolutionary vision impregnated with the realities of Algerian politics. From the mid-1990s, however, it became more and more an expression of social and political conservatism, distinct from an obsession with the conquest of the state. This shift towards an apolitical and pietist Salafism can be explained by two factors: the marginalisation of political Salafism under Algerian influence and the emergence of a new centre of influence in the Arabian Peninsula.[2]

Simultaneous with the decline of Algerian Salafism was the development, from the mid-1990s, of a new centre of influence in Salafism, stemming from Saudi Arabia and the Arabian Peninsula more broadly (the *dar al-hadith* (Islamic university) in Dammaj in Yemen, under the direction of Sheik Mûqbil, the al-Albani centre in Amman and the sharia department in Damascus). Within this framework, it was less a case of the decline of Algerian Salafism than of the rise of Saudi Salafism. This shift was partly owing to the policy of the Saudi royalty, who decided as early as the 1960s to establish themselves as a "religious superpower".[3] The expansion of this doctrine was essentially the work of proselytising by European students returning from Saudi Islamic universities (and training centres in Yemen), especially those in Medina. In France, it was thanks to the predication of the first generations of European graduates – who had gone to Saudi Arabia to study theology – that Saudi Salafism gained a foothold on the Continent.[4] This was the case for example of Abdelkader Bouziane, who was behind the development of the movement in the region around Lyon. Before becoming an imam in various mosques in the Rhône-Alpes region of France in the 1990s, he spent two years in Medina studying Islam with Salafist theologians. It is worth noting that Saudi Arabia has three Islamic

---

[2] Saudi Arabia played a central role, but countries like Jordan where Sheik Nassir ud-dîn al-Albani lived, and Yemen, with Sheik Mûqbil ibn Hadi, also contributed to the spread of Salafism in Europe and in France.

[3] See S. Amghar, "Islam de France et acteurs internationaux", *Politique étrangère*, No. 1, 2005. Numerous pro-Saudi international institutions were created and the Muslim World League (Rabitat al-islamiyya al-'alamiyya), created in 1963, is one of the largest Saudi institutions to participate in the expansion of Salafism in the world.

[4] This is true of Reunion, for example. Salafism is present through two mosques, the imams of which were educated at the University of Medina.

universities (Medina, Riyadh and Mecca), although non-Saudi foreigners may only study in Medina. Numerous French students are attracted by the quality and reputation of the Saudi teaching as well as the scholarships on offer.

Moreover, encouraged by certain French students, religious teachers of a Salafist persuasion came to France from Saudi Arabia, Egypt or Jordan. Sheik Abdel Salam al-Bourjis (a disciple of the former mufti of Saudi Arabia) or Sheik Muhammed Bazmoul, who was Egyptian and a professor at the University of Mecca, participated in several religious conferences in France (as well as in Belgium, the UK and the US). Until 2001, a pious form of Salafism developed and was successful in France, especially with the arrival of Saudi teachers. Mosques were built (or taken over), and there was even talk of setting up an axis of Salafism in France. There were roughly 20 Salafist cultural centres in France (Marseille, Paris, Lyon, Roubaix, Valence, Romans-sur-Isère, Aix-en-Provence, Stains, etc.) that organised many events. Every year since 1998, a large Salafist convention has been organised in the Parisian suburbs by a middle-aged Dutchman named Yacoub Leenen, who now lives in Saudi Arabia and directs a publishing house that translates works from Arabic into French. In 2001, this gathering attracted close to 1,000 participants from all over France, but also from Germany. Following the attacks of 11 September 2001, the French police authorities decided to limit the development of the movement they saw as being behind the terrorist attacks perpetrated against the West, particularly as Salafism was beginning to develop internationally and establish an organisational structure. Salafist sheiks were therefore refused entry to France; a Salafist convention to be held in June 2001 was suspended and the theologians who had come to address it were arrested at the Charles de Gaulle airport and sent back to their countries. Moreover, numerous imams were expelled or placed under surveillance. The imam who was behind the introduction of Salafism in Lyon, Abdelkader Bouziane, was sent back to Algeria for misogynist imprecations. The imam of the mosque in Argenteuil, Ali Yashar, of Iraqi origin, was dismissed; he now lives under surveillance in the region of Lozère.

Ahbâch

Originating in Lebanon, this movement was founded by Sheik Abdallah al-Habachi in the 1950s before developing in France in the 1990s. The movement developed thanks to the proselytism of students from Lebanon studying in France. In 1988, a young science student of Lebanese origin,

Khaled al-Zanat, created an association in Montpellier. In that town, the Ahbâch controlled a 400-seat mosque in a converted abbey: the al-Tawba Mosque. Simultaneously, in Paris, an Ahbâch activist network was set up by a Lebanese computer scientist named Tamim Abdelnasser. In 1991, he co-founded the Association for Islamic Charity (Association bienfaisance islamique, AIB). With the arrival of the leader of this movement, Sheik al-Habachi, in 1996, the Parisian leaders decided to federate all these associations to create the French division of the Ahbâch: the Association for Islamic Charity Projects in France (l'Association des projets de bienfaisance islamique en France, APBIF). In this new structure, the Lebanese members (notably Khaled al-Zanat in Montpellier, Walid Dabbous[5] in Nice and Tamim Abdelnasser in Paris) formed the ideological and administrative backbone, although they were surrounded by young persons from Muslim immigrant families (from north and sub-Saharan Africa). The group has 20 or so centres at its disposal (in Saint-Etienne, Saint-Dizier, Nice, etc.), which are particularly well anchored in the south of France (Narbonne, Perpignan and Avignon) and in Paris, where they have a 300-seat mosque. Very dynamic, the movement has opened a number of places of Islamic teaching and learning as well places of worship over the last few years (in Marseille, Toulouse, Lyon, Strasbourg and Alès). As a place of postulation, France is of strategic interest for the Ahbâch because the French Muslim community is the largest in Western Europe; indeed, it is larger than the Muslim population of Lebanon. As proof of the particular attention paid to French Muslims, Sheik al-Habachi (who died in September 2008) came regularly to France, as did the president of the Lebanese branch, Houssam Qaraqira (himself married to a French woman who is also a member of the movement).

Tabligh

This movement was founded by Muhammad Ilyas in 1927, in Mewat in India, then under British administration. Responding to a desire to re-Islamise the local populations that he judged only superficially Islamised,

---

[5] Walid Dabbous is currently president of the French branch of the Ahbâch, the APBIF. Having arrived in France in the mid-1990s to study, he graduated with a Doctorate in Computer Science. The author of numerous articles, he is currently a researcher at the National Institute of Research in Technology and Computer Science.

the founder of this movement sought to preserve Indian Islamic identity through religious postulation, and protect it from what he saw as the dangers of the English presence and Hindu hegemony. Before establishing itself in France, the movement had a significant impact on the entire Indian sub-continent, such that many individuals were converted or re-Islamised through contact with the proselytism of the Tabligh.

In 1944, upon the death of the founder, Ilyas's son decided to internationalise the movement by taking its proselytising beyond the borders of the Indian sub-continent and setting up permanent missions throughout the world. At the beginning of the 1950s, the movement settled on the pilgrimage routes in the Middle East and in East Africa. In the 1960s, it spread to West Africa and South East Asia. In the space of a few years, the Tabligh became a religious multinational, following the example of the Muslim Brotherhood. Wherever it is found, the organisation operates a policy of systematic management of the Islamic domain through the control or the construction of mosques, and through the numerous preaching activities that it organises. The internationalisation of the movement, which led to its presence in a number of countries, was the response of its leaders to their desire to spread the universal message of Islam, following the logic of proselytism. At the end of the 1940s, when the movement reached its peak on the sub-continent, it was also a matter of ensuring the continued development of the organisation by not hesitating to recruit in other parts of the world. Indeed, even at that time, there was a high turnover in the structure of the organisation: many of those who were re-Islamised through contact with the Tabligh left it after a certain number of years. In this context, it became vital for a movement as structured as this one was to find new populations to seduce in order to ensure the continuation of the movement.

In the 1960s, the movement was also established in the UK through the Indo-Pakistani population, and it then increasingly turned towards Europe as a new land of postulation. Thus it was that the early Tabligh missions emerged at the same time as immigrants from the sub-continent settled in the UK. The leaders of the movement set up their European centre in Dewsbury in Yorkshire. They then spread to France in 1968 following a mission run by Pakistani preachers operating with immigrant workers, in what is probably the oldest re-Islamisation movement in France. Under the authority of Sheik Hammami, the movement was officially established in 1972 with the creation of the Muslim association Faith and Practice (Foi et Pratique). Not long afterwards, the movement founded the mosque of Abou Bakr on the boulevard Belleville in Paris, in 1973. The mosque can hold 800 faithful and is one of the largest in the capital. Other mosques were created (in Mantes la Jolie, Creil, Goussainville, Le Mans, Rouen, Lyon, Toulouse, Marseille, Roubaix, etc.).

In the middle of the 1980s, the movement underwent a crisis as a result of an internal conflict, when the authority of the charismatic figure of Sheik Hammami was contested. Under the instigation of a young Lebanese man, a dissident association was set up called 'Tabligh wa daoua ila llah'. In 1985, it organised a large gathering in Lille. Despite being a new association, it managed to draw a certain number of the founding members of the Tabligh and the auspices of Indo-Pakistani leaders into its wake. At the end of the 1980s, this association had become the official representative of the movement in France. Its leaders founded their French centre in Saint-Denis in the Parisian suburbs, where they could accommodate close to 500 faithful. Faith and Practice and Tabligh wa daoua ila llah control roughly 50 places of worship in France (Marseille, Saint-Denis, Dreux, Montereau, Mulhouse, etc.). In spite of having few mosques under their authority, the influence of the Tabligh extends beyond these places of worship. Indeed, a non-negligible number of first-generation immigrants were re-Islamised through the predication of the Tabligh. Today, many of those in this first generation are imams or leaders of 'independent mosques' and even those who are no longer official members of the Tabligh maintain friendly relations with Tabligh missionaries. Thus, Tabligh missionaries are authorised to preach in certain mosques. For example, in the mosque–cathedral in Evry-Courcouronne, the rector Khalid Merroun (himself a former member of the Tabligh) regularly hosts Tabligh meetings. In Sens, a town of 30,000 residents, Tabligh missionaries from Auxerre preach with the agreement of the managers of the mosque.

1.2 *The content of the radicalism of these movements*

These movements set up a sort of 'safety barrier' between their militants and society, between a community that is conceived of as pure and French society that is seen as corrupt. This endows the movement with a number of the features that are characteristic of a sect in the sense that the German sociologists Ernst Troeltsch and Max Weber[6] understood it. These

---

[6] See E. Troeltsch, *The Social Teaching of Christian Churches,* Basingstoke: Macmillan, 1931.

movements developed a "negative attitude" towards France:[7] they did not recognise the dominant values of society as legitimate. Indifferent to projects of social reform or to the political solutions to social problems – even when they concern Muslims – these movements have all the qualities of pietist sects as defined by the sociologist of religions, Bryan R. Wilson.[8] Proponents of these movements prefer to withdraw from the world in order to bask in the self-assurance of their own personal sanctity and the feeling of belonging to a chosen people. They are opposed to all forms of political participation in French society by Muslim populations, on the pretext that such participation is contrary to Islam. Democracy is thus assimilated into a form of associationism (*shirk*), which gives way to heresy because French ministers legislate in the name of values that are not those of sharia, and which occasionally even contravene Islamic norms – such as the 2004 law on the wearing of religious symbols at school. In France, they defend the idea of reticence, bordering on indifference, with regard to official politics, even when the debates concern French Muslims. During the demonstrations against the proposed law banning religious symbols at school that were organised by Muslim associations in December 2003 and January 2004, members of these movements were rare among the several thousand participants, according to personal observations. More recently, in 2005 and 2006, the demonstrations organised in support of Lebanon during the Israeli bombing or against the cartoons of the Prophet Mohammed did not attract many Salafist or Tabligh participants. Along these lines, Salafist websites encouraged individuals to refrain from participating in these gatherings. The conspicuous absence of these movements from these marches, which contrasted with the presence of militants and sympathisers close to the Muslim Brotherhood, should be interpreted as a form of generalised indifference to the questions of citizenship and foreign policy that affect Muslims in France and the Arab world. In the words of one Salafist from the Parisian suburbs, "when there are demonstrations by Muslims to defend other Muslims, my brothers and I never go along. We shouldn't use Western methods to make our voices

---

[7] See M.E. Marty, "Sects and Cults", *Annals of American Academy of Political and Social Science*, No. 332, November 1960, pp. 125-134.

[8] See B.R. Wilson, "Typologie des sectes dans une perspective dynamique et comparative", *Archives des sciences sociales des religions*, Vol. 16, 1963, p. 58.

heard. I don't want to mix Islam up with the politics of the French. The [s]heiks tell us not to go." [9]

For these movements, Islam is thus above political parties and issues. Consequently, the Muslim religion cannot be restrained through negotiation with the state, which implies that questions of secularism (laïcité) do not concern them. Their interpretation of religious faith as being based on the primacy of Islam over all other systems – especially secular ones – prevents them from considering themselves actors in a non-Muslim political system. Participation implies recognising an identical status between social questions and Islamic ones. An Ahbâch in Paris stated: "If I demonstrate or sign petitions or if I vote, it's as though I'm putting Islam, the best of religious and the best of humanity, in with the political baseness of the French. Never in my life! I prefer to do nothing. In any case, that's not how you should act."[10]

Although the Salafists, the Tabligh or even the Ahbâch are perceived by the French authorities as just a step away from violent action, one cannot help but notice that they do not constitute a vector of political radicalisation in the name of Islam – even if they are very critical of France. This form of religiosity is opposed to any form of political engagement in the name of Islam. Lacking in any will to involve themselves in French society and without a political project other than messianic expectation (with no immediate implications), they defend an apolitical and non-violent vision of Islam. This is founded on a desire to organise all of their existence around the advice of their religious leaders.

Out of fear of *fitna* [division] and anarchy, they advocate the non-contestation of political authority, even when the power is in the hands of non-Muslims. The Salafist preacher Sheik al-Albani, who was of Syrian origin and who died in 1999, argued that the only solution to the problems of Muslims was not the Islamisation of the state but what he called *"al-tasfiyatu wa-tarbiyya"*: the purification of education. On the one hand, this suggests the purification of the Muslim religion from all the forms of 'innovation' that have marred its precepts and dogmas, in order to return to the original religion such as it was conveyed to the Prophet. On the other hand, it implies educating Muslims so that they conform to this purified

---

[9] Derived from an interview with Abdelkrim, aged 19, Paris, 23 February 2004.

[10] Derived from an interview with Abdelkader, aged 34, Paris, 25 February 2004.

religion and leave behind their bad habits. Persuaded of the inevitability of Allah's reign on earth, they deem that the establishment of Koranic law will follow a number of stages. Through education, they aim at creating an Islamic consciousness, and through predication at provoking a total reversal of the social hierarchical organisation of the world that will leave them collectively dominant. Hence, they are waiting for a future social and political revolution, as only then will the return of the true Islam lead to the emergence of a social movement that will allow the development of an Islamic state. [11]

Still, are these movements as apolitical and as pious as they pretend? It seems clear that the relations they maintain with the public sphere are not based on a strictly religious vision of Islam. Their discourse is in many ways very politically charged. In the Arab world, the appearance of neutrality presented by these movements with regard to political life conceals their support for the regimes in place.[12] In Lebanon, the Ahbâch benefited from the support of the Syrian regime in exchange for the movements defending pro-Syrian positions. In Algeria, President Abdelazziz Bouteflika encouraged the development of Salafism to combat the development of jihadist Salafism. He institutionalised and operationalised many actors within this movement, and in Algeria, an exponential growth of this form of Salafism has been observed. From Algiers to Constantine and Béjaïa, Salafism has become the primary re-Islamisation movement in the country, well ahead of the Muslim Brothers and the Sufi Brotherhood. Although the Saudi theologians advocate a pious vision of Islam, they openly support the monarchy, which they consider the best guarantee of Islamic values and the national cohesion of the country. A young person becoming Salafist reproduces the ideological positions of the Salafist clerics in France, and thus s/he also becomes pro-Saudi. One young person who has turned to Salafism told us that

---

[11] See S. Amghar, "Le salafisme en France : de la révolution islamique à la révolution conservatrice", *Critique internationale,* no. 40, août-juillet 2008.

[12] Algerian Salafist preachers have always supported the Algerian regime and this is particularly true of that of Abdelazziz Bouteflika, who encouraged the development of the movement. Even the Saudi Sheik Uthaymin, before his death in 2001, had been the object of praise by the Algerian president for his policy of national reconciliation, through his civil agreement.

> Saudi Arabia is a magnificent country. I've never been but one day, God-willing, I'll go. It's magnificent, it's a country that defends Muslims throughout the world in contempt of the West. When you see documentaries on TV on Saudi Arabia that show how it's a bizarre society or that it's corrupt, it's just propaganda and manipulation by journalists. Saudi Arabia is the land of Muslims, is my country in a way, if I can say that.[13]

In this context, the numerous French youth who embrace Salafism constitute a loyal client network that is uncritical with regard to Saudi Arabia. Through these Salafist theologians, the Saudi monarchy facilitates the greater visibility of Saudi foreign policy by portraying themselves as a patron of European Muslims – while simultaneously discrediting the demands of certain Islamists for a more equitable repartition of oil revenue. A young French person wishing to study in Saudi Arabia will often benefit from scholarships and lodgings from the Saudi authorities. This strategy enables Saudi Arabia to inscribe itself in the minds of the French Salafists as the only religious and political power that benefits European Muslims. Through their pro-Saudi position, the Salafists contribute to maintaining the symbolic influence of that country in the construction of an ideological and religious zone of influence. Eventually, the objective is to defend the national and strategic interests of the Saudi kingdom through the promotion of a vision of Islam that is favourable to Saudi Arabia.

While in the Arab world they have developed a form of loyalty and established non-conflictual relations with the authorities, in France these movements represent a powerful critical voice vis-à-vis the political system. Both their preachers and the Arab world more broadly rail regularly against the political, moral and social values of France. Salafists encourage the faithful to leave France, which they consider a land of *kufr* [unbelievers], for a Muslim country. They condemned the 2005 law on the wearing of ostentatious religious symbols at school. Although this discourse might lead young Salafists to refuse the examination of their wives by a male doctor or to physically threaten an imam whom they consider too conciliatory in his attitudes towards France, the trend tends simply to be avoidance. Salafists or Tabligh members have a tendency to flee from contact that might lead to clashes. Instead of continuing to go to

---

[13] Derived from an interview with Nadir, aged 27, 28 May 2003, Saint Denis.

the mosque of an imam of whom he is critical, a Salafist or a Tabligh member will move to a place of worship that better corresponds to his religious and ideological expectations. Rather than accompanying his wife to a hospital where he knows a male doctor will examine her, he will opt for a clinic where he can choose the doctor.

Yet, neither their verbal violence towards France, nor their orthodox conception of Islam should be taken as the prelude to an engagement in jihad (even if this was the case in the 1990s). On the contrary, this form of religious radicalism and the anti-French tirades of its militants act as a sort of 'safety valve' that diverts the militants from direct action. Hence, violence is no longer necessary. Moreover, the Salafists, the Tabligh and the Ahbâch living in France continue to affirm that they respect the laws in force in their host country. According to them, they do not call for violence and rebellion each time their movement is accused of terrorism. A Salafist in the Lyon region explained to us that "the minhaj salafi [Salafism] has nothing to do with terrorism. The expectations of Salafists, the real ones, are never attained. The Sheiks teach us peace and good behaviour. It annoys me that Salafism is confused with terrorism." [14]

2. Politico-religious radicalism (jihadism)

Since 2002, a hundred activists have been jailed in the fight against terrorism, according to the figures given to members of parliament by the then Minister of the Interior Nicholas Sarkozy on 23 November 2005. Actions of the French security services included the neutralisation of a 'Chechen group' in the suburbs of Lyon and Paris in 2002, the dismantling of Farid Benyettou's group in the 19th district of Paris in January 2005, and the identification and arrest of volunteers leaving for Iraq in 2005. There were also arrests of militants associated with the Salafist Group for Preaching and Combat (Groupe salafiste pour la prédication et le combat, GSPC), in September 2005 in the Yvelines. This armed Algerian movement has been directed by Safé Bourrada, himself already associated with the 1995 bombings in Paris.

As noted earlier, far from representing a homogenous and well-structured trend, the politico-religious radicalism of these movements is made up of several tendencies and sensibilities. It stems from a composite,

---

[14] Derived from an interview with Jamel, age 23, 31 March 2004, Vénissieux.

heterogeneous group, based on the diverse projects (not always coordinated) of individuals acting alone or in small groups, or of autonomous organisations. A trend that is both complex and evolving, it covers a large spectrum of political sensibilities. From the different examples of Islamic-inspired terrorism that can be seen in France, we can identify three types of radical or jihadist mobilisations of a politico-religious persuasion. We should also emphasise the great diversity of positions within this form of radicalism.

2.1 Islamo-nationalist radicalism: The construction of an Islamic state or a caliphate in immigrants' countries of origin

The first trend among these movements that can be seen in France concerns groups that seek to conquer power in order to establish an Islamic state (*dawla islamiyya*) in their countries of origin. Many organisations follow this kind of jihad, such as the GIA, the Takfir wal hijra (Anathema and Exile), and the GSPC, of which some members distinguished themselves in Afghanistan. Before it developed its terrorist actions in Algeria, the armed violence of the GIA struck French residents in Algeria. Shortly after the attacks, foreign residents were instructed to leave the country on pain of execution.[15] On the 24th of December 1994, the GIA struck outside Algeria: a commando hijacked an aeroplane leaving from Algiers, with the apparent intention of crashing it into the Eiffel Tower. Because of its colonial past, France appeared to be a scapegoat on which the jihadists of the GIA pinned the responsibility for Algeria's woes. These actions were designed to demonstrate that the Algerian state was not capable of ensuring the security of those whom it was supposed to be protecting, to make an impact on public opinion internationally and to make Western governments question the appropriateness of their support for the Algerian government. Because of their link to the problems of Algerian politics, these structures are principally composed of persons of Algerian origin, including some who were members or sympathisers of the FIS, such as Mohamed Chalabi. They also include new immigrants, such as Chellali Benchellali, and young persons of immigrant origin, such as Khaled Kelkal and Jamel Beghal. In 1995, the GIA organised a series of bomb attacks in the stations at Saint-Michel and Maison-Blanche in Paris. In 1998, to

---

[15] The first foreign victims were French: land surveyors killed in Sidi Bel-Abbès on the 18th of October 1993.

prevent possible attacks during the football World Cup, a hundred members of the GIA were arrested. On the 11th of June 1999, by way of a threatening letter to the press, the GIA announced a jihad on French territory.

Expressing the return to a former political order that was perceived as ideal, these movements are prone to seeking Islamisation of the state by force. Often incarnating the most radical of the different currents of Islamism, this form of radicalism is the product of both state repression in the countries of origin and deception born of the vote-catching strategies of Islamism. Its central core is often composed of former mujahideen fighters who had joined the Islamist opposition in their own countries at the end of the war in Afghanistan. Within the Islamist opposition in Muslim countries, these militants were allied with those groups that had the most experience with political strategies. This form of radicalism believes that the jihad constitutes the only instrument capable of Islamising the state and then society if the political option does not work. Faced with state repression and the closure of the political sphere, the partisans of this movement encourage the whole Islamist movement and the wider population to take arms and rise up against the state. Considered the only obstacle to the establishment of an Islamic regime, the state is accused of *taghut*.[16] The urgency is thus placed on the mobilisation of combatants rather than on the political strategies of the Islamists, who are criticised for having negated the effects of an Islamic revolution. Although they continually attack political Islam, of which they are extremely critical, this movement does consider its objectives in line with those of the Islamists: the establishment of an Islamic state.

The terrorist attacks became progressively more frequent. Fearing for the political stability of the region, France acted by multiplying its declarations of support and its supply of material aid to the Arab governments. In fact, France was concerned that the insurrectionist rationale of the jihadists would bring the Islamists to power. The jihadists saw France as being a barrier to the establishment of the Islamic state, in

---

[16] *Taghut* is the name that the Islamists give the state. In the jihadist vocabulary, it means 'tyrant', 'oppressor' and 'false god worshipped out of fear'. See L. Martinez, "Le cheminement de la violence islamiste en Algérie", *Critique internationale*, no. 20, juillet 2003.

cohort with the authoritarian regimes that curb the Islamic revolution. From then on, the jihadists sought to convince France to withdraw its support for the Arab regimes – and particularly Algeria – by direct action. France was not directly targeted but the attacks were seen as a way of destabilising and then overthrowing the regimes in the various countries of origin. The aim was to export the political crises of these countries into France to the 5 million or so Muslims residing there.

Embodying an important anti-colonial message, this form of radicalism accused France, a former colonial power, of having designs on the economic, cultural and political domination of the region and of continuing to support the Arab regimes. In these countries, this accusation was accompanied by violent action directed against political, economic and military personnel seen as being the manifestation of the state structure. Advancing the idea of the destruction of all non-Islamic authority and the rejection of the order of things, this form of jihadism assumes an anarchist and nihilistic dimension. The dominant figure of this jihadist militancy is that of the mujahideen. The jihadist Salafists consider themselves combatants for justice who are fighting for a legitimate cause: the construction of the Islamic state that is to precede the coming of divine justice on earth. This feeling of fighting for a noble cause is reinforced by certain religious authorities who authorise this type of jihad, whereas others, without explicitly legitimising it, do so by not condemning it.[17] Moreover, they believe that they have the support of Muslim communities in Europe, of whom they consider themselves the representatives. In polarising the attention of the masses through their actions, their objective is to awaken the popular consciousness of Muslims in Europe.

2.2 The politico-religious radicalism of al-Qaeda: Fighting American imperialism

Many organisations claim to belong to the same kind of jihadist Salafism as the 'Gang of Roubaix'. In 1995, Christophe Caze and Lionel Dumont, two French converts, went to Bosnia with friends of Algerian origin to fight against the Serbs. When they returned to France, they embarked on recruiting their friends and did not stop until they had convinced all of

---

[17] Youssouf al-Qardawi never condemned this kind of jihad. See M. el Oifi, "La guerre en Algérie vue du monde arabe: le cas de la chaîne satellitaire d'al Jazeera", *Pouvoirs*, No. 86, Le Seuil, 1998.

them to take part in the jihad in Bosnia. The following year they launched a number of attacks in the north of France, against businesses and armoured vans to collect funds to finance the jihad, before they were shot by police. Several years later, in 2002, another group of a dozen or so individuals was arrested in the suburbs around Lyon. The police suspected them of preparing terrorist attacks against France. This group was organised around the Benchellali family, of Algerian origin, of which the father was an imam in the working-class area of Minguettes. Just before 1990, he created a humanitarian association called 'Openness' (Ouverture) with a friend who was a nurse. These two men collected funds, medicine and supplies 'for the Chechen cause'. They went regularly to Bosnia in a truck carrying humanitarian aid. On one of these trips in 1993, Benchellali was captured by the Croatians, who suspected him of being an Islamic soldier. He was released some months later, after undergoing torture. His son, on the other hand, left with some friends for Chechnya to fight the Russian army.

This form of radicalism is incarnated for the most part by al-Qaeda, and all the organisational structures that have set up allegiances with it in France, such as the GSPC. These are organisations that originally operated within a nationalist paradigm (often Algerian nationalism), and which are now reorienting their activism according to the jihadist ideology advanced by al-Qaeda. This recycling of the Algerian jihadists into the al-Qaeda network is explained by the strong links between those who are active in France and the members of Osama bin Laden's organisation. In many cases, the Algerian jihadists first took up arms in the war in Afghanistan. Moreover, there was a lack of well-known Algerian spiritual guides – some of whom had been assassinated, such as Mohammed Saïd – capable of influencing the ideological direction of the jihad in Algeria. This lack led the Algerian jihadists to turn to leaders of other nationalities, who were also active in other forms of jihad and often moved by internationalist visions. Finally, the pressure for security by the Algerian army and the French secret services led the Algerian emirs to reconsider their strategy and find another ideology for the fight. It was thus that in 1998, the emir of the GSPC, Hassan Hattab, swore allegiance to the World Islamic Front for Jihad against Jews and Crusaders, created by Osama bin Laden.

Although the terrorist attacks perpetrated by the first form of jihadist radicalism are part of a process of extending the activism of Islamo-nationalist radical movements in foreign countries, the violent action of the second kind of jihadist mobilisation is no longer an imported reality. It now concerns French (European) residents and draws on an anti-imperialist Islamised discourse, fed by the questions of Palestine and Iraq, as well as the question of discrimination in France.[18] The combat is now of a different nature. Whereas the first form of jihadist radicalism aimed at seizing power and establishing an Islamic state in a given country, the second form is part of a larger confrontation with the enemies of the resolutely transnational Islamic community (umma). Contrary to the first kind of mobilisation, which had a nationalist dimension, the second is part of an international rationale that sanctions the transfer of the oppositional struggles in the Arab world to the international scene. Several factors are behind the emergence of this kind of violent radicalism. Faced with police action from the secret services, the lack of success in mobilising Muslim populations living in France (as well as in Europe) in support of insurrection, and incapable of changing the foreign policy of Western countries in their support of Arab regimes threatened with Islamic terrorism, this form of Islamo-nationalist jihadism has progressively reoriented itself towards international networks. The enemy is ever less specific countries that support Arab states and ever more the new world order dominated by the US, the government of which makes demonstrative use of Christian religious references. Even if the choice of targets remains the same, the reasons for targeting them have changed. Unlike the first type of jihadism, in which the criticism of France was part of an anti-colonialist rationale, the second is characterised by its anti-imperialist dimension. The globalisation of American power is increasingly answered by the internationalisation and the re-territorialisation of armed combat.[19] According to its supporters, the universal battle must set in opposition a coalition composed of jihadist movements from the different lands of Islam and a clearly defined enemy – Western countries such as France and the US (the latter being the principle enemy to be defeated).

While the first form of jihad followed a political logic of negotiation by violence aimed at pressuring states and eventually overthrowing them,

---

[18] See the report by the International Crisis Group, "La France face à l'islam : émeutes, jihadisme et dépolitisation", Brussels, March 2006.

[19] See F. Burgat, "La génération al-Qaïda. Les courants islamistes entre dénominateur commun identitaire et internationalisation de la résistance islamique", *Mouvements*, no. 36, novembre-décembre 2004, p. 84.

the second form of jihad does not seek to negotiate or compromise but annihilate the opposition. Motivated by an extremist logic, their action seeks neither to change political power relations nor to overthrow the regime but to upset the social order profoundly. The combatant feels compelled by a mission: saving an endangered Islam and the project of an Islamic state is merely a necessary utopia that serves to maintain a tension that liberates bellicose energy. From that point on, violence is understood as a sacrifice cloaked with meta-political significance. Indeed, jihadist violence has risen above politics to become a vector of meaning that gives it an air of intransigence, of non-negotiability and the religious impact of absolutism. This is de-territorialised violence, beyond borders, and the issues that it targets are so vital to its militants that they are willing to sacrifice their very existence for them.

Although it is not in the logic of political negotiation, this is not apolitical violence: the political elements of its objectives are just associated and subordinated to other goals, defined in cultural and religious terms, which will suffer no concession. This violence is about identities, which is foreign to the political sphere. This jihadist militantism applies the sectarian disqualification to those it means to fight: Muslims, who in their eyes are not sufficiently Muslim, as well as Jews and Christians. Faced with another Muslim, the rhetoric of takfir [excommunication] is mobilised to deny the adversary the guarantees of legitimate belonging. Faced with a non-Muslim, the person is disqualified through recourse to the identity of the unbeliever (kufr). Whereas the first kind of radicalism is aimed against the taghut state, the second form of radicalism is aimed at the society that is accused of impiousness. Excommunication, takfir, is the response in this case. The movement holds that the society is in the jahiliyya (a period before the Islamic divine revelation) and the combatant is not regarded as noble (as a jihadist would normally be), but as a pure figure in a sullied world. The jihadist militant is no longer a mujâhid [warrior of the holy war] but a shahid [martyr]. In this kind of jihad, the repertoire of action in combat is not taken from the guerrilla logics of bombing and so forth, but from that of suicide attacks. The objective is not to set up an Islamic state but to create hell on this world for all those who, for one reason or another, are not considered Muslim.[20]

---

[20] See O. Roy, *L'islamisme mondialisé*, Paris: Seuil, 2002.

The first form of jihad found the justification to overthrow the state in certain fatwas, approved by some of the Muslim population who saw democratic virtues in the holy war. The second form, however, is unanimously condemned by the entire body of Muslim theologians and Muslim populations of Europe. Thus, the day after the attacks in New York on 11 September 2001 and after the attacks in Madrid on 11 March 2004, the religious authorities of Islam in both the West and the Muslim world condemned these acts, which according to them had nothing to do with Islam. It is worth noting that some of these clerics simultaneously justified the first form of radicalism.

Stemming from a feeling of belonging to the global umma, and not being linked to any country of origin, the defenders of this kind of jihad take little account of nationalities and national reasoning. This movement is transnational because the networks have become global and intertwined with the international operators of jihadism. This undoubtedly explains the diverse national origins among these jihadists, compared with those of the first category, and their recognition of themselves more easily in internationalist claims. Therefore, compared with the first form of jihad in which there was an over-representation of persons of Algerian origin, this second form of jihadist radicalism mobilises individuals of different origins (e.g. Moroccans and Tunisians). This jihad also facilitates the conversion of French-born members, the centrepiece of the jihadist operation in France since 1995 and an increasingly important one. These new networks evolve in a 'de-territorialised' imaginary space.

2.3 *Radicalism mobilising the defence of Muslims' agenda*

The third movement of jihadist radicalism does not seek to fight against 'Jews and Crusaders' by direct action and the use of violence, nor does its action seek the establishment of an Islamic state and society, as it is not concerned with the question of dawla islamiyya. The jihad actually waged by this group aims at defending and supporting Muslim populations whose territorial, political and physical integrity is threatened by foreign powers. For its members, the use of violence is legitimate if it is consecrated to the defence of Muslims put in danger by non-Muslim armies. In the name of transnational Islamic solidarity, they have an obligation to provide military and financial assistance to their brothers in arms, in the defence of dar al-Islam and in maintaining the cohesion of an imaginary umma. Within the logic of patriotism and Islamic independence, this jihadist radicalism takes the form of a national war of liberation, in mobilising a sovereigntist discourse.[21] Comparing himself with the International Brigade, a jihadist told us during an interview that "we are for the jihad in Iraq or anywhere because our brothers are in mortal danger. We want to defend them and France doesn't understand, even though some French people did the same thing in the 1930s to defend the Spanish democrats against the dictator Franco." Therefore, while the dominant figure of the second type of jihadism is that of the kamikaze, the third type is characterised by the figure of the *mûhtal* or the *mûnâdil* [resistance fighter] or the *mûqatil al-oumma* [the fighter of the *umma*] fighting against occupation. They consider themselves the protectors of Islamic unity and fight to save the morality and piety of Muslims who could no longer live their Islamic way of life under the occupation of impious armies. These jihadists wage a sacred war to defend a sacred nation, a belief that reinforces in their mind their feeling of performing a higher task. Contrary to the kamikaze, death is not the goal of these jihadists, but rather military victory against the occupying armies. This is what constitutes the ultimate objective of this form of jihad. It is heavily marked by mythologised stories of a war in which the Afghans "threw rocks at the [S]oviet tanks and made them explode, where an army of mountain people defeated the most powerful army in the world", according to one former soldier who today runs a Koranic school in Paris. He suggests that this holy war is part of a logic of negotiation by force: to cause the opposing army to capitulate so that it leaves *dar al-Islam*. The soldiers of the opposing armies are undoubtedly deemed impious but this religious disqualification is only relevant in the context of the war.

The jihad does not happen in the West; instead, it is deployed in all the conflict zones in which Muslims and non-Muslims are in opposition (Bosnia, Chechnya, Kashmir, Afghanistan and Iraq). Although these jihadists are very critical of the West and they condemn its bellicose politics towards Muslim countries, this movement maintains peaceful relations with Europe. It draws a parallel between the situations of Muslims in war against foreign armies where it is necessary to go and fight on the one

---

[21] This support operates on several levels: first, it involves the collection of funds to help Muslim populations that are victims of war to buy weapons; second, the aim is to gain media coverage for the conflict to facilitate the exchange of opinions. Finally, this logistical support is complimented by the sending of militia troops to join national forces.

hand, and on the other hand the conditions of Muslims in Europe who, although they are subject to discriminations, are not threatened militarily by the armies of the Old World. Farid Benyettou told us, before he was arrested for having been behind the Iraqi group, that

> France is a country of unbelievers. I don't like this country. It doesn't respect Muslims, there is discrimination and Islamophobia. We must fight in France to defend Muslims but we must do so by legal means. We must turn democracy against France. But we must not use arms or lay bombs. France has not declared war on us.

It is thus that he demonstrated (peacefully) against the American military intervention in Iraq in March of 2003. To the question of which Muslim country he would choose in order to live his Islam fully, he replied "You think I'm going to say Saudi Arabia, Yemen or Algeria. These are not countries that are benevolent towards Islam. I would choose the United Kingdom or the United States. There they respect Muslims and I could be active in the defence of the Muslims of the world." Whereas the jihadists of the second group live their engagement as a deviance and a social transgression that is punishable by the security forces, the third category is convinced of the legitimacy of its cause. This feeling is all the stronger for the fact that Arab countries tolerate imams who rail against "non-Muslim armies that attack impious Muslims", to take the words of a religious leader and public servant during a Friday service in an Algerian city. In the eyes of these jihadists, this holy war is all the more legitimate because it benefits from the support of Muslim populations living in Europe (but also in the Muslim world) and has the backing of theologians. In fact, theologians encourage their followers through numerous fatwas to 'go and fight the impious armies that are attacking Muslims'. From Youssouf al-Qardawi to the Salafist theologians in Saudi Arabia, they all justify this jihad, considering it an act of rightful defence and resistance. Because armed combat is part of the defence of the *umma*, the ethnic origin of the jihadist combatants is highly variable as was the case for the second group. As such, we find young persons of different origins (e.g. Moroccan and Tunisian) as well as converts in this group. The core of this third group, however, remains of Algerian origin (Benchellali, Benyettou and Fateh Kamel).

3. Secular political radicalism

This kind of radicalism or radicalisation is carried out by political groups and individuals of Muslim origin who do not incorporate a religious argument into their radical position. Their rhetoric is based on secular politics. It is in the name of political and ideological values that the partisans of this form of radicalism attempt to defend their position by force. This concerns groups such as those involved in the urban riots in the French suburbs in November and December 2005, and extreme left, rap groups.

The riots in the suburbs are the first form of this a-religious political radicalisation. This violence can be analysed as the eruption of an accumulated tension from daily frustrations and general annoyance about economic difficulties and precarious living conditions, the absence of opportunities, the perceived contempt of the political class, discrimination in housing, work and daily life, and so forth. For others, they were also witness to the general unhappiness over the policies of Nicolas Sarkozy. Most of the early acts of vandalism were spontaneous and isolated movements of idle youth in the streets among the housing estates. These acts then became veritable riots, notably involving direct combat with the riot squad. The riots were sparked by the death of two young men who were being chased by the police in Clichy-sous-Bois in the Parisian suburbs. They were also clearly the product of a yearning to break with what was seen as a repressive situation, linked to the inflationary security policies that had been in force in these areas for many years (Minguettes in 1983, Vaulx-en-Velin near Lyon in 1990, the suburbs north of Marseille and riots in the suburbs in November and December 2005). More than through the temptation of jihadism, it is through popular revolt that political claims are made when the citizenship structures are lacking.

The blaze in the suburbs at the end of 2005 was an episode without religious content or actors. In spite of a number of attempts to bring calm to the situation, the Muslim organisations did not play the role of social regulator expected of them. This showed that Muslim actors do not organise the riots, nor do the neighbourhoods, although sometimes they are active in the latter on a local level. These riots were manifestly the result of a desire to fight against an order perceived as authoritarian and repressive, especially stemming from the security policy in place in these areas since 2002.

This movement is part of a demand for social recognition, through the use of violence. In choosing to attack institutions, it is the state that is targeted for its shortcomings, e.g. the police for its repression, the bus stations because of geographical isolation and schools because they reproduce social failure.

The second element within this radical mobilisation is rap music. Part of the French rap scene aims at being radical. Its messages are provocative and seem to signify a desire for rupture, often by violence. In thematic compilations (e.g. "Patrimoine du ghetto", 2005; "Yzo", 2005; "Prison", 2005) or through albums of groups such as Sniper, Bakar or Médine, the rappers point the finger at those guilty for social misery and exclusion. Among the accused, the state is represented as an oppressive machine, of which the armed presence is the police, the number one enemy. Constant identity checks, blunders, arbitrary arrests and so on, lead rappers to think of the police as an organised gang. Behind their critique of the institution of the police force, the state is incriminated, accused according to a vision of the world that resembles a conspiracy theory. Below are some extracts of their songs:

> For the kids with hands of vengeance
> To burn the police state and send
> The Republic to burn at the same stake, yeah...
> Why are we waitin' to screw up their game,
> Why are we waitin' to not play by their rules
>
> ("What are we waiting for?", NTM)

> Fuck the system; they'll get fire 'cos they spread hate
> Burn them, hang them, throw them in the Seine
> The youth of the ghetto have rage in their veins
> Gotta break the chains
>
> ("The System", Sniper)

Despite the dimension of extreme protest calling for an insurrectional uprising, these texts essentially play a role in channelling that violence. The violence expressed in these texts has a cathartic effect on rappers and the youth who listen to this music.

The third group that defends the idea of secular political violence concerns individuals belonging to movements on the extreme left. In the 1960s, there were already signs that small groups on the extreme left were trying to organise Muslim immigrant workers. Other structures for students of Middle-Eastern origin (e.g. Lebanese and Pakistani) who were close to the national liberation movements occupied themselves with radical political activities (political assassinations and hostages). Today, the 'Islamic extreme left' is principally incarnated by the Movement for Immigration and the Suburbs (Mouvement de l'immigration et des banlieues, MIB), which regroups former Maoists and uses direct action against discrimination in the legal system and against police violence, of which youth in the suburbs are often the victims.

Conclusions

The forms of radicalism among the Muslim populations in France are multiple and varied. To overplay the religious variable would prevent us from seeing the great plasticity of the phenomena of radicalisation. Political violence can take its source from religious justifications, or religious references can impede radicalisation, or Islam is absent altogether, even though the radicalism is practised by Muslims. Beyond this, it is necessary to recognise that all these different forms of radicalism are the product of experiences of injustice and exclusion, which can be directly linked to realities on the ground or to the political trauma of young persons having known delinquency and homelessness, personal failure, long-term unemployment and so on.

Yet, the link between Muslim populations and radicalism cannot be reduced to an economic equation in which poverty is the common denominator. It seems more likely to be the inadequacies of social and political regulation that is a problem, along with the lack of recognition, contempt and "the great wall" – in the words of Khaled Kelkal[22] (one of the perpetrators of the terrorist attacks in 1995) – separating the estates where most of France's Muslims live and the rest of the towns.

---

[22] See the article, "Moi, Khaled Kelkal", *Le Monde*, 7 Octobre 1995.

4. Political, Religious and Ethnic Radicalisation among Muslims in Belgium

Theodoros Koutroubas, Ward Vloeberghs & Zeynep Yanasmayan

Were we to believe alarmist reports on Islam in Belgium, such as that of the Dutch journalist Arthur van Amerongen, a major terrorist attack against Brussels is only "a matter of time".[1] A bit further away from Europe's capital, other journalists keep announcing the imminent introduction of the sharia in Flemish municipalities,[2] who trembled some years ago at the prospect of Muslim patrols antagonising the police. Responsible for the security of the several international institutions established on its soil and eager to avoid a repetition of the terrorist attacks experienced by other states, the Belgian authorities in fact already take such threats seriously. In December 2007, following the receipt of intelligence reports of an alleged plot to liberate Tunisian-born al-Qaeda-related convict Nizar Trabelsi, extraordinary measures were adopted in

---

[1] See for example the interviews of Arthur van Amerongen in *Knack*, "Aanslag in Brussel is kwestie van tijd" (Attack on Brussels is matter of time), 8 August 2007 and in *De Morgen*, "De islam woekert hier als een roos op een mestvaalt" (Islam thrives here like a rose on a dung heap), 27 January 2008. A Dutch journalist, Mr van Amerongen claims to have infiltrated Brussels Moroccan Islamist circles and to have lived among them during a whole year, an experience he chronicles in a book *Brussel: Eurabia*, published by Uitgeverij Atlas (Amsterdam) in February 2008.

[2] See "Ooit wordt de sharia hier ingevoerd" (One day, the sharia will be introduced here), *Knack*, 12 March 2008.

order to protect the capital from an imminent threat.³ Some months afterwards, in May 2008, the Moroccan authorities announced the dismantlement of a small Islamist group, based in their country but involving a Belgian resident Moroccan as well, allegedly aiming at bombing buildings of the European Commission in Brussels.⁴

Notwithstanding the accuracy of such information, both its impact and the frequency with which it occurs prove at least that there is a broad perception of the 'Muslim community'⁵ of Belgium as being increasingly radicalised.

Whether or not this perception is accurate is of course a matter for debate, as several other observers seem to refute such an evolution, pointing rather towards the emergence of a distinctively 'Belgian' or 'European' Islam, well integrated in the Western cultural values.⁶

What is clear, however, is that the time is past when it was sufficient that issues relating to this community could be successfully managed – or so it seemed – by a handful of charismatic mayors and personalities responsible for areas with a high concentration of Turkish and North African populations.⁷ Individuals with leadership and vision can certainly

---

³ See for example *Le Soir*, 22 December 2007, "La menace terroriste sous le sapin de Noël" (The terrorist threat under the Christmas tree). Fourteen persons were arrested in relation to this alleged plot, only to be released two days afterwards for insufficient proof (*Le Soir*, 24-25 December 2007). See also http://www.lefigaro.fr/international/2007/12/22/01003-20071222ARTFIG00126-alerte-antiterroriste-a-bruxelles-.php

⁴ See for example *Le Soir*, 19-20 May 2008 (also in http://www.lesoir.be/actualite/belgique/demantelement-d-un-reseau-2008-05-19-599389.shtml

⁵ The term is used here to describe both believers in Islam and persons coming from a Muslim cultural background.

⁶ See e.g. *La Libre Belgique*, "L'islam s'intègre bien chez nous" (Islam is well integrated among us), 12 March 2008. Also see Felice Dassetto, Brigitte Maréchal and Silvio Ferrari, *Islam in the European Union: What's at stake in the future?*, study prepared for the European Parliament (IP/B/CULT/ST/2006_061), May 2007 (PE 390.031).

⁷ Such as for example former mayors such as Guy Cudell of Sint Joost ten Node or the Socialist Party's heavyweight Philippe Moureaux of Molenbeek St Jean. To a less successful extent, the same applies to the city of Antwerp, with figures such as Bob Cools and, more recently and more efficiently, Antwerp's mayor, Patrick

still produce good work, but with only 54 of the at least 333 mosques operating legally in Belgium, it is obvious that more carefully designed, long-term efforts are needed.[8]

In this paper, we propose to discuss a number of different types of radicalisation that have been observed among persons of Islamic faith or culture in Belgium, highlighting the conflicts it has caused or it could become the cause of. Of course, the authors are well aware that there are numerous other issues, completely unrelated to the presence of a 'Muslim' community, that can cause conflict at a micro level in Belgium.

1. Political radicalisation

1.1 The country's political context

Religion has never been absent from Belgium's political life. Since its declaration of independence from the Netherlands in 1830, the small country has in fact almost always counted a 'Christian' party amongst the components of its successive coalition governments, whilst the consensual model that still characterises the country's governance is based on a perpetually renewed balance between the Catholic (Socio-Christian), the Liberal (originally strongly linked to Free-Masonry and rather anti-clerical) and the Socialist political families. At the same time, the Belgian royal family, whose constitutional powers and influence continue to be quite important, has never made a secret of its strong links with the Roman Catholic Church. Thus, issues such as the financing of faith-based schools or the legalisation of abortion, have become landmarks in the history of the lengthy and subtle negotiations that Belgian politicians are famous for, with inventive solutions of compromise assuring every time the continuation of internal peace and the stability of the regime. Notwithstanding how difficult and sometimes divisive such issues might have been, it is interesting to point out that, neither these nor the ever-present grievances and rivalries between the Flemish North and the Wallonian South have caused any serious violent conflict in the land. This tradition of non-violent co-existence between people of different

---

Janssens. On the impact of Cudell, see F. Dassetto, *Immigrés et communes. Equilibres difficiles. Le cas de Saint-Josse-ten-Noode*, Louvain-la-Neuve: Academia, 1991.

[8] *De Standaard*, "Vlaanderen erkent moskeeën" (Flanders recognises mosques), 22-23 December 2007, pp. 14-15.

convictions, culture, faiths or language is still a major source of pride amongst Belgians.

As is the case in most countries of Western Europe, the last 20 years have witnessed a progress of secularism in the Belgian society. By the mid-2000s, the once rather conservative country was amongst the first countries to legalise marriage between same-sex persons and euthanasia with a broad consensus. With the numbers constantly diminishing of those regularly attending church services, joining the clergy or baptising their children, the two 'Christian' parties have begun to play down their Roman-Catholic identity, putting forward a 'humanistic' profile and vocally dissociating themselves from Vatican guidelines on 'moral' issues.

This period also witnessed the emergence of a growing involvement of Muslims and other persons coming from an Islamic cultural background in Belgian politics, first at the local and then at the regional and the federal levels. Most of these citizens were of Moroccan or Turkish origin whilst Algeria and Tunisia constituted respectively their third and fourth source.[9] The access of citizens of foreign origin to elected office was far from being a taboo in the country at the time 'Muslims' started becoming interesting potential candidates for political parties.[10] Despite common beliefs that religious practice and values are higher among citizens hailing (or having parents who hail) from predominantly Muslim countries,[11] it is the traditionally agnostic and morally liberal Socialist Party (both in the South and in the North of the country) that seems to take the biggest share of their vote and counts most of those elected within their ranks. It is interesting to note that during all recent debates and votes on legislation strongly rejected by the official representatives of the most organised religions recognised by the Belgian state,[12] 'Muslim' members and officials of political parties have

---

[9] Open Society Institute, EU Monitoring and Advocacy Programme, *Muslims in the EU: Cities Report – Belgium*, Preliminary research report and literature survey, 2007.

[10] An example amongst many others, Dr. Elio di Rupo, a son of Italian immigrants, who has occupied several ministerial seats including the position of Vice-Prime Minister, and was Minister-President of Wallonia in the 2000s. Dr. di Rupo is currently the President of the French-speaking Socialist Party (PS).

[11] According to the preliminary research report of the Open Society Institute, op. cit., there is a lack of academic knowledge regarding religious practice and beliefs among Muslims in Belgium.

[12] Islam has this status since 1974.

chosen not to differentiate themselves from party lines (at least openly), even when those lines where clearly opposed to the opinions of their community's religious leaders.

In the pages to come, we are going to discuss the attempts of some of the members of Belgium's Muslim community to establish Islamic or community-based political parties, their discourse and the tensions they have or could create.

1.2 Islamic political parties

The first attempt to set up an Islamic political party in Belgium took place in Flanders, with the creation of the Moslim Volkspartij van Brussel en Vlaanderen in 1992. The party never submitted a list to elections at any level and was rather quickly disbanded.

More organised than the leaders of the 'Moslim Volkspartij', Mr. Redouane Ahrouch has founded Noor – Le Parti Islamique in 1999. The party, self-defined as an 'Islamic movement', was created out of concern for the fact that "the Jewish / Christian values are no longer the foundations of the political orientations that have determined the future for all over the centuries" and with the belief that "religion provides the solution" for the problems society is facing.

Its short 'manifesto', figuring in the initial page of what is a very basic (six pages only), non-interactive website (http://noor.ovh.org), uses a discourse often proposed by radical religious groups/movements of all denominations. The party's programme, distributed in mailboxes during electoral campaigns, contains 40 points, presented as simple headlines with no further explanation. A small number of these points express ideas that do seem radical in the current Belgian socio-political context, such as the "re-establishment of capital punishment",[13] or the promise to "favour marriage in adolescence". Other points address concerns common to several religious-minded voters such as the "real protection of the family", the "struggle against alcoholism, smoking, drugs and debauchery" or the need to render divorce more difficult.

---

[13] The author makes it precise: "for odious crimes (murders of innocents)" (http://noor.ovh.org/Français/program.htm).

Most of the programme, however, seems to contain promises obviously aimed at pleasing voters in a country with a high level of taxation (abolition of the VAT, the tax on work, etc.).

Absent from the federal elections of June 2007, Noor, which didn't manage to get more than 0.02% of the votes in those of 2003, seems today almost dismantled. Initially designed to contain pages in French, Dutch, Arabic and Turkish, its website was, in May 2008, unavailable in most languages and it was obvious that no updating had been done for a long time. No activity of the party was mentioned in the country's written, electronic or radio-televised press for the last two years, thus rendering its visibility almost non-existent.

Noor's (rather discreet) existence did not prevent the Belgian convert to Islam, Jean-François Abdullah Bastin, to found, together with another group of converts and Muslims coming from Muslim families, the Parti Citoyenneté Prosperité (PCP) in 2003.

The party became quickly visible thanks to its active opposition to the ban of the Islamic scarf or *hijab* in school premises by an institute of secondary education in one of Brussels' municipalities (Laeken), and its vocal defence of the female students who defied that decision. The interdiction of wearing the *hijab* during school hours, adopted by several other schools in Brussels and Wallonia during the years 2003–04 became indeed an issue of tension and controversy in Belgium at that time, and PCP's militancy did bear fruit in the federal elections of 2003. The (new) party, which had presented lists only in the Brussels-Halle-Vilvorde district, scored a mere 0.13% at the national level. It did however manage to obtain almost 3% of the vote in a number of the capital's communities with a high percentage of 'Muslim' population,[14] thanks to a programme including a lot of specifically 'Islamic' proposals, such as the right of Muslim women to wear the Islamic scarf both in class and in their identity card picture, the inclusion of halal menus in school cantinas, the creation of Islamic cemeteries, etc.

Considered to be radical because of its founders' often controversial statements (discussed later in this paper) the party was nevertheless declaring that "it does not contest the legitimacy of the government or any democratically constituted authority in the country" and explicitly

---

[14] See, for example, *Le Monde diplomatique,* June 2004.

denounced "any terrorist activity, any armed or violent expression of a religious, ideological or political revendication".

Almost one year after PCP's foundation, Jean-François Abdullah Bastin has resigned from membership denouncing the party's "sectarian and arrogant re-orientation" of its ideology by its 'spiritual guide', Sheikh Bassam Ayachi. A few months after his departure, "Citoyenneté et Prosperité" took part in the June 2004 elections for the regional government of Brussels-Capital, realising a score of 3.281 votes, or 0.84% of the French-speaking electorate with a list including an important number of 'new' Muslims (converts to Islam).

By May 2008 however, this party was also all but extinct according to all indications: it did not present lists for the June 2006 federal elections, it had no presence on the web and in the media and no activity was reported even in those of the capitals' municipalities that used to constitute its stronghold.

Last in the list of inactive Muslim political parties in Belgium, the ephemeral Moslim Democratische Partij was founded by the then leader of the Arab European League (AEL), Dyab Abou Jahjah, in an effort to translate the League's alleged popularity among youths of Arabic origin in Flanders into elected representation at the local, regional and federal levels.

An advocate of Arab nationalism,[15] Abou Jahjah had already participated in the federal elections of 2003 as a candidate of the far left coalition RESIST obtaining 0.90% of the vote in the city of Antwerp, headquarters of AEL. Given the rather non-religious political discourse of the League (to be discussed in the following pages) and its (very) secular political allies within RESIST (the 'Parti du Travail de Belgique'), the choice of 'Muslim' as an adjective describing the nature of the new party was rather surprising, and is certainly characteristic of a tendency among 'Muslim' candidates (and not only) to often confuse religious affiliation with national origin in order to serve their agendas. Anyhow and despite its founders' hopes,[16] the Moslim Democratische Partij got worse results

---

[15] See his lengthy interview to the 'Open Democracy' (http://www.opendemocracy.net/faith-europe_islam/article_1908.jsp).

[16] In his interview to the 'Open Democracy', op. cit., Abou Jahjah was predicting that the new party would grow so much that by 2006 it would be able to "have a higher vote and perhaps win one or two representatives in city hall".

than RESIST in Flanders (Antwerp and East Flanders) at the regional elections of 2004 (0.27% in Antwerp and 0.14% in East Flanders) and is now completely disbanded.

The only Islamic party really active in Belgium by May 2008, when this chapter was written, was the Parti Jeunes Musulmans (PJM), founded in 2004 by Jean-François Abdullah Bastin after his resignation from the PCP. PJM considers itself to be "the party of all Muslims and of all the generations that have definitively turned the page of colonialism and humiliations" and according to its statutes "conceives its activities in total harmony with the rules of democracy and the applying legislation in the Kingdom of Belgium".[17]

Much like Noor and several other radical Christian political movements in Europe, the party deplores "a world that has banished the sacred in a stupid and dangerous way" and calls upon "all men and women of good will who (are) scandalised by the programmed disappearance of every moral sense".[18] Like its 'predecessor', the PCP, PJM also supports the right of Muslims to wear the *hijab* in schools, insist upon *halal* menus in cantinas, have holidays during Islamic feasts and be educated in religious schools respectful of the principle of separation between the sexes. At the same time, it pleads for the right of parents to have the ultimate choice on all activities proposed to their children in the framework of their school curriculum (including, for example, museum visits) and promises a free of charge and less 'West-centred' compulsory education.[19]

Its allegiance to the rules of democracy and the Belgian laws seem however much less sincere after a careful study of the ideas proposed in its website. When presenting the democratic nature of the party, for example, the authors of the electronic portal of PJM admit that the latter "plays the game (of democracy)…respects scrupulously its rules …but this does not prevent it from promoting another game, another form of governance, more elaborate, more appropriate to the destiny of Muslims, of Islam, of humanity in general and whose rules are not fixed by men but by God. When the day will come, it will stand up from the table of the game, along

---

[17] http://www.mvjm.be

[18] See the Statutes of the party, updated June 2006, on its website, op. cit.

[19] Op. cit., «Enseignement».

with all the Muslims who have played beside it in the most civilized manner, it will thank its hosts and it will re-join its country (its State)".[20] Some (web)pages further, state that the party its objective "is obviously, in no way to install an Islamic State in Belgium", only to observe immediately afterwards that it is "perfectly conscious of the fact that the Muslims cannot live but elsewhere, and in due time, when God shall decide, (there will be) an Islam integrally re-established in its original authenticity, in a really Islamic and independent State, perfectly respectful of and respected by the other States of the international community".[21]

At the same time, PJM's leaders are often using in public a provocative discourse, likely to raise tensions or create conflict both within the community they have pleaded to defend and between the different components of Belgian society. As an example, during the time of the 2007 electoral campaign, the party's chairman, Mr Bastin, has caused significant controversy by declaring in an interview with TV Brussel that "there is a Muslim party and thus all Muslims must defend their party...", claiming that "all learned men of Islam and not only the Salafists…have condemned in the most explicit way as being haram all Muslim votes for a non-Islamic party where the possibility of that choice exists".[22] Bastin often uses an ironic, aggressive and bitter tone, against those 'Muslims' who do not support his party and have denounced his politics and discourse as being un-Islamic, challenging the sincerity of his conversion. His attitude is not very different from that of many of PJM representatives who often participate in public debates on issues relating to religion and secularism, and defend their views in an aggressive way. Their reports published afterwards in http://www.mvjm.be are all but polite towards those who express different ideas.[23]

---

[20] Op. cit., «Parti Démocrate».

[21] Op. cit., «Etat islamique».

[22] «Lettre ouverte à Monsieur Jean-François Abdullah Bastin, Parti Jeunes Musulmans» and «Réponse de Abdullah Bastin à la lettre ouverte de Salim Haouach», op. cit.

[23] See, for example, in the page "Le PJM y était" the party's coverage of the conference on the issue, "La laïcité, rampart contre les intégrismes le racisme, l'antisémitisme, la misogyny et l'homophobie", organised in Brussels in December

Aggressive campaigning didn't succeed, however, to raise PJM's popularity. Despite being the only Islamic party competing in the latest federal elections (with candidates in the district of Brussels-Halle-Vilvorde like the PCP four years before) the 'Young Muslims' obtained a mere 0.07% of the vote at the national level. Their score was even inferior to that of the PCP in 2003 (0.13%),[24] when Mr Bastin was still the leader of 'Citizenship and Prosperity'.

Born to parents of Belgian origin (his father was a University professor), PJM's chairman has become a familiar and rather picturesque figure in Belgian households thanks (at least partially) to his oriental dress, headgear and long beard, that constitute a striking antithesis with the western clothing of almost all politicians with Arabic or Turkish origin in the country. The later often point out the important presence of converts in PJM's lists (5 out of 14 candidates in 2007), as well as Bastin's own origins, in order to contest his right to represent a Muslim community still quite divided along ethnic lines. The verbal vehemence with which Mr Bastin usually attacks his 'coreligionist' political opponents have made him 'persona non grata' in numerous manifestations on community-related issues and in several mosques.[25] Last but not least, his active support to radical Christian organisations at the time of the discussion of the law opening adoption to same-sex couples in Belgium earned PJM a reputation of extreme right-wing movement. It is interesting to note here that some of these organisations, like Belgique et Chrétienté[26] do not hesitate to use a strong anti-Muslim discourse in their 'defence' of the country's 'Christian roots', in spite of their alliance with the PJM against the "*destruction of the last ramparts of civilisation*".[27]

Often a cause of (micro)tension mostly within the 'Muslim' community, the Parti Jeunes Musulmans did not appear to have the

---

2005 by the Free University of Brussels (ULB) and Secular Jewish Community Centre (CCLJ).

[24] See the comparative results of the 2003 and 2007 federal elections in the Belgian government's federal web portal (http://polling2007.belgium.be/fr/cha/results/results_graph_etop.html).

[25] See, as an example, his own complaints in his answer to Salim Haouach, op. cit.

[26] See http://www.bechrist.be

[27] See the "Marche pour la Famille" page in the PJM website, op. cit.

potential for the creation of serious conflict or violence between communities in Belgium at the time these lines were written. As the electoral results demonstrate, its influence was diminishing among voters and its presence in the media seemed to be more due to its leaders' dress code than to the party's real importance. PJM's radical discourse however, and especially the parts relating to a future 'Islamic State' to be founded on an unidentified space, can be used as a weapon by the country's extreme right-wing parties which are constantly growing in popularity in the North.

Not really a political party, but important enough to make the headlines of the international press, Malika El-Aroud, a Belgian of Moroccan origin, spouse of the Tunisian Abdessatar Dahmane and one of the assassins of Afghanistan's anti-Taliban leader, Ahmad Chah Massoud, is also worth mentioning here. Viewed as the *"Belgian woman who wages war for al-Qaeda on the web"*,[28] Ms El-Aroun is managing to successfully manipulate Belgium's legal requirements on e-publishing in order to diffuse particularly heinous discourse against the West and to overtly encourage terrorist activities, rallying, notably, Muslim women to support them.[29] Allegedly unwilling to arrest her in order to avoid attracting further publicity around her name,[30] the Belgian authorities are closely monitoring her actions. At the time these lines were written, a serious study on the impact of El-Aroud's message amongst the population of Islamic culture or faith in Belgium was yet to be carried out.

1.3 Non-religious political radicalisation

The Arab-European League (AEL)

Founded in 2000 by Dyab Abou Jahjah, the Arab-European League defines itself as "a political and social movement that stands for the Rights of the Arab and Muslim communities in Europe and the Arab causes in general. ".[31] The movement, which proclaims that it also stands for "solidarity with all Muslim peoples and communities and all the oppressed peoples of the world", declares that its members' objective is to abide and strive for 19

---

[28] See for example the *International Herald Tribune*, 27 May 2008 (http://www.iht.com/articles/2008/05/27/europe/terror.php?page=2).

[29] See for example http://minbar-sos.com/

[30] See *Le Monde*, 17 June 2008.

[31] See its website (http://www.arabeuropean.org).

principles and goals, 6 of which concern the Arab Diaspora and 13 the Arab world in general.

The goals of the League regarding Arabs in Europe are not radically different from those of many an immigrant-friendly political party or NGO in modern-day Belgium. AEL pleads in fact for the right of Arab immigrants to cultivate their cultural identity "while engaging actively as European citizens in the countries of residence, with equal rights and treatment", and vows to combat racism, Islamophobia, discrimination in the fields of employment, housing and education, as well as attempts to breach their freedom of expression, religion, religious practice or any other of their human rights.

It is however the "Arab Nation", and not so much its Diaspora in Europe, that seems to be the target of the movement's manifesto. AEL's 13 declarations "towards the Arab world" are in fact nothing less than a project for the creation of an Empire, redrafting the current map "in order to give birth to the "Unity of the Arab people in one democratic federal State." (points 7 & 8). The League's vision includes a whole constitution for its ideal future 'Arab homeland', the borders of which would extend from the Atlantic to Iran. Political freedom, freedom of expression, social rights, eradication of poverty, measures against the concentration of power including the field of the media, rights for linguistic minorities, internal autonomy for the 'provinces' of Rif, Sous and Kabilya, no detail has been left out from the movement's ambitious plan!

The son of a Muslim father and a Christian mother, Abou Jahjah calls for a secular State that "will also respect religious diversity… provide all individuals and groups the freedom to practice their religion (and) grant its citizens the protection in order to be able of changing religion, or practicing no religion at all without being persecuted or discriminated." (point 11). Despite that, and probably for historical reasons or in order not to completely alienate religious-minded from potential AEL membership, the movement affirms that "the Arab Constitution will refer to Islam as the Religion of the Arab State". It is obvious however that we are here far away from the PJM's imaginative future Islamic realm. For the League in fact, democracy is "the only acceptable system of government" and has links to the Arab tradition. In that context, AEL makes clear its disapproval of the current Arab regimes – albeit falling short from openly denouncing them (point 6).

These ambitious declarations of intentions would have certainly not justified the classification of the Arab-European League among the examples, of political radicalisation within Belgium's 'Muslim community',[32] if it weren't for the discourse and activities with which it has chosen to promote its goals, and, of course, for its attitude regarding the State of Israel. Already in the fourth point of its declarations of intentions, the movement defines itself as "an anti-colonial and anti-Zionist organisation". Point 6 becomes even more explicit: "We reject the Zionist project in Palestine and we call for the dismantling of the Zionist entity and the establishing of a united Palestinian democratic state in all historical Palestine." The terminology of the League is very close to that often used by the Hamas, or the Hizbullah, even if Abou Jahjah's movement does not (at least officially) wish to see the entire Jewish population extinct from an 'historical Palestine' but rather calls for an Arab state where "Arabs and Jews can coexist peacefully enjoying equal rights without any discrimination.".

With an important part of its activities in Belgium concentrated in the city of Antwerp, which also serves as a traditional centre of the country's orthodox Jewish community, the absence of tensions between the latter and the Arab-European League would have been indeed a surprise. In April 2002, the AEL made its debut in the Belgian media by organising a pro-Palestinian demonstration close to Antwerp's Jewish neighbourhood. Condemned by the city's union of mosques, the event degenerated into violence and soon Dyab Abou Jahjah became a household figure in a context marked by the growing popularity of the openly anti-immigrant, far-right-wing party Vlaams Blok in Flanders.[33] It was one of this party's MPs, Filip Dewinter, who triggered the event that gave the movement a visibility without precedent in Belgian annals. A confidential note of the police, announcing an intensification of controls towards youths of Moroccan origin, was in fact transmitted to the Flemish press by the extremist parliamentarian, who was obviously aiming at raising inter-community tension in order to serve his party's scaremongering goals. AEL reacted almost immediately by announcing the creation of Arab squads

---

[32] The term 'Muslim community' of Belgium signifies here not only the believers in Islam but all those who have origins in countries where Islam is the dominant religion and/or cultural tradition.

[33] See *Le Soir*, 23-24 November 2002.

composed of young men who would patrol the city with cameras in order to monitor police excesses against Antwerp's (mainly North African) Arab community. The appearance of the first AEL patrols (dressed in black) on the streets of the Flemish metropolis caused a wave of outrage among all Belgian political parties, greatly increasing the perceived importance of what was in reality a group with no more than 800 members (according to its own estimations).[34] A dreadful coincidence, the assassination of a Moroccan-born young schoolteacher by a 66-year-old pensioner (described as being mentally unstable by the prosecutors) just days after the setting up of the patrols, pushed Antwerp into at least two days of violent riots in which the League played a prominent role. Accusing the AEL of attempting to create areas of no-go for the police, the authorities arrested Abou Jahjah, charging him with conspiracy to cause disorder, whilst Prime-Minister Guy Verhofstadt was announcing an investigation on his movement and the Parliament was debating how to handle the affair.[35]

Eventually, the unrest in Flanders's biggest city calmed down, no incriminating evidence was found regarding AEL's finances nor any links to terrorist groups (a suspicion initiated, again, by the Vlaams Blok, nowadays re-named Vlaams Belang) and Dyab Abou Jahjah was released[36] with a brand new reputation as 'Belgium's Malcolm X'"[37] and a storm of invitations for interviews by media from all over Europe. In the years that followed, the League and its President have fully exploited their prestige as champions of the immigrant youth's cause, establishing a strong branch in

---

[34] BBC News was referring to Abou Jahjah at the time as "Belgium's Arab Leader" (http://news.bbc.co.uk/2/hi/europe/2529683.stm).

[35] To get an idea of how these events were covered by the Belgian and international media, see for example *Le Soir* of 23-24 November 2002, op. cit., *La Libre Belgique* (http://www.lalibre.be/index.php?view=article&art_id=90032
and http://www.lalibre.be/index.php?view=article&art_id=92644), *De Standaard* (http://www.standaard.be/Artikel/Detail.aspx?artikelId=DST21112002_008&word=Dyab+Abou+Jahjah),
or BBC News (http://news.bbc.co.uk/2/hi/europe/2526895.stm,
and http://news.bbc.co.uk/2/hi/europe/2522987.stm)

[36] His trial for these events before the appeals court of Antwerp was still going on at the time these lines were written.

[37] See BBC News:
(http://news.bbc.co.uk/2/hi/programmes/crossing_continents/2847621.stm).

the Netherlands and profiting from different controversial debates in order to make their voice heard.

As mentioned in the previous pages, the AEL did try to translate its visibility into votes by forming a cartel with the Marxist-Leninist Parti du travail de Belgique - Partij van de Arbeid van België (PTB - PVDA) and was not discouraged by its poor electoral results in the federal elections of 2003.[38] Acting in a way that could be viewed as political opportunism given the organisation's and his own secular credo, Abou Jahjah founded soon afterwards the Moslim Democratische Partij (MDP). A month before MDP's first (and last) electoral test, in an interview with "Open Democracy", he was defining himself as a "moderate Muslim", albeit insisting on his Arab-nationalist ideology:

> It is easier to mobilise if you talk only about Islam. But we chose a more difficult and complex route. Having taken up that challenge, we are succeeding despite the obstacles. This is because when you talk to people for a while they realise that their identity is more complex than just their religion. They know it in themselves.[39]

Voters did not seem to share his views, however, and the MDP had a very short existence. After this second electoral defeat, the movement began to concentrate on the political developments in the Middle East, organising demonstrations against the war in Iraq or Israeli occupation of "historical Palestine" and using an increasingly radicalised discourse. During the controversy caused by the caricatures of Muhammad published by a Danish newspaper, the League encouraged the drawing of anti-Semitic, anti-gay or anti-European cartoons in retaliation, and its current website still hosts a couple of particularly heinous ones under the cynical title: "Freedom of speech Campaign".[40] The League had already become so vehemently anti-Israel by then that it didn't hesitate to publish its support for some of the most extremist enemies of the Jewish State.[41]

---

[38] See Dyab Abou Jahjah's interview with Rosemary Bechler of "Open Democracy", op. cit. (http://www.opendemocracy.net).
[39] Ibid.
[40] http://www.arabeuropean.org/newsdetail.php?ID=95
[41] See for example: "*Zionism is racism: Ahmadinajad said it but we mean it*" (http://www.arabeuropean.org/article.php?ID=49).

At the time of the Hizbullah–Israeli conflict of 2006, Dyab Abou Jahjah resigned from the AEL leadership and left for Lebanon in order to join the fighting. He delivered a particularly theatrical adieu to his "comrades":

> This might be the last thing I'll write before going home on a trip that might be my last…I lived my life for this Nation and not a hair in me will hesitate in laying it down for this Nation too. When oppression rises above the sun to cover it, and injustice defies the wind and the Wicked and the Evil feast on the Flesh of innocent men, women and children, from within the darkness and the orgy of blood, a sword will shine, and the brave will murmur: "What a beautiful day to die.[42]

At the end, Mr Abou Jahjah didn't die a martyr, nor did he realise his dreams to see the AEL expanding in France, gaining seats in Antwerp and Utrecht city councils and becoming a European trans-national party.[43] He did continue to write though, with the same militant attitude. His personal diary, *Dagboek Beiroet Brussel*, parts of which were published in the Dutch newspaper *Trouw*[44] betrays however a certain fatigue towards his fellow Arab-Belgian 'compatriots', considered by him to be "very conservative in matters of religion …(and) strictly following an approach that excludes any rationality (een kritiekloze benadering) when it comes to faith in its most orthodox form". Still active within the movement, AEL's former President nowadays has his own blog,[45] from where he keeps attacking 'Zionism', and those of his fellow Belgians of Arab origins who were luckier than him with the voters, or less critical of their country of adoption.[46]

The Arab-European League was still active by May 2008, mostly in Flanders. Its discourse hasn't changed much from its days of glory (the latest item posted on the website was a call for demonstration "against the crimes of the Zionist entity") but its presence in the media was severely

---

[42] http://www.arabeuropean.org/article.php?ID=117
[43] See interview with "Open Democracy", op. cit.
[44] http://www.trouw.nl/deverdieping/overigeartikelen/article690699.ece/Dyab_Abou_Jahjah_Maro
[45] http://www.aboujahjah.com
[46] http://www.aboujahjah.com/?p=110#more-110

reduced and it has never tried to put forward candidates in elections since 2004.

The movement still represents a potential source of severe tension and violent conflict in Brussels and the North of the country, albeit less than it used to, but it seems to have lost a great deal of its credibility among the immigrant youth and to have become rather marginalised within the Belgian Muslim community.

2. Religious, non-political radicalisation

Non-political religious radicalisation can be observed among Belgian Muslims both at an individual and at a collective level. By May 2008, a number of organised radical religious groups without known or openly expressed political ambitions were active in the country. We discuss below the more important and visible among them.

It is, at this point, necessary to keep in mind that the existence of organised groups animated by and practising a 'radical' form of religion – one that totally or partially rejects the ways of society and proposes a conservative interpretation of sacred texts as absolute rules for everyday life – is a phenomenon as old as organised religion itself. Some of these groups have a 'mystic', monastic approach to their self-appointed mission (constantly praying for the salvation of humanity for example), and some other a militant one (proselytising the 'infidels' and calling upon the 'sinners' to repent, in ways that vary, from preaching to coercion). Extreme militancy in a number of these groups leads to violent or even terrorist activities.

It goes of course without saying that immigrants and their sons and daughters are far from being the only category of persons that could be tempted to join these groups. It is interesting to note in this context that converts, born to non-Muslim 'autochthon' parents, constitute a privileged target for some of the most militant among the radical Islamic religious groups in Belgium. It is a sad fact that the only Belgian Muslim who ever committed a suicide attack, Muriel Degauque (in Iraq in 2005), was a convert to Islam of Belgian origin.

By May 2008, a highly diversified but not always inter-related network of Islamic associations was operating in Belgium. The country's capital was home to approximately 39% of all Belgian 'Muslims', 70% of whom were of Moroccan origin.[47] The community was geographically very concentrated (75% of its members were residing in 5 of the 19 municipalities of the Brussels region) and well organised. One could observe that Muslims of Turkish origin have the tendency to more easily set up organisations than their co-religionists of Arab or Berber background.

Milli Görüş

Today a major, if not *the* major movement among religious-minded persons of Turkish origin in Western Europe, Milli constitutes a significant actor in Belgium's Islamic scene. Even though the literal translation of its name, National Vision,[48] bears no mention of Islam, the word Milli does in fact not refer to the Turkish nation but to the Qur'anic notion of 'Millet'.[49]

In Belgium, the organisation has never demonstrated political ambitions. Its actions evolve around strengthening and inspiring Islamic practices among families and youth. It also runs a number of educational institutions and boarding schools. Unlike official Turkish Islam, the Milli Görüş preaches what it considers to be a 'filter-less religion',[50] understood as a close following of the literal meaning of the sacred texts of Islam. It could be said in fact that it takes a rather holistic approach to religion and claims that Islam provides all necessary guiding principles for a Muslim's (everyday) life. These ideas have given the organisation a political dimension in Turkey, where it has traditionally supported political parties sharing its vision.

Despite its Turkish frame of reference, Milli Görüş does place religious identity higher than national affiliation and works for the dissemination of a traditionalist Islamic ideology in a European context. Its discourse and activities seem to progressively take into consideration the

---

[47] See Corinne Torrekens, "Concentration des populations musulmanes et structuration de l'associatif musulman à Bruxelles", *Brussels Studies*, No. 4, 5 March 2007, pp. 1-15.

[48] The name of the organisation refers to the title of a pamphlet published in 1973 by Turkish politician Necmettin Erbakan.

[49] For further information, see http://www.igmg.de/verband/islamic-community-milli-goerues/what-does-milli-goerues-mean.html.

[50] Interview by the authors with a representative of Milli Görüş in Belgium.

need of the community's full integration in Belgian society and it has recently began to propose Koranic courses in French and Dutch.

Currently, the organisation has a significant number of adherents in the provinces of Limburg (Flanders), Hainaut (Wallonia) and in the Brussels-Capital region. They all operate under the name *Belçika-Islam Federasyonu*, the Islamic Federation of Belgium, established in 1986. It estimates that its members constitute up to 30% of all persons of Turkish origin living in Belgium, and attributes its influence to its operating of some 30 mosques.

Süleymancilar

Founded in Turkey during the 1940s by Süleyman Hilmi Tunahan, Süleymancilar began its activities in Western Europe in 1973. Its followers, the Süleymancis, attribute saintly powers to the founder and call themselves the 'disciples of Süleyman', being often accused of being heretics despite the fact that they claim not to constitute a sect.

The movement is thought to be the first of its kind established among the Turkish immigrants living in Europe. An Islamic judge under the Ottoman Süleyman Hilmi Tunahan was disenchanted by the attitude of the secular Turkish Republic towards Islam. His (and the movement's) activities have thus taken the form of opposition to the new regime, responsible for the abolition of the Islamic Caliphate, which Süleymancilar still strives to restore albeit by non-violent means. In Turkey, its Koranic schools oppose the official Imam-Hatip schools that are under the control of the secular authorities, and they are often identified with (right-wing) radical extremism.[51] Notwithstanding that, the organisation has no (known) political activities or ambitions in Belgium.

Today, Its members concentrate on changing secular practices among the society through the setting up of new mosques and education facilities, as well as through publications and lectures, notably in Antwerp, in Brussels and in the province of Limburg. The movement is in fact running approximately 13 Islamic cultural centres throughout Belgium, called Belçika Islam Kültür Merkezleri Birliği. Unlike Milli Görüş, it is very discreet when it comes to publicity and it does not seek many contacts with

---

[51] Jørgen Nielsen, *Muslims in Western Europe*, Edinburgh: Edinburgh University Press, 3rd Edition, 2004, p. 150.

other organisations or the political authorities. Hence, it is not considered to be a major actor in the national debates concerning Islam or the integration of Turkish immigrants in Belgian society.[52]

Tablighi

Jama'at al-Tabligh was founded by Mohamed Ilyas (1885-1944) in the first half of the 20th century in Northern India. The centre of the movement is located in Nizam ud-Din, in the vicinity of Delhi.

This religious movement has at times been labelled as "Islam's Jehovah's Witnesses", mainly because of its organisational structure and activities, which evolve around mobile Koranic schools (*madrassa's*), door-to door proselytising and continuously renewed preaching teams, formed by volunteers trained to reach even those parts of the population generally ignored by similar other groups.

Peaceful behaviour constitutes a key notion for the Tablighi, since according to their founder a religious act can never result from coercion. As a consequence, the movement claims not to be interested in any quest for (political) power and its members observe strict neutrality towards political parties, viewing them as a cause of division among Muslims. Tablighis practice a radical form of Islam, studying the scripture and transmitting[53] the faith. They believe in a struggle to imitate the way of life of the prophet, with poverty, simple ways and a meticulous regulation of corporeal facts and gestures. The nucleus of the organisation is in fact formed by a relatively small number of such missionaries.

In Belgium Tablighi is active within different mosques and non-profit-making associations, the first and most central of which was established in 1975. Since the 1980s it has became more visible in all parts of Belgium and has obtained a legally recognised status.[54] Because of their strong organisation, the movement has quickly managed to become the first effective and successful alternative for an 'Islam of the people' in the

---

[52] Meryem Kanmaz, "Des organisations turques aux fédérations flamandes: 40 ans de vie associative en Flandre", *Nouvelle Tribune*, No. 34, December 2003.

[53] *Tablîgh* (Arabic) can be translated as "transmission" or as "conveyance" and hence as conveyance or transmission of a message.

[54] See Felice Dassetto, *Le Tabligh en Belgique. Diffuser l'Islam sur les traces du Prophète*, Louvain-la-Neuve: Academia, Sydibi papers, Vol. 2, 1988, p. 14, fn 15.

country and by 1985 it was able to set up a Federation of Mosques and Cultural Islamic Organisations (Fédération des Mosquées et des Associations Culturelles et Islamiques de Belgique). This federation gradually evolved, cunningly using the attention of the media, into a very influential element within Belgian Islam. Since the 1990s, however, the movement appears to have lost some of its influence, notably amongst the younger generation.[55] Most of its members today seem to be of Moroccan origin, although the organisation can still count on the loyalty of many well connected Pakistanis as well.

Muslim Brotherhood

The Jama'iyyat al-ikhwân al-muslimîn, very well known for its actions in the Middle East, is particularly active among Muslims of Arab origin in Belgium. Composed of a myriad of fractions, the 'brothers' are also divided between an Egyptian and a Syrian 'obedience'. The organisation seems to raise members and sympathisers by proposing an authentic religious discourse that does not resent the reform of some of the most antiquated traditions and encourages the merging of the faithful within their host societies. Its activities in Belgium mainly evolve around preaching and education with an emphasis on the renewal of moral norms.

Hizbullah

The 'party of God' is also present in Belgium, albeit not significantly so. Its members seem to be working to raise funds to finance its Lebanese activities. It is mentioned here mainly because of its purely religious activities, which include preaching and dissemination of sermons. Even these endeavours however are most often framed within a discourse denouncing the Israeli occupation of Palestine,[56] whilst issues proper to the Muslim community of Belgium do not seem to belong to its top priorities. It is interesting to mention that Hizbullah is one of the few Shiite organisations in the overwhelmingly Sunni landscape of Islamic movements in Europe.

---

[55] Brigitte Maréchal, "Courants fondamentalistes en Belgique", *Journal d'étude des relations internationales au Moyen-Orient (MERIA)*, Vol. 3, No. 1, March 2008, pp. 65-78.

[56] The most recent (small) demonstration with a 'free Palestine' theme organised by the movement took place in the centre of Brussels on Sunday, 4 May 2008.

Other Groups

Belgian citizens or residents belonging to Sufi orders have organised themselves according to different traditions of Islamic mysticism. The most significant ones include the Naqshbandiyya (with different branches), the Barelwi (originating from the Indian peninsula), the Deobandi (reformist soufis focusing on traditional learning) and the Nurcu (attaching particular attention to personal devotion and the compatibility of Islamic revelation with discoveries in natural science). Very few Belgian Muslims (of Turkish origin concentrated mainly in Liège) are believed to be members of Kaplancilar,[57] an Islamic movement outlawed in Germany.

3.   National/Ethnic Tensions

Our analysis of the landscape of the Belgian Muslim community could not be complete without the discussion of groups whose activities are related to the politics of the countries of origin of its members. Such groups are particularly present in the associative life of Turkish immigrants: It is believed in fact that the combination of interlinked dynamics such as economic exclusion due to rural origins, cultural and linguistic marginalisation and residential concentration made it possible for Turkish immigrants to keep very close links with their home country.[58]

Indeed, for many among the Turkish community in Brussels, nationalism provides an overarching framework for self-definition. To quote a Belgian politician of Turkish descent, "regardless of their stance in the political spectrum, everyone is a bit of a nationalist here".[59] The results of a survey[60] very recently conducted indicate in fact that 42% of Belgian-Turks feel equally close to their country of residence and to that of origin. According to the same research, their close attachment to the home country does not seem to decrease according to the length of the period they have been residing abroad or according to their political affiliation. Thus, even

---

[57] Ural Manço, "Des organisations socio-politiques comme solidarités islamiques dans l'immigration turque en Europe", *Les Annales de l'Autre Islam*, Institut national des Langues et des Civilisations orientales, No. 4, 1997, pp. 97-133.

[58] Ibid.

[59] Interview with the authors, our translation.

[60] Ayhan Kaya and Ferhat Kentel,*Belgian-Turks: A Bridge or a Breach between Turkey and the European Union?*, Brussels: King Baudouin Foundation, 2007, p. 52.

groups such as the Milli Görüş, which aim to address Belgian Muslims rather than Belgian Turks, would have had a hard time recruiting members if they'd dare to completely estrange themselves from the notion of Turkishness.

Milli Görüş' participation in the organisation of a demonstration entitled "Condemning the terror – Invitation to solidarity" can be seen as an acknowledgement of this fact. The event in question took place in Brussels on 3 November 2007, and its analysis is very helpful in understanding the current feelings within the Turkish community in Belgium.

At the end of October 2007, the killing of 12 soldiers by PKK in an ambush in the Southeast of Turkey led to violent reactions throughout Europe. In Brussels, Turkish youngsters, mostly teenagers, demonstrated their anger in the streets of Schaarbeek – mainly along the Chaussée de Haecht which is heavily populated by Turkish immigrants. The protest degenerated into acts of vandalism (breaking the glass windows of cafés, throwing stones at the police, beating up journalists, etc.), widely attributed by the Belgian media to ultra-nationalist groups. Even though such groups were also to be blamed for the aggression, the media coverage of the events underestimated the complex nature of the youngsters' behaviour.

Of course, the deep-rooted rivalries between the Turkish and the Kurdish populations have played a significant role in the genesis of the violence and so have done the extreme-right wing organisations. It is not by coincidence that the Turkish youngsters attacked cafés and shops known to be owned by Kurds. These intolerable acts were indeed committed by a band of Turkish ultra-nationalists and a number of ill-advised teenagers who received SMS and e-mails about the venue and time of the demonstration from sources they have refused to name. The Turkish associations of Brussels said to be unaware of the senders of these messages and claimed that they believed the manifestation to be spontaneous. Both the silence of the youngsters and their elders, and the fact that many inhabitants of the area have shown their sympathy to those arrested by driving around in cars bearing Grey Wolves stickers[61] is an indicator of the vulnerability of the Turkish population in Schaarbeek to radical nationalist discourse.

---

[61] Kaya and Kentel, op. cit., p. 40. See below for more on the Grey Wolves.

But the youngsters who demonstrated against the PKK have been also particularly aggressive towards the Belgian police. Far from being impulsive behaviour, this reflects a wider frustration caused by their perception of the way the Belgian authorities dealt with the issue. Many Belgian Turks felt in fact that they had been unfairly treated and that their grief had not been respected, an impression shared and spread by the major community organisations. Moreover, several Turkish-speaking media have accused Belgium of being tolerant towards the activities of organisations considered to be terroristic in Turkey.[62] The escape of Fehriye Erdal, from the hands of the Belgian justice whilst she was wanted for murder in Turkey, has contributed to this feeling.

One of the reasons many within the Turkish community are eager to condone nationalistic discourse is their economic and educational situation, which seems to be worse than that of other immigrant groups.[63] Coupled with the Belgian Turks' tendency to concentrate their residencies,[64] this situation provides the perfect ground for nationalist discourses to flourish. Hence, a triggering event such as the killing of soldiers in the Southeast of

---

[62] See for example, http://yenisafak.com.tr/arsiv/2002/mayis/05/g7.html, http://www.belturk.be/go.php?go=3031562&do=details&return=summary, http://www.euractiv.com.tr/ab-ve-turkiye/article/belcikada-okullarda-pkk-propagandasi, http://www.belturk.be/go.php?go=3030952&do=details&return=summary&pg=125.

[63] A number of studies confirm this; see in particular Ural Manço and Altay Manço, "La scolarité des enfants issus de l'immigration musulmane: difficultés et actions positives", in U. Manço (ed.), *Voix et voies musulmanes de Belgique*, Brussels: Publications des Facultés Universitaires, 2000.

Saint-Louis, pp. 41–54., Ural Manço (2001), *Populations musulmanes de Belgique et la stratification du marché du travail*, Hasan Bousetta and Laure-Anne Bernes (2007), "Muslims in the EU: Cities Report, Belgium", Open Society Institute, EU Monitoring and Advocacy Program, Ayhan Kaya and Ferhat Kentel (2007), *Belgian-Turks: A Bridge or a Breach between Turkey and the European Union?*, Brussels: King Baudouin Foundation.

[64] To understand how the policies of the municipality in which the Turkish community lives can contribute to their marginalisation, see Ural Manço and Meryem Kanmaz, "From Conflict to Co-operation between Muslims and Local Authorities in a Brussels Borough: Schaerbeek", *Journal of Ethnic and Migration Studies*, 31 (6), 2005, pp. 1105-1123.

Turkey, combined with a provocation orchestrated by the ultra-nationalist groups, is sufficient to provoke serious tensions. Failing to understand the complexity of these sociological dynamics could largely undermine the effectiveness of policies aiming at addressing the issues creating them and their (more visible) effects.

Tensions between a big part of the Belgian Turkish community and the Turkish authorities in Belgium should be also taken into consideration in the analysis of the November 2007 events. Many have in fact criticised the Turkish embassy for downplaying their national sensitivities. At the same time, the embassy's failure to address in a sensitive manner the community's feelings has facilitated the stirring up of these feelings by the ultra-nationalists, leading eventually to the violent demonstrations.[65] Criticism has also been addressed to Belgian politicians of Turkish descent. Instead of intervening in order to calm feelings, a number of them have allegedly tried to increase their popularity by using a 'double discourse', including statements such as "We are all soldiers".[66]

We have tried to demonstrate that radical nationalistic groups are not solely responsible for the violence and conflict within Belgium's Turkish community. In the sections that follow we discuss a number of movements that exalt ethnic identity among Belgians of immigrant origin and that might become a source of serious tensions in the years to come.

Grey Wolves

Although its formal name in Turkish is Ülkücüler, the youth organisation of the Turkish Nationalist Movement Party (MHP) is better known as the 'Grey Wolves', a reference to a Turkic legend in which a female wolf is believed to have fed a wounded boy and to have helped him reproduce a new generation of Turks.

The Ülkücü ideology puts accent on Turkish history insisting on its glorious days and exploiting events such as the establishment of the first Turkish States in Central Asia, almost tracing a 'Turkish race'.[67] At the

---

[65] This might actually reveal a wider trend for the survey study of Kaya and Kentel, op. cit., p. 40, show that only 7% of the Belgian-Turks reported that they appreciate the efforts of official Turkish bodies in Belgium.

[66] Evening news bulletin of the Belgian channel *La Une* on 26 October 2007.

[67] See the official webside of the Ülkücü (http://www.ulkuocaklari.org.tr/).

same time, its conception of the Turkish nation is blended with Islam. The principle of what they consider to be the synthesis of Turkishness and Islam is very dominant in their rhetoric and activities. Mottos like "Your doctor will be a Turk and your medicine will be Islam" reflect their feelings on the issue. The Wolves are also characterised by a strong emphasis on leadership and hierarchical, military-like organisation.

In Belgium, the largest among the organisations considered to be affiliated with or sympathetic to the Wolves is the Belçika Türk Federasyonu (BTF). BTF came under considerable criticism during the 2006 regional and local elections when mainstream parties such as the Parti Socialiste (PS) and the Centre Démocrate Humaniste (CDH) chose to include BTF members or sympathisers on their lists of candidates and were thus accused by Belgian media at belonging to a fascist ultra-nationalistic movement.[68] In fact, some of these candidates have regularly attended organised events of a nationalistic character, such as the ceremony to commemorate the death of the "Great Turkish Idealist leader"[69] Alparslan Türkeş, founder of the Nationalist Movement Party in Turkey.

The official aim of the Grey Wolves in Belgium is to foster loyalty among young people of Turkish origin to their ancestral culture, religion and history and to keep alive the Turkish identity in Europe.[70] BTF claims to oppose not the integration of Belgian-Turks into their host society but rather their assimilation by it. Most of its activities seem to be centred on issues relevant to Turkish national sensitivities. It has a strong stance towards the Armenian genocide controversy and the Kurdish question and its demonstrations, such as, for example the one against the erection of an Armenian monument in Brussels, have often led to violence and/or tensions between members of different communities.

---

[68] To read a few press articles, see http://archive.indymedia.be/news/2003/07/70265.html, http://www.lesoir.be/regions/bruxelles/2006/08/25/article_van_gorp_chez_l_extreme_droite_turque.shtml

[69] Our translation from the speech of the President of the BTF.

[70] Emre Arslan, "Turkish Ultra-nationalism in Germany: Its Transnational Dimension", in Thomas Faist and Eyüp Özveren (eds), *Transnational Social Spaces: Agents, Networks and Institutions*, Ashgate Publishing, 2004, p. 134.

Kurdish Institute of Brussels

The association was established in 1978 in order to raise awareness of the Kurdish cause and to help the integration process of Kurdish immigrants. Its activities have always been in line with this double objective. The institute organises many cultural events such as concerts and folkloric dance shows in order to better acquaint Belgian society with Kurdish civilisation. Largely dominated by Turkish Kurds, it also assists the immigrants by offering French, Dutch and Kurdish language courses. In parallel to these activities, the Kurdish Institute has a very explicit political agenda, served by other actions, such as press conferences or demonstrations, designed to draw attention to violations of human rights in Turkey and the precarious situation of the Kurdish people in the Southeast of the Republic. These actions are sometimes organised jointly with other associations of immigrant groups with issues against past and present Turkish policies, such as its stance vis-à-vis the Armenians.

Belgium also hosts other Kurdish organisations active in promoting the Kurdish national cause, such as the Kurdish Cultural Centre or the Confederation of Kurdish Associations in Europe. At the time of publication, the latter was pursuing a campaign to prevent Europeans from going to Turkey for holidays arguing that their money would be financing the war against Kurds. The campaign in question is an example of how issues relating to the homeland politics can cause tension in the host country.

All these organisations are looked upon with suspicion by Belgium's Turkish associations. The latter believe them to be supporters or sympathisers of the PKK, and demand that they denounce it as a terrorist organisation before entering into dialogue with them.[71] The Kurdish organisations refrain from condemning PKK's acts but they often underline that their problem is not with the Turkish people as such but with the politics of Turkey.[72] Thus, for the time being a constructive dialogue between the two communities seems rather unlikely. This lack of

---

[71] As remarked in interviews with representatives of local Turkish associations and the comments by the secretary-general of the EYAD in a broadcasted debate on Télé-Bruxelles on 4 November 2007, following the violent events.

[72] As stated by the representative of the Kurdish Cultural Centre in a Broadcasted debate on Télé-Bruxelles on 4 November 2007, following the violent events.

communication is further accelerated by physical separation. While Belgian Turks predominantly live and socialise in Schaarbeek, Kurds reside in the neighbourhood of Saint Josse.

Conclusions

Our research and interviews suggest that the majority of Muslim Belgians seem to have embraced the spirit of compromise and moderation prevalent in the country's political scene. Despite the presence of several radical movements within its borders, Belgium in fact was largely spared the very serious violence and conflict that were recently experienced by some of the neighbouring countries with large populations of Islamic cultural backgrounds.

Nevertheless, a number of the groups and movements discussed have indeed represented a challenge to the peaceful co-existence between Belgian society's cultural components and the attempt to create a distinctively Belgian Islam is far from bearing fruit.

One of the most important conclusions to draw from this brief study is the considerable antithesis between the visibility and mediatisation of radical movements and the very poor results they have obtained every time they have tried to transform their alleged popularity into electoral gains. It seems to us in fact that the attention often given by the media to such movements is attributable more to a quest for the dramatic and sensational than to a genuine wish to raise awareness about the different tendencies within Belgium's relatively large Muslim community.

Even the most radical organisations in the country's Muslim community have never really been the cause of an incident more serious than the usual tensions one witnesses at the end of football competitions between long-standing rivals. At the same time, however, an important number of initiatives and activities launched and carried out by other groups originating from the same community but striving for much less provocative or spectacular effects are barely mentioned, with the excuse that they concern only a minority of Belgian Muslims. It is our belief however, that electoral results are a very reliable test of real popularity and one that none of the radical groups that often occupy the national and regional television channels or newspaper front pages has managed to pass.

Many Belgian citizens of Islamic cultural background in fact deeply disapprove of radicalisation tendencies within their community and wholeheartedly condemn all criminal acts. These citizens appreciate what they experience as being the benefits of living in Belgium (freedom of religion, freedom of speech,...). And unfortunately, these citizens are the first victims of the stigmatisation of "the Muslims in Belgium" or the "Moroccans/Turks in Belgium", as a consequence of unfounded generalisations, or manipulation of public opinion by extreme right-wing political parties, such as the Vlaams Belang.

As is well known, religion can be both a personal 'mystical' experience and a collective one. In Belgium, as in several other countries, many youngsters born to immigrant parents (and not only) feel alienated by both the cultural values of their families and those of the society surrounding them. In search of stronger beliefs that could provide them with a feeling of belonging, these youngsters are often tempted by radical groups, where such a feeling is particularly stressed. Inside such groups their energy is channelled into activities designed to make them feel accepted, important and even self-righteous, when many among their 'autochthon' compatriots are quick to collectively hold them responsible for anti-social behaviour or an alleged rise of criminality.[73] At the same time, membership/participation in such movements offers them the opportunity to express their discontentment, in a way that is 'dignified' by the prestige of a great religious/cultural tradition, with what they perceive as being unfair treatment by Belgian authorities and society as well as with their own parents' attitude towards them (and towards life in general). This is not an unavoidable or irreversible process, however, and it is important to keep in mind, as we have already discussed elsewhere,[74] that, far from being static, identity is a dynamic process, a conception that is lived and experienced day by day in an ever-changing/evolving society and throughout life. As such, identity has by definition a changing nature. It is something that can be easily claimed but cannot be authoritatively attributed.

---

[73] On this topic, see Ed Husain, *The Islamist: Why I joined radical Islam in Britain, what I saw inside and why I left*, London: Penguin Books, 2007.

[74] See Theodoros Koutroubas and Ward Vloeberghs, "De l'identité imputée: à propos de l'islam comme appartenance ethnique", *La Revue Générale*, February 2008, pp. 33-38.

In a multicultural society such as ours the risk of micro conflicts is always present and in fact unavoidable. The realities we have analysed can easily lead us to predict that issues such as evolution of the political situation in Iraq and the related reaction of Turkey is likely to create tensions between the Turkish and Kurdish communities living in Belgium. Likewise, the liberation of Palestine will continue to be a major issue of mobilisation and tension for Belgian residents with Arab sensibilities and groups such as the ones we have observed will certainly try to capitalise on the unrest. And of course, xenophobic and fear-mongering parties in both the North and the South of the country are likely to use tensions (or an eventual terrorist attack) as grounds for promoting their own agendas.

On the whole, however, Belgium's Muslims are likely to remain no more radicalised than their Christian or their Jewish compatriots. At a time when religious radicalisation has become almost synonymous with Islamic radicalisation, it is important to remember that the need for political parties that express religious concerns or are inspired by a faith-based world view is present in all communities and is not likely to disappear as long as there are persons who place faith high among their priorities. As for political radicalisation, the phenomenon does occur in Belgium in many contexts, and unfortunately no faith, language, culture or any other element-based community is immune.[75]

Can we say that everything is ok then? No, it is not. Youngsters of immigrant origin, who feel excluded from both their parents' culture and their autochthon compatriots' world, constitute a huge potential source of tension and an easy prey for radical groups. There are many of them in Belgium, but fortunately they are not yet lost to our society.

---

[75] As witness to this statement, a book published in Brussels by the city's Dutch-speaking free university in 2001 discusses the rise and fall of radicalisation in Belgium (seen as leftist – liberal thought) without even mentioning Islam as a relevant issue. See Johan Basiliades, "De lotgevallen van het radicalisme in België. Het ontstaan, de opkomst en de ondergang van een negentiende-eeuwse links-liberale stroming", in Sven Gatz and Patrick Stouthuysen (eds), *Een vierde weg? Links-liberalisme als traditie en als oriëntatiepunt*, Brussel: VUB Press, 2001, pp. 33-62.

5. MUSLIMS IN THE NETHERLANDS: TENSIONS AND VIOLENT CONFLICT
TINKA VELDHUIS & EDWIN BAKKER

The release of the anti-Islam movie "Fitna" by the Dutch Member of Parliament Geert Wilders, early 2008, aroused anxious fears of angry responses by Muslims communities. As happened in the Danish cartoon crisis, people expected the movie to trigger violent demonstrations, boycotts, the burning of flags and other aggressive responses by Muslim communities, both in the Netherlands and around the world. Months prior to the actual release of the movie, the Dutch prime minister already spoke of a crisis, predicting violent confrontations between Muslims and non-Muslims, and devastating consequences for Muslim integration in Dutch society.

Contrary to the wide anticipation that Muslims would respond violently to the movie, there were few incidents. In the Netherlands, there were no noticeable incidents at all. Eloquent young Muslims stepped forward as representatives for their communities and of Islam, explicitly distancing themselves from radical or violent action by Muslims in answer to the film. Likewise, orthodox Muslims made strong pleas to react in a non-violent and dignified way to "Fitna". Outside the Netherlands, there were only a few incidents, like the attack on a Dutch consulate in Indonesia by a group of students and the expected burning of the Dutch flag in countries like Afghanistan.

Nevertheless, the Dutch fear of violence involving Muslims typifies the implicit association that people easily seem to make between Muslims and violence. Almost irrespective of the actual level of violent incidents, Muslims seem to project an image of responding violently to every political incident. How did this image come into being? In the Netherlands, what types of incidents and developments have occurred that led to potentially violent tensions and conflicts in which Muslims were involved?

This chapter seeks to answer this question. For that purpose, it first elaborates on radicalisation and on tensions and violent conflicts, both within and between social groups, and on the underlying mechanisms that are responsible for causing inter-group conflicts. Thereafter, we give an overview of radicalisation and tensions and violent conflicts involving (elements of) Muslim communities in the Netherlands. We focus on three different categories of events: Muslims 'attacking' non-Muslims, non-Muslims 'attacking' Muslims and confrontations between or within Muslim communities. In the concluding part, we elaborate on global trends regarding the peaceful or not-so-peaceful co-existence of different social groups and focus on the current situation in the Netherlands.

1.   Tensions, conflicts and radicalisation

Essentially, we are interested in types of incidents and developments that have or may have posed a threat to a) the democratic order, b) society at large or c) that have or may have otherwise undermined integration of minorities or relations between and within social groups in the Netherlands. That is, the focus lies on violent incidents, or incidents that may potentially have led to violent outcomes.

For example, in October 2007, Bilal Bajaka, a young Dutch Muslim from Moroccan descent, entered a police station in Amsterdam, pulled a knife and stabbed two police officers. In self-defence, one of the officers shot the man who died on the spot. Immediately, the incident prompted questions about the perpetrator's motivations. Was Bajaka a radical Islamist, inspired by fundamentalist ideologies and beliefs that instructed him to attack any representation of the Dutch state? Was this an act of terrorism or was the perpetrator simply a criminal whose acts were not religiously or politically charged? It was rapidly publicised that Bajaka was probably not radicalised; apparently, he was a suicidal schizophrenic who had just left a psychiatric clinic where he had been treated for mental problems. Nevertheless, especially after it turned out that in 2005, Bajaka had had loose contacts with some of the members of the Hofstadgroep – the radical network that included the murderer of filmmaker Theo van Gogh – the media started speculating about whether Bajaka was a radical Islamist and whether the Netherlands was the target of a terrorist attack. Although the Bajaka case was unrelated to radicalisation or terrorism, the incident triggered riots among young Muslims in immigrant neighbourhoods in Amsterdam and fuelled tensions between Muslim and the non-Muslim communities in the Netherlands.

The foregoing example illustrates the implicit association that is often made between incidents involving Muslims and radicalisation, although this link is often not justified. Particularly after the assassination of Theo van Gogh, who was murdered by a radical Islamist named Mohammed Bouyeri, radicalisation of Muslim youth received extensive attention by Dutch media, policy-makers, politicians and academics. Radicalisation is only one manifestation of intergroup conflicts, however, and in contrast to what often seems to be popular belief, most Muslim-involving tensions and conflicts are not associated with radicalisation. In fact, radicalisation of Muslims is a very rare phenomenon. In comparison with other European countries, the Netherlands is home to a relatively large Muslim community: according to the latest estimations, over 857,000 Muslims live in the Netherlands, comprising approximately 5% of the total population.[1] According to the Dutch Minister of Integration, between 20,000 and 30,000 of them are potentially attracted to Salafi ideologies, and yet another 2,500 might be susceptible to violent radicalisation.[2] The latter figure represents only a mere 0.3 percent of the total Muslim population. Although radicalisation of Muslims can have profound societal consequences, it is quite rare.

1.1 *Defining radicalisation*

What is radicalisation exactly? Despite the increased scientific attention to radicalisation and its causes and consequences, scholars have not yet developed a generally accepted definition. Nevertheless, faced with pressure to tackle radicalisation, policy-makers have developed a few definitions. In particular, the European Commission came up with a clear and frequently applied definition of violent radicalisation: "The phenomenon of people embracing opinions, views, and ideas which could

---

[1] Centraal Bureau voor de Statistiek (2007), "Naar een nieuwe schatting van het aantal islamieten in Nederland" (Towards a new estimate of the number of islamists in the Netherlands), CBS (http://www.cbs.nl).

[2] R. Kloor (2007), *Radicale Islamstroming Islamisme Rukt Op* (Radical Islam movement Islamism progresses), Elsevier, 5 September.

lead to acts of terrorism".[3] This definition accounts for a few distinct features of radicalisation that illustrate the differences with other types of tensions and conflicts.

Primarily, although it can occur very rapidly, radicalisation is a gradual process that has no strictly specified beginning or end. It is a twofold process including a shift in thinking towards fundamentalism and a heightened readiness to act on behalf of a cause. Secondly, its gradual nature indicates that in most cases, the direct causes or triggers of radicalisation are unclear and can even be unknown to the radicalising person. Rather, radicalisation is the product of a combination of causal factors that interact and that is unique for every individual.[4] People are drawn to radical movements or ideologies for different reasons, of which some are more conscious than others. Whereas some are primarily inspired by ideological or political motivations, others might simply be attracted by action and adventure or seek group membership to obtain a positive identity. Even more so, radicalisation can occur beyond the consciousness of the relevant person, who might not be aware that he or she is in a process of radicalisation.

Again, the Bajaka case, which was unrelated to radicalisation but triggered violent behaviour by young Muslims in Amsterdam, illustrates how radicalisation is only one factor in the emergence of tensions and conflicts involving Muslims. Therefore, the present study aims to widen the scope and focuses on a broad spectrum of incidents and developments that, over the last three decades, have led to tensions and conflicts, including cases of radicalisation, in which elements of the Muslim community have been involved. In doing so, however, one essential question deserves further exploration. How do tensions and conflicts between social groups emerge and under what circumstances are they likely to be sustained and result in violent outcomes?

---

[3] European Commission (2006), Terrorist recruitment: Commission Communication addressing the factors contributing to violent radicalisation, MEMO/05/329.

[4] T.M. Veldhuis and E. Bakker (2007), "Causale factoren van radicalisering en hun onderlinge samenhang" (Causal factors of radicalisering and their mutual consistency), *Vrede & Veiligheid*, 36 (4): 447-470.

1.2 Inter-group tensions and violent conflicts

The first academic notions on the origins of inter-group tensions and conflicts date back several decades. Initially, the main premise was that realistic competition between groups leads to favouritism of the own group (in-group) and hostility towards other groups (out-groups).[5] Since that time, however, our understanding of the wellspring of inter-group conflicts has grown considerably sophisticated. Decades of empirical investigations of the roots of inter-group conflict have reached the conclusion that, irrespective of the presence of competition or conflicting group interests, the mere act of categorising individuals into groups can generate tensions and conflicts between groups.[6] According to social identity approaches and self-categorisation theories,[7] people define themselves not so much in terms of self, but rather in terms of group membership. People are driven by a powerful need to belong,[8] and simply categorising people based on random, meaningless associations like colour preference or even by the flip of a coin, can trigger the sense of belongingness in people. To feel good about themselves, people thus need to feel good about the group and seek collective self-esteem.[9] In doing so, people make biased judgments. For

---

[5] See for example, M. Sherif and C.W. Sherif (1953), "Groups in harmony and tension", New York, NY: Harper & Row; M. Sherif (1966), *In common predicament: Social psychology of intergroup conflict and cooperation*, Boston: Houghton-Mifflin.

[6] E.g. H. Tajfel (1970), "Experiments in inter-group discrimination", *Scientific American*, 223, pp. 96-102; Tajfel and Turner, 1989.

[7] H. Tajfel and J.C. Turner (1979), "An integrative theory of intergroup conflict", in W.G. Austin and S. Worchel (eds), *The social psychology of intergroup relations*, Monterey, CA: Brooks-Cole, pp. 33–47; N. Ellemers, R. Spears and B. Doosje (2002), "Self and Social Identity", *Annual Review of Psychology*, Vol. 53, pp. 161-186; J.C. Turner (1982), "Towards a cognitive redefinition of the social group", in H. Tajfel (ed.), *Social identity and intergroup relations*, Cambridge: Cambridge University Press, pp. 15-40; J.C. Turner (1984), "Social identification and psychological group formation", in H. Tajfel (ed.), *The social dimension: European developments in social psychology*, Cambridge: Cambridge University Press, pp. 518–538.

[8] R.F. Baumeister and M.R. Leary (1995), "The need to belong: Desire for interpersonal attachments as a fundamental human motivation", *Psychological Bulletin*, Vol. 117, No. 3, pp. 497-529.

[9] J. Crocker and R. Luhtanen (1990), "Collective self-esteem and ingroup bias", *Journal of Personality and Social Psychology*, 58, pp. 60-67.

example, they tend to attribute superiority to the in-group over out-groups and derogate other groups and their characteristics as inferior. In addition, they tend to believe that whereas the in-group is heterogeneous, members of the out-group are all similar to one another[10] and very different from members of the in-group.[11] Hence, the mere perception that one belongs to a social group can be sufficient to activate stereotypes and discrimination of out-groups and can eventually result in violence between groups.

Having said this, two important implications become clear if we look at how conflicts involving Muslims can emerge. First, an identity crisis can have profound consequences for people's well-being and behaviour. An identity crisis can arise under various circumstances, for example, when the group we wish to affiliate with rejects us or when we are unsure which group we identify with. Scholars often suggest that many young, second-generation Muslims in the West face an identity crisis.[12] On the one hand, they face a generational conflict with their parents. On the other, they do not feel fully accepted by Dutch society. Buijs and his colleagues,[13] for example, suggest that Moroccan youngsters in the Netherlands feel alienated from both their parents and Dutch society and have a hybrid-identity that is not recognised and accepted by their direct environment. Consequently, they find a satisfactory identity in the *Ummah* that connects them with other Muslims and for which nationality, be it Moroccan or Dutch, becomes irrelevant.

---

[10] P.W. Linville and E.E. Jones (1980), "Polarised appraisals of out-group member", *Journal of Personality and Social Psychology*, 38, pp. 689-703; P.W. Linville, G.W. Fischer and P. Salovey (1989), "Perceived distributions of the characteristics of ingroup and outgroup members", *Journal of Personality and Social Psychology*, 57, pp. 165-188.

[11] T.F. Pettigrew (1997), "The affective component of prejudice: Empirical support for the new view", in S.A. Tuch and J.K. Martin (eds), *Racial attitudes in the 1990s: Continuity and change*, Westport, CT: Praeger, pp. 76-90.

[12] T. Choudhury (2007), *The Role of Muslim Identity Politics in Radicalisation (A Study in Progress)*, London: Department for Communities and Local Government; S. Malik (2007), "My brother the bomber", *Prospect Magazine*, 31 May.

[13] F.J. Buijs, F. Demant and A. Hamdy (2006), *Strijders van eigen bodem. Radicale en democratische moslims in Nederland* (Worriers of own soil. Radical and democratic Muslims in the Netherlands), Amsterdam: Amsterdam University Press.

Second, once people have categorised themselves into a social group and this group has become an important part of their social identity, issues that concern the group also concern the individual. This implies that members of a group will perceive and treat a threat to the group as a personal threat.[14] Given that Muslims perceived the anti-Islam film "Fitna" as an illegitimate assault on Islam, the release of the movie definitely had the potential to result in violent outcomes. Indeed, prior to the release of "Fitna" the public, the media and even the government suspiciously eyed the Muslim community in anxious anticipation of violent responses. Fortunately, violent manifestations remained absent but the release illustrates how incidents that prompt a sense of being threatened among Muslims can easily erupt in violent outbursts or otherwise negatively affect inter-group relations with Muslim communities.

2. Radicalisation and organised groups

In the Netherlands of today, Muslim communities are – rightly or wrongly – associated with tensions, violence and radicalisation. It should be stressed that this is a rather new perception. In the past Muslims were at first associated with work many Dutch no longer wanted to do. During the 1960s and 1970s, the larger Dutch companies recruited a considerable number of so-called 'guest workers' from Turkey and Morocco. Additionally, refugees and immigrants from former colonies like the Antilles, Suriname and Indonesia were arriving in substantial numbers and creating large communities of immigrants in the Netherlands. Initially, guest workers were encouraged to return home as soon as the Dutch labour market no longer required their services, but most did not. On the contrary, a process of family reunification took place, bringing thousands of new immigrants, mainly women and children. Since the early 1980s, sizable communities emerged from Morocco, Turkey, and Suriname, mainly concentrated in the larger cities and industrial areas. During this period, the Netherlands experienced its first encounters with radical Islam and tensions between Muslims and non-Muslims. Naturally, the societal

---

[14] See e.g. E.R. Smith (1993), "Social Identity and Social Emotions: Toward new conceptualisations of prejudice", in D.M. Mackie and D.L. Hamilton (eds), *Affect, cognition, and stereotyping: Interactive processes in group perception*, Oxford: Blackwell, pp. 183-196.

context as it is today is a product of developments and incidents that occurred over decades. In other words, in order to understand the contemporary relationships between Muslims and non-Muslims in the Netherlands, it is essential to take into account the historical context in which these relationships developed. For that reason, we include incidents of tensions and conflicts involving Muslims in the Netherlands that occurred within a time span of approximately three decades; from the 1980s until today. First, however, we discuss the rise and increase of radicalisation in Muslim communities.

2.1 Radicalisation in practice

Radicalisation among Muslims in the Netherlands is not a post-9/11 phenomenon. However, since the attacks on the United States in 2001, this process and in particular radical Islamism has been generally regarded as a threat to the state, Dutch society and Muslim immigrant communities in general. This feeling was intensified by a series of terrorist incidents and numerous scandals in the Netherlands that revealed extremist, discriminatory and illegal practices by a number of radical Islamist groups and institutions.

The first signs of radicalisation date back to the 1980s, when individuals and groups started to organise themselves around issues such the start of the first Palestinian intifada in 1987, and the row over Salman Rushdie's *Satanic Verses* in 1988. The demonstrations related to these events alarmed the Dutch Minister of the Interior, who was aware that these incidents could lead to increasing tensions in the Netherlands with regard to Islamism.

Following the Rushdie affair, fears regarding the influence of radical Islamism within Muslim communities increased. This concern led to publication of the first public reports on radical Islamist groups' activities, produced by the Dutch General Intelligence and Security Service (then known simply as the Security Service). In 1991, the Service revealed the existence of small groups of militant fundamentalists and expressed concern regarding their consequences for the integration of Muslims into mainstream society; the Service indicated the possibility that these militants might offer their services to foreign powers or that these countries were already directing them.

Partly based on the idea that the existence of such groups could hamper the integration process, the Erasmus University of Rotterdam was asked to investigate this potential threat. Their classified study, whose main conclusions were made public in 1994, found that radical Islamists had indeed attempted to impede this process but had not been very successful in their endeavour. Furthermore, it concluded that very few Muslims wanted to challenge existing social structures in the Netherlands.

In its 1995 annual report, the Service reaffirmed the idea that the threat of radical Islamism was rather limited. It stated that there was no real threat from Islamic society in the Netherlands. However, it noted serious prejudices toward Islam that had a negative impact on the integration of Muslims into mainstream society. Various terrorist attacks by Islamists – including those in France (attacks by the Algerian Groupe Islamique Armé), Israel (suicide attacks on buses in Jerusalem) and the United States (the 1993 attack on the World Trade Center) – were among the factors leading to such negative stereotypes.

After 1995, the Dutch General Intelligence and Security Services abandoned the idea that the threat posed by radical Islamism was insignificant. From 1996 onwards, all public documents on this issue repeated warnings about the potential danger. Moreover, the 1996 annual report spoke for the first time of information on possible attacks in the Netherlands, by Hizballah, which had been investigated by the Service.

In response to the increase in Islamist terrorist activities worldwide as well as growing concern over domestic developments, in 1998 the Service published a report on political Islam in the Netherlands. It described the various political organisations based on Islam. Most of them, in one way or another, rejected Western society and the integration of Muslims into that society. Yet the report revealed that only small groups of Muslims had radical opinions and were prepared to pursue their ideal of an Islamic state or world order through violent means. With regard to mosques, the report depicted them as political arenas in which many different political actors operated. The main political issues were integration and education. Some of the actors were supported or influenced by foreign powers, with Iran, Libya and Saudi Arabia being mentioned as examples. In addition, the governments of some of the mother countries of Muslim migrants were known to be interfering in the political-religious lives of their (former) nationals in the Netherlands – something particularly evident in the cases of Morocco and Turkey.

The interference of external forces was also apparent in the field of education. For instance, the Libyan al-Da'wa movement (which is linked to the Islamic Call Society), was involved in the establishment of an Islamic university in Rotterdam. The same holds for the Turkish government's Directorate for Religious Affairs (Diyanet Iserli Baskanligi).

Concerning political-religious organisations, the report showed that most were established on a national basis. Their focus of interest mainly pertained to their countries of origin and not the fate of the Muslims in the West. However, they did try to gain support from this Diaspora by way of taking a strong anti-Western, anti-integration and isolationist position. Although anti-Western feelings and resistance to integration were relatively widespread, the Service concluded that political Islam played a minor role within Muslim communities. Moreover, it did not anticipate that the more radical variants of political Islamism in the Netherlands would gain in power and size. However, it did warn that ongoing marginalisation of Muslim immigrants would possibly pose a long-term threat with regard to the growth of radical groups. Ideological polarisation between Muslims and their surrounding society was considered a likely consequence, which could possibly lead to a negative impact on the integration process, as well as undermine the peaceful and democratic coexistence of different cultures in the Netherlands.

By the end of the 1990s, the threat of radical Islamism in the Netherlands was still more or less a distant one. Threat perceptions were dominated by events taking place both outside the Netherlands and even beyond Europe. Moreover, on its territory, the main players were 'foreign' in the sense that the groups mainly consisted of foreign nationals who predominantly focused on their mother countries without receiving active support within the local Muslim communities. Nonetheless, the diversity of these groups continued to grow.

One of the leading causes of this growth was the increase in both legal and illegal immigrants with an Islamist background, including asylum seekers from Algeria, Bosnia, Chechnya, Egypt, Iraq and Syria. In the Netherlands, these individuals established political-religious organisations that were strongly oriented towards their mother countries. Examples include fundraising organisations for the Palestinians, Bosnia, Chechnya, Afghanistan and Algeria; some of these groups emphasised both ties to their mother countries and a strong rejection of the Western society in which they lived.

After the attacks on the United States on 11 September 2001, the idea that Muslims posed a threat to Dutch society – even to the extent of considering them a Trojan horse or a fifth column – was gaining ground. This perception was bolstered by reports about the deaths at the hands of Indian security forces in Kashmir of two Dutch citizens of Moroccan descent who were believed to be jihadists. The boys who died in December 2001 shortly after their arrival in the troubled Indian territory were associated with one of the most radical mosques in the Netherlands, the Al-Fourqaan mosque in the city of Eindhoven.

These incidents also worried many politicians and policy-makers, leading them to request information about the extent and nature of Islamist terrorism in the Netherlands from the Dutch General Intelligence and Security Services. In a report published in March 2004, the Service estimated the numerical strength of radical Islamists to be between 100 and 200 activists. According to the General Intelligence and Security Services, this group included so-called 'veterans' from Afghanistan and Chechnya, who played an important role in the conversion of young Muslims into potential jihadists. Moreover, the Service contended that there were several dozen young Muslims preparing for jihad. This jihad includes both conflict areas in the Muslim world and potential targets in Europe.

Furthermore, the role of these 'veterans' is not the decisive factor in the development of new recruits. Indeed, internal dynamics within groups of radical young Islamists play an important developmental role as well. This was observed through intensive Internet discussions among young Muslims on the developing patterns of strife in arenas of conflict such as Chechnya, Afghanistan and Iraq, which resulted in the development of increasingly radical opinions. Additionally, anti-Muslim feelings – brought on by incidents in the Netherlands as well as the Madrid bombings and other Islamist terrorist attacks abroad – also contributed to this radicalisation. Consequently, a number of these Muslim youths developed an exceedingly hostile attitude towards the Dutch state and society to the extent that these youngsters, predominantly of Moroccan descent, developed views so extreme as to embrace the use of violence. In November 2004, one of them, Mohammed Bouyeri, killed Dutch filmmaker Theo van Gogh. This young Moroccan, born and raised in Amsterdam, was a member of the Hofstadgroep, a loose-knit radical Islamist group of mostly young Dutch Muslims.

2.2 Radical groups

The Hofstadgroep is probably the most extreme and infamous radical Muslim organisation in the Netherlands. There are, however, quite a number of other organisations that can be regarded as radical Muslim organisations. These include political groups, religious groups and all kinds of mixes between these two categories. Below is a list of the most important formal organisations and informal groups – in alphabetical order. It should be stressed that a number of these organisations do not consider themselves as radical. Nonetheless, they are generally considered as such by the authorities or scholars.

Al-Jama'a al-Islamia (AJAI)

Al-Jama'a al-Islamia, or the Egyptian Islamic Jihad, is an Islamist group active since the late 1970s, with origins in the Muslim Brotherhood. The organisation's primary goal is to overthrow the Egyptian government and replace it with an Islamic state. The organisation is responsible for several terrorist attacks against high-level Egyptian government personnel and official US and Egyptian facilities. A few key members of AJAI live in the Netherlands, among them Usama Rushdie Ali Kalifa (who lived there until 2003).

Arab European League (AEL)

The Arab European League is a pan-Arabist political and social movement that is active in Belgium and the Netherlands. The AEL was founded and is led by Dyab Abou Jahjah, a Lebanese-born Shiá Muslim who emigrated from Lebanon in 1991 to study political science in Belgium. The organisation strives to develop an Arab Muslim communalist movement in Europe. Particularly in Belgium, mainstream political parties sharply attacked the AEL for anti-integrative ideas, alleged anti-Semitism and for disturbing the social peace. In 2002, its leader was arrested and detained for several days after he allegedly organised riots and called for violence (see chapter on Belgium). In the Netherlands, the AEL was never associated with violence. Nonetheless, the organisation was under observation of the Dutch General Intelligence and Security Service (AIVD).

Groupe Islamique Armé (GIA)

The Armed Islamic Group is a militant Islamist organisation with the declared aim of overthrowing the Algerian government and replacing it with an Islamic state. The GIA adopted violent tactics in 1992, after the

Algerian military government voided the victory of the Islamic Salvation Front in the first round of legislative elections held in December 1991. It conducted a violent campaign of civilian massacres in Algeria. The GIA has also established a presence in Europe. In France, it was responsible for several terrorist attacks, and some of its members who were wanted by French authorities reportedly are hiding in the Netherlands.

Hamas/al-Aqsa Foundation

Hamas, or the Islamic Resistance Movement, is a Palestinian Sunni Islamist organisation. At the beginning of the first intifada in 1987, Hamas was established by Shaikh Ahmad Yassin of the Gaza wing of the Muslim Brotherhood. The European Union lists it as a terrorist organisation. About a dozen individuals of Palestinian descent are actively involved in Hamas in the Netherlands, receiving financial support from a few hundred sympathisers. One of the institutions that channelled these funds was the al-Aqsa Foundation, which had a local branch in the Netherlands until the EU put it on the list of terrorist organisations and it was banned as an illegal organisation.

Hizb al-Tahrir

Established in 1953 by Shaikh Taqiuddin al-Nabhani, Hizb al-Tahrir (Party of Liberation) is an Islamist political party whose goal is to re-establish the caliphate. The party has been banned in many Arab countries, Central Asia and a few Western countries (such as Germany). Its activities in Europe are concentrated in the United Kingdom, though the organisation also has a branch in the Netherlands. Most of its supporters are of Turkish or Moroccan background. They are organised in small groups numbering a few dozen people each. Their activities include the organisation of (protest) meetings against alleged attacks on Islam, such as the Danish cartoons, and the activities of the Dutch Member of Parliament Geert Wilders. These events have always been non-violent.

Hofstadgroep

The Hofstadgroep is an Islamist organisation of mostly young Dutch Muslims of mainly Moroccan descent. The name 'Hofstad' was originally the codename the Netherlands secret service used for the network and leaked to the media. The name refers to the nickname of the city of The Hague, where some of the members used to live. In total, a few dozen of people were part of this loose-knit network of radicals. In the end, only a dozen of them were tried on membership of a terrorist organisation. Other charges included obstructing the work of Members of Parliament, including Ayaan Hirsi Ali, and the illegal possession of firearms. Some members were acquitted for lack of evidence, while others were found guilty and sentenced ranging from one to fifteen years imprisonment. Mohammed Bouyeri, the murderer of Van Gogh, was also sentenced for membership of the group. In January 2008, however, the Dutch Court of Appeals overturned a number of the convictions in the Hofstadgroep case. Although the Court of Appeals concluded that the alleged network members embraced and incited radical attitudes and ideologies, it stated that it could not be proven that the Hofstadgroep was a terrorist organisation and that these acts would inevitably result in terrorist engagement.[15]

According to the Ministry of Interior, there exists a number of other loose-knit informal groups similar to the Hofstadgroep. Not very much is known about these radical groupings. The exception is the group around Samir Azzouz, also described as the 'Piranha Group', which is further described below.

İslami Büyükdoğu Akıncılar Cephesi (IBDA-C)

The Great Eastern Islamic Raiders Front follows the 'Great East' ideology of Necip Fazil Kisaktürek, a well-known Turkish author and Islamist ideologue. This organisation's goal is the creation of a Sunni Islamist federal state in the Middle East and the re-establishment of the caliphate. The Front is responsible for a series of terrorist attacks in Turkey, including the dual synagogue bombings in Istanbul in November 2003 as well as the subsequent attack on the HSBC Bank and the British consulate. While support for this movement exists in the Netherlands, it has been limited in scope.

Milli Görüs

Milli Görüs, or 'National Vision', is a Turkish orthodox-Islamic movement that has clear political aspirations. Its aim is to Islamise the Turkish state and society through democratic ways. Milli Görüs has approximately 40,000 members in the Netherlands. The movement is part of the European

---

[15] F. Jensma (2008), "Niet zomaar te straffen voor terrorisme" (Not to punish just like that for terrorism), *NRC Handelsblad*, 24 January.

Milli Görüs organisation whose headquarters are located in Cologne, Germany. The movement is widely considered to be of a politico-religious nature. The Dutch branch is considered more moderate than the German and Turkish branch.

Piranha Group/Samir Azzouz

In October 2005, the police arrested a young Dutch national of Moroccan descent, Samir Azzouz, on suspicion of attempting to procure firearms and planning terrorist attacks in the Netherlands, a case that was codenamed 'Piranha Group'.[16] Azzouz had been apprehended twice before on suspicion of terrorist activities, but had not been convicted. This time he and two others ended up in jail. In December 2006, Azzouz received a sentence of eight years for membership of an organisation with terrorist intentions, for preparing an attack and recruiting followers. He was not sentenced for membership of the Hofstadgroep, although he had close contacts with some of its members, including Mohammed Bouyeri.[17] Azzouz is also known for his failed attempt to join the jihad in Chechnya. At 17 years of age, he and a friend were arrested at the border between Russia and Ukraine and sent back to the Netherlands.

Teblig movement (Islami Cemiyet ve Cemaatlar Birligi)

The Teblig movement, also known as Kaplanci's, is a radical splinter group of the Milli Görüs movement. Its goal is the establishment of an Islamist Turkish state, using force if necessary. Following the death of its spiritual leader Cemaleddin Kaplan in 1995, the organisation broke up into different factions. In the Netherlands, and today there are about 200 Muslims active within two separate Kaplan factions.

3. Types of tensions and violent conflicts

As mentioned earlier, we look at three types of tensions and violent conflicts involving Muslims: incidents in which Muslims attack non-Muslims and vice versa, as well as incidents within and between Muslim communities. We look at politically inspired events, as well as political-

---

[16] District Court of Rotterdam, 7 December 2006, 10/600052-05, 10/600108-05, 10/600134-05, 10/600109-05, 10/600122-05, 10/600023-06, 10/600100-06.

[17] A. Benschop (2005), "Chronicle of a political murder foretold, Jihad in the Netherlands", University of Amsterdam, SocioSite (www.sociosite.org).

religious and apolitical-religious or pseudo-religious violence. It should be stressed that it is sometimes rather difficult to make distinctions along these two lines. As in most conflicts, when two or more groups clash it is never easy to distinguish the perpetrators from the victims. The same holds for the nature of incidents. When is something politically inspired or more of a political-religious nature? Is a violent demonstration of Muslims against the occupation of Palestine purely political, and what if some of the demonstrators wear burqas and djelabas?

Regarding the Netherlands, most of the violent attacks of Muslims against non-Muslims are associated with violent Islamists, who are considered political-religious. Most of the violent attacks by non-Muslims on Muslims are of a right-wing political nature, although the low level of political awareness of some of these groups and individuals raises questions. The tensions and violent conflicts between Muslim communities are both of a political and a-political nature. The same holds for confrontations within the same community.

We have singled out the incidents that attracted the most attention and that had most impact on communities and Dutch society as a whole. In the following sections, we first look at non-violent tensions, followed by violent incidents. Relatively much attention is paid to the only deadly incident, the murder of Theo van Gogh.

3.1 Muslims versus non-Muslims

The al-Moumni affair

In May 2001, a Moroccan imam, Khalid al-Moumni of the al-Nasr Mosque in Rotterdam, was interviewed on television. The interview took place against a backdrop of growing discrimination against homosexuals by Moroccan youth. When questioned about homosexuality, al-Moumni described it as a disease that was pandemic the world over and that posed a threat to Muslim youth. The interview led to a public outcry, causing leading members of parliament, NGOs and ministers to hold weighty discussions. Following this incident, a news agency began investigating al-Moumni's past. The agency revealed that the controversial imam was forced to leave Morocco because of his fundamentalist views and sermons in which he described Christians as pigs. The interview and article about al-Moumni led to debates in Parliament that called for closing Islamist mosques and possibly expelling radical imams. Even key members of liberal Muslim groups supported the idea of the closure of certain mosques.

Resulting from this and other comparable incidents, the Dutch government received a lot of pressure from Parliament, the media and the public to take a tougher stance on Islamism than it did before. After the al-Moumni incident, more would follow and a few radical Imams were indeed extradited from the Netherlands.

Cheering young Moroccans on 9/11

In the city of Ede, a group of young Muslims of mainly Moroccan descent allegedly was loudly celebrating the attacks on the United States on 11 September 2001. Journalists were shooting pictures of some young man who had quickly printed a picture of Osama bin Laden. It remains unclear to what extent members of the media incited this small group of teenagers to produce this picture. Nonetheless, the incident provoked a lot of criticism and could be considered one of the starting point for journalists to hunt 'scoops' like this by finding out all kinds of worrisome developments within Muslims communities. At one official state-sponsored Islamic school, for instance, journalists found Hamas propaganda and posters glorifying attacks against the West.

Foiled attack on the US embassy in Paris

In July 2001, a Frenchmen of Algerian descent, Djamel Beghal, was arrested in Dubai. He subsequently confessed to plotting an attack against the American embassy in Paris and was extradited to France in September 2001. His network included Kamel Daoudi, a number of other (French) Algerians and three French converts. In multiple court cases, in France and elsewhere, members of this network were sentenced to prison terms between one and 10 years. In The Netherlands, two persons were convicted on terrorism charges. One was a French convert, the other an Algerian living in France.

Plot to threaten Dutch politicians and to make an explosive device

In September 2004, two youngsters of Moroccan descent were arrested and accused of terrorist activities. On 14 February 2005, a court sentenced one of them, Yehya Kadouri, to 140 days jail and forced admission to a psychiatric institution. He was convicted of publishing death threats on the internet towards Dutch politicians and collecting information and raw materials to make an explosive device. The individual was radicalised almost entirely via the internet.

The murder on filmmaker Theo van Gogh

In spring 2004, against the backdrop of growing anti-Muslim sentiment and increasing radicalisation among certain groups of Muslims, the Dutch General Intelligence and Security Service issued a clear and unprecedented warning in its report *Background of Jihad Recruits in the Netherlands* (10 March 2004). The report warned about "a growing number of Muslims who feel [that they are] treated disrespectfully by opinion-makers and opinion-leaders… In addition, from their perspective, the government's attitude is [either] not impartial enough or not impartial at all." These feelings were deeply shared by a small group of radical Islamists, but they also existed among the larger community of Muslim individuals who felt loyal to the democratic principles of the Dutch state. In particular, young second-generation and third-generation Muslim immigrants appeared to feel strongly about the alleged alienation between society and Muslim citizens. In particular, it was found that this group of Muslim youth felt that they were treated disrespectfully, which potentially made them a vulnerable target for radicalisation and possibly recruitment efforts.

One of these opinion-makers was the filmmaker Theo van Gogh, who had earned a reputation in the Netherlands as an outspoken provocateur. In his short film *Submission*, shown on Dutch television, van Gogh adopted an adversarial stance concerning Islamism. It challenged the abuse of women in the Islamic world based on verses from the Koran, which were projected onto the bodies of naked women wearing only veils. A Dutch parliamentary deputy, Ayaan Hirsi Ali, a woman of Muslim Somali origin, wrote the script. A member of the liberal Freedom and Democracy Party, Hirsi Ali is a known critic of Islamism. Following the showing of the film *Submission*, both Hirsi Ali and Theo van Gogh received death threats via the internet.

One such individual who took the issuance of these threats very seriously was a young man of Moroccan descent by the name of Muhammad Bouyeri, who was born in 1978 and raised in the Netherlands. Friends and acquaintances described him as a shy but intelligent man.[18] Bouyeri had been an eager and successful student in secondary school[19]

---

[18] J. Alberts, J. Chorus, S. Derix and A. Olgun (2005), "De wereld van Mohammed B" (The world of Mohammed B), *NRC Handelsblad*, 9 July (www.nrc.nl).

[19] Albert Benschop (2005), *Chronicle of a Political Murder Foretold*, Utrecht: Forum.

and easily advanced on to studying at college. Nevertheless, although he started several studies he never finished any of them until finally, after five years, he dropped out of college all together.[20] In the same period, his mother died and a number of his ideas to improve the situation of youngsters in his neighbourhood failed to get the support of the authorities. For whatever precise reason, he started to become radicalised. He spent months attempting to gain a more in-depth knowledge of Islam and radical interpretations of the Koran. Often, he would lock himself up in his home and sit behind his computer for hours, downloading, reading and translating radical Islamist texts, writing articles and distributing his work via the internet under a pseudonym. Meanwhile, Bouyeri became embedded in a network of similar-minded peers all of whom frequented the same mosque and met at regular basis at Bouyeri´s home to discuss Islam-related issues. During these meetings, Bouyeri played videos of decapitations in the Middle East and attempted to persuade his friends to participate in violent jihad against the West.[21]

By the summer of 2003, Bouyeri had become so radicalised that he even rejected the most prototypical orthodox al-Tawhid Mosque as being too liberal. In his radicalisation, Bouyeri adopted an ideology contending that violence against both non-believers and moderate Muslims – often characterised as renegades – was justified. On 2 November 2004, Bouyeri assassinated Theo van Gogh. In a threat letter, which he stabbed with a knife to Van Gogh's body, Bouyeri expressed anger and disgust against Western societies and their governments' foreign policies. He accused the Dutch Liberal Party of being anti-Islamic and accused Member of Parliament Ayaan Hirsi Ali of terrorising Islam.[22] Bouyeri was apprehended by police while attempting to die a martyr's death – a fact confirmed by a farewell letter, which was found on him. While Bouyeri

---

[20] E. Vermaat (2005), *The Hofstadgroup: A radical Islamic network*, Soesterberg: Uitgeverij Aspekt; E. Vermaat (2006), *Nederlandse Jihad. Het proces tegen de Hofstadgroep* (Dutch Jihad. The trial against the Hofstadgroep), Soesterberg: Uitgeverij Aspekt

[21] Alberts et al., 2005.

[22] H. Jansen (2005), "De brief van Mohammed B., bevestigd aan het lijk van Theo van Gogh" (The letter of Mohammed B., stuck to the body of Theo van Gogh), *Tijdschrift voor Geschiedenis*, Vol. 118, No. 3, pp. 483-491.

may have failed to become a martyr, he succeeded in underscoring the home-grown terrorist threat to the Netherlands.

Soon after the murder of Van Gogh, it became clear that although Bouyeri proclaimed to have acted independently, he was one of the central figures in the Hofstadgroep. The event very much shocked the Netherlands. It became obvious that extreme ideologies as vented by al-Qaeda and other radical terrorist organisations had gained ground in the Netherlands, even among those born and raised in the country. It also became clear that radicalism among Muslims in the Netherlands had a 'home-grown' terrorist dimension that could no longer be ignored, as had been the case with the Kadouri case and a number of other thwarted plots.

Violent arrests and convictions

In the investigation following the murder of Van Gogh, the police arrested several youngsters allegedly embedded in the radical network surrounding Bouyeri. Approximately one week after Bouyeri´s arrest, the police set out to investigate a building in a neighbourhood called the Laakkwartier in The Hague. Jason Walters and Ismail Akhnikh, two members of the Hofstadgroep, were inside the building. One of them threw a grenade at the police, injuring four police officers of whom two were seriously hurt. The incident was the start of a 14-hour stand-off during which several attempts to arrest the suspects failed. Ultimately, the police used tear gas to force the two suspects out of the building and shot one in the shoulder.

In the year following the murder of Van Gogh, more than a dozen alleged members of the Hofstadgroep stood trial. In March 2006, the court convicted nine of them and sentenced them to between one and 15 years imprisonment. In its verdict, the court stated that the Hofstadgroep aimed at destroying existing Dutch structures and terrorising Dutch society. At that time, Bouyeri was already sentenced to life imprisonment in a separate court case.

Plot to prepare a terrorist attack and attempt to recruit a fellow-prisoner

In February 2006, Bilal Lamrani, a young Dutch Muslim was given a three-year sentence.[23] According to the court in Rotterdam, Lamrani was

---

[23] LJN: AV1652, Rechtbank Rotterdam, 10/600017-05; Buro Jansen & Janssen, Overzicht terrorisme, angst of aan terrorisme gerelateerde arrestaties in Nederland sinds 11 september (Overview of terrorism, fear or terrorism-related arrests in the

preparing a terrorist attack and had tried to recruit a fellow prisoner while in jail for threatening a leading Dutch Member of Parliament. In his home, the police found hundreds of (digital) copies of radical Islamist texts and information on how to make explosive devices. The 21-year old had close contact with some members of the Hofstadgroep and Mohammed Bouyeri who murdered Theo van Gogh.

Plot to attack politicians and a government building

Samir Azzouz, a long-time suspect of terrorism, was arrested with nine others in October 2005, on suspicion of preparing terrorist attacks on politicians and a government building. Azzouz was close to most of the members of the Hofstadgroep. One of the other suspects in this case had already been sentenced for membership of the Hofstadgroep. Of the 10 persons arrested in October 2005, three were convicted. As mentioned earlier, Azzouz and the other two were given sentences for membership of an organisation with terrorist intentions, for preparing a terrorist attack and for their recruiting activities.

Dutch jihadi terrorists abroad

Besides the loose-knit, home-grown terrorist networks, the Netherlands has been confronted with a number of locally embedded international networks controlled from abroad, or in a manner whereby foreign recruiters residing in the Netherlands play a key role. These networks and recruiters have managed to find young Muslims in the Netherlands willing and able to go on jihad. In the past decade, two of them, associated with a radical Salafi mosque in the city of Eindhoven, died in Kashmir. Some Dutch Muslims are believed to be fighting in Iraq. Six of them, from the city of The Hague, were ostensibly on a journey to Chechnya or Dagestand. Religious leaders and family members successfully persuaded them to return from Azerbaijan and not to continue their assumed journey. It is not clear whether this 'trip' was organised by an internationally operating

---

Netherlands as from 11 september), 12 July 2006; NOS Journaal, Drie jaar cel voor Bilal L. (Three years of jail for Bilal L.), 14 February 2006; "Hofstadgroep plande aanslag op Wallen" (Hofstadgroup planned an attack on Wallen), *De Telegraaf*, 10 December 2004; A. Benschop (2005), "Kroniek van een Aangekondigde Politieke Moord. Jihad in Nederland" (Chronicle of a Political Murder Foretold. Jihad in the Netherlands), op. cit..

network or a more autonomously decided 'adventure'. The latter seemed to have been the case with the earlier mentioned failed attempt by Samir Azzouz to join the jihad in Chechnya.

3.2 Non-Muslims versus Muslims

Following the attacks of 11 September 2001, growing anti-Muslim sentiments in reaction to cases such as the al-Moumni affair escalated. Newspaper reports about a group of nine adolescents of Moroccan descent "celebrating" the terrorist attacks caused public fury and rendered substantial damage to the image of Muslims in the Netherlands. In addition, a series of arrests of suspected Islamist terrorists led some to question the loyalty of Muslim communities towards the Dutch state, norms and values. Spurious findings by opinion polls employing questionable methodologies further added fuel to the fire by fostering the notion that there was indeed a lack of loyalty exhibited in the Dutch Muslim population. Moreover, in the weeks following the attacks, the media revealed many scandals and potential threats, thereby exacerbating the situation. For example, there was a report about propaganda in Islamic schools that glorified terrorism and quoted from radical anti-Western speeches by Salafi imams. Although many of these reports later turned out to be based on hearsay or misinterpretations of texts and events, with most of the suspected terrorists being released within days or weeks, the damage had already been done.

The impact of September 11th and the previously mentioned incidents was profound, resulting in a tougher tone of debate. While in the past, few in the Netherlands dared to speak out against Islamist radicalism, the Dutch community suddenly became unbridled in its (often negative) expressions regarding Islamism.

A number of public opinion polls in the months following these attacks consequently revealed strong anti-Muslim sentiment and a fear of Islam. One survey indicated that about three-quarters of the Dutch population were in favour of providing military support to the United States. At the same time, 60% also feared that this might lead to terrorist attacks in the Netherlands. Another poll showed that a clear majority of the Dutch wanted to expel Muslims with anti-Western opinions from the country. A survey among Muslims that appeared in a multi-cultural weekly further fed these opinions and fears. The results of the survey showed that the majority of those interviewed believed there was at least some justification for the attacks on the United States.

Pim Fortuyn

As the relationship between non-Muslims and Muslims in the Netherlands grew increasingly tense, the flamboyant right-wing Pim Fortuyn entered the Dutch political arena. Being a former member of the Social-Democratic Party, he became the head of the populist party Leefbaar Nederland (Liveable Netherlands) in 2001. Fortuyn, who was openly gay and appeared to enjoy controversy, was forced to leave this party after some very provocative statements regarding Muslims and Islam in the Netherlands. More specifically, he emphasised that the Netherlands should put a hold on immigrant flows from, in particular, Islamic countries. He proclaimed that if he were to be elected into the next government, he would grant citizenship to large groups of Muslims already residing in the Netherlands, but at the same time would heavily restrict Muslim influx. He considered Islam a backward culture that had never undergone a period of Enlightment and was therefore unfit to integrate into modern western societies.[24]

After being rejected by LN, Fortuyn founded his own political party, Lijst Pim Fortuyn (LPF) in February 2002, and was running for the upcoming governmental elections that were to be held in May that year. During his political career, Fortuyn continued to make provocative statements, hereby fuelling existing tensions between Muslims and non-Muslims. The taboo on conservatism and right-wing politics seemed to disappear, and Fortuyn appeared to have triggered a revival of extreme-right lobbying groups and organisations. On 6 May 2002, approximately one week prior to the governmental elections for which he was running, Pim Fortuyn was assassinated after having given a radio-interview in Hilversum. Initially, the common assumption among the Dutch public seemed to be that Fortuyn had become the victim of radical Islamists seeking revenge for his anti-Islam statements. Even though it was soon publicised that Fortuyn's murderer, Volkert van der Graaf, was a left-wing environmental activist, the killing of Fortuyn increased the tension between

---

[24] Frank Poorthuis and Hans Wansink, "De islam is een achterlijke cultuur" (Islam is a retarded culture), *De Volkskrant*, 9 February 2002.

Dutch and non-Dutch populations, particularly focusing on Muslims. During the days after the murder, representatives of the radical right-wing vented anti-Islam sentiments and in cities in the eastern part of the country incidents were reported of harassment of immigrant youngsters by right-wing extremists.[25] Despite the assassination, the elections continued one week later with Fortuyn as a posthumous candidate winning 26 out of 150 seats in the Parliament. Nevertheless, the LPF's success was not to remain; after the next elections in 2004, it lost 18 seats and by 2006, the party was elected out of the parliament. Ultimately, the party fell apart by January 2008. Nevertheless, although Fortuyn's political career was relatively short, his provocative statements contributed significantly to the debate about multiculturalism in general and multiculturalism in the Netherlands in particular.

Violent reactions to the Van Gogh murder

Immediately after the murder of Van Gogh, the authorities realised it might provoke violent reactions by non-Muslims, but they did not react with a strong statement urging everyone to remain calm. And the situation did not remain calm. Dutch society was shocked not only by the crime itself, but also by the manner in which the basic principles of the Netherlands' democratic constitutional state had been so brutally attacked. Not only did Dutch society exhibit outrage over the murder, but many also sought violent revenge against 'those Muslims'. Youngsters with racist and right-wing ideas exploited the situation to incite hatred and violence against Moroccans, Muslims and immigrants in general. As Albert Benschop elaborates in *Chronicle of a Political Murder Foretold*, "the Islam-inspired murder of van Gogh was grist to the political mill of extremely nationalist and racist groups... [who] seized the event to give vent to their violent and venomous opinions."[26] Consequently, the Netherlands has witnessed a growing climate of intolerance in its non-Muslim community followed by increased episodes of attacks against Muslims and cases of discrimination. In the days following the murder of the film maker, there were more than 100 incidents of arson and assault directed at mosques, Islamic schools and

---

[25] "Blanke terreur in de Kempen" (White terror in the Kempen), *NRC Handelsblad*, 2 June 2003.

[26] Benschop, op. cit.

individual Muslims. In reaction, young Muslims also attacked a number of churches and individuals.

Attacks by right-wing youngsters

In the context of the inflamed racial tensions that followed the Van Gogh murder, right-wing extremists launched a renewed assault on the Dutch Muslim communities in 2005. In particular, the so-called 'Lonsdale youth' received extensive attention by the media as well as by politicians. Lonsdale is a popular clothing brand among right-wing elements of the 'gabber' youth, a subgroup that is largely defined by a preference for house music. In a study of the Lonsdale issue, Van Donselaar[27] concluded that the Lonsdale subgroup is very diverse in both nature and size. Between 2002 and 2005, the authors counted more than 100 groups in the Netherlands that were either right-wing-oriented or had been involved in extreme right-wing or racist incidents. After a fight between right-wing and immigrant youngsters in Venray and an attack on an Islamic primary school in Uden, early in 2005, the Intelligence Service started an investigation into Lonsdale youth.[28] In the report, the Service concluded that at present, Lonsdale youth do not pose a considerable threat to the democratic order, and that the subgroup mostly consists of unorganised, loosely-knit structures that are not defined by political ideologies. The threat for society is mostly long term, in the sense that provocative statements and symbolism prompt frequent confrontations with immigrant youngsters and can erode social cohesion and multicultural relations within the Dutch society.

Geert Wilders

In recent years, Member of Parliament Geert Wilders has made a name for himself as the leading politician on immigration and integration issues. Many Muslims (and non-Muslims) perceive MP Geert Wilders as having an anti-Muslim agenda. The earlier-mentioned movie "Fitna" was not his first provocative statement concerning Islam. Other well-known statements of his include comparing the immigration of Muslims with a tsunami wave,

---

[27] Jaap Van Donselaar (ed.), *Monitor racisme en extremisme: zevende rapportage* (Monitor racism and extremism: seventh report), Amsterdam: Anne Frank Stichting; Leiden: Universiteit Leiden, 2006.

[28] AIVD, *Lonsdale jongeren in Nederland* (Lonsdale youngsters in the Netherlands), The Hague, 2005.

comparing the Koran with Hitler's *Mein Kampf* accompanied with a plea for a ban on the Koran, and questioning the 'loyalty' of Dutch politicians with a Moroccan or Turkish background. His alleged anti-Muslim attitude and remarks have led to several charges against Wilders for inciting hatred of Muslims or insulting them. He was never convicted in court, however, and repeatedly has stated that he respects the rule of law. Nonetheless, he is generally regarded as contributing to a harsh, polarised debate on the integration of Muslim communities in the Netherlands. The popularity of Geert Wilders and his ideas did result in his Partij voor de Vrijheid (PVV, Party For Freedom) winning nine (out of 150) seats in Parliament.

3.3 *Muslims versus Muslims*

Kurds and Turks

There are many different levels and types of tensions and violent conflicts between Muslims. If we look at incidents between Muslim communities, the most striking ones are of a political nature, especially concerning tensions and violence between Turks and Kurds. Both have their own groups and organisations. Think of the Kurdish Workers Party (PKK) or the Turkish nationalist 'Grey Wolves'. This is not to say that tensions and incidents are always 'formally' organised through groups like these. There are also quite a number of locally organised or 'spontaneous' incidents, such as provocative behaviour of young Kurds in front of a Turkish coffeehouse just after an important European football match in which *Galatasaray* or *Besiktas* were beaten. In addition, the invasion of Turkish troops in Iraq in early 2008 caused an increase of tensions between the two groups, both accusing the other of terrorism and organising protest meetings or demonstrations. There have been a number of arson bombings of Turkish and Kurdish targets. However, it remains unclear whether these incidents were of a political nature or criminals fighting criminals. The latter type of tensions and violence is perhaps one of the most serious ones, at least in terms of people killed or injured, but falls beyond the scope of this study.

Customary and pseudo-religious violence

Within some Muslim communities, dramatic incidents have occurred involving family members beating up and even killing girls and women. These 'honour crimes' have added to the earlier-mentioned association between Muslims and radical behaviour and violence, in particular towards women. Of course, this kind of pseudo-religious behaviour not only gives Islam and the Muslim communities a bad-image problem, but it is also a very serious social problem within communities – between generations. The problem is even more serious within families – between parents and children and between couples of which one partner is born and raised in the Netherlands and the other is the 'imported' partner.

Whereas in the past, these kinds of crimes were more or less ignored or considered as crimes of passion, today they are given widespread attention in the media and receive special attention by social workers, the police and public prosecutors. The exact number of honour crimes is unknown but in recent years, more than a dozen cases have led to hefty debates, including in Parliament. In fact, political parties are currently pushing the authorities to restart investigations into the murder of a young Kurdish woman by her ex-husband (who committed suicide immediately after killing her).

Conclusions

In recent decades, the world has witnessed a trend of globalisation that brought forth an increase in interaction, interdependency and networking between social groups. However, one of the side effects of these developments is that they also led to an increased awareness of social heterogeneity. Cultural diversity becomes increasingly salient, not only across borders but also within them. For social groups with different values, different norms, different historical backgrounds and different beliefs to coexist peacefully, it is important that they can agree on a basic set of common rules and values and that there is a minimum level of mutual respect and understanding.

In the Netherlands, many different cultural, ethnic and religious groups have lived together peacefully and successfully for decades. The country has experienced hardly any violence between social groups. In contrast to countries like France and the United Kingdom, the Netherlands has not been confronted with many serious terrorist attacks. There have not been riots like those in Paris or Bradford, and there have not been violent confrontations with extreme-right groups like there have been in Germany. In other words, the Dutch experience with inter-group violent conflict is, fortunately, rather limited.

However, in recent years, a few incidents and developments have occurred that have led to tensions and conflicts between Muslims and non-

Muslims and that have eroded the idea of the Netherlands as a peaceful and tolerant country. This new image of the Netherlands as a place of harsh debates, polarisation and violence did not only take root outside the country, but also among many Dutch citizens. There are as yet no convincing explanations of how and why this happened. The single incidents that probably added to the polarised political and social climate are the attacks on the United States in 2001, the 'discoveries' by the media of extreme radical behaviour among Muslims and the murder of Theo van Gogh in 2004. These and other incidents inflamed inter-cultural and inter-ethnic tensions between different social groups and have led, in some occasions, to violent outbursts. They also contributed to political polarisation over issues related to Muslims (and other immigrants), as well as to the implicit association that presently seems to be easily made between Muslims and violence. The fact that the release of the anti-Islam movie 'Fitna' did not lead to angry responses by Muslim communities may indicate two things. Either the idea of intolerance and polarisation has been exaggerated, or that Dutch society has gradually rediscovered its traditions and the importance of adhering to common rules and values and showing a minimum level of mutual respect and understanding. Probably it is a bit of both.

6. Radicalisation among Muslims in the UK
Rachel Briggs & Jonathan Birdwell

Muslim communities in the UK have come under intense scrutiny in recent years, but especially since 7 July 2005 (7/7). The emergence of a home-grown threat raised concerns not just about the threat of future attacks, but it also played on deeper anxieties about Britain's growing diversity and apparent loss of a cohesive identity. The current terrorist threat and the UK's responses to it should be viewed against this wider backdrop. Since 7/7, the extent of the problem has become clearer as new plots have been unearthed and a succession of trials has provided rare glimpses into the lives of the radicals. This chapter outlines the details of the main plots.

Many theories have been offered about the drivers or causes of radicalisation, but they are rarely able to prove more than the exception, never the rule. In fact, it is almost impossible to say with any certainty what the causes are as it is so difficult to know whether a factor is instrumental, or merely present. It is perhaps more helpful to think about 'radicalising agents' – factors that are present (though not necessarily causal) and which appear frequently across different cases. This chapter highlights a number: key places, charismatic leaders, relationship links, experiences and stated and assumed grievances.

One of the most frequent theories about radicalisation is that certain organisations or movements play central roles in indoctrinating individuals into a set of fundamental beliefs and an acceptance that violence is a legitimate tool for solving their problems. This collaborative research project divides Muslim organisations into three broad categories for the purposes of this study: non-political religious groups, religious and political groups and non-religious political groups. This chapter provides a brief synopsis of the main organisations and movements under each heading and offers, where it exists, evidence about their links to violence.

It should be acknowledged that this is a problematic framework. Few groups fit neatly into one category and often move between them over time or depending on their activities. It is also highly unlikely that they would self-categorise themselves in these terms. It also assumes that organisations – as corporate entities – are important players within the radicalisation process, rather than the individuals who pass through them. In fact, in many cases individuals go in and out of these organisations, often leaving when they do not find what they are looking for. To conclude that their presence confirms the organisation's role would be misleading. Finally, these organisations can find themselves being used as convenient spaces for individuals to convene – often in the margins – where the culpability of the organisation is due more to its poor visibility and governance than a commitment to violence.

This chapter sets out the position of Muslims in the UK, the threat to the UK from al-Qaeda-linked and -inspired terrorism through an account of the main terror plots, outlines the main radical groups and movements under the three-pronged categorisation outlined above and closes with an explanation of latest UK government policy responses. It concludes with a note of caution about misinterpreting the nature and intention of these groups and notes the role that many – with some notable exceptions – could play in the effort to tackle radicalisation in the UK.

1. Muslim communities in the UK

There are around 2 million Muslims in the UK, the largest faith group after Christians.[1] Most trace their roots to migration and settlement after the Second World War, although their presence dates back as far as the 17th century. Almost half (46%) were born in the UK,[2] with three-quarters having South Asian heritage. The community is becoming more diverse:

---

[1] Z. Bunglawala, M. Halstead, M. Malik, and B. Spalek, "Muslims in the UK: Policies for Engaged Citizens", Open Society Institute, EU Monitoring and Advocacy Program, November 2004, p. 12.

[2] Ibid.

there are now 56 nationalities represented and 70 languages spoken.[3] Muslims have the youngest age profile of all faith groups; in 2001, one-third (33.8%) were under the age of 16, compared to one-fifth of the population overall (20.2%).The average age is 28, 13 years below the national average.[4] This has a bearing on the extent of political activism within the community, with most being youth-led.

Muslims constitute some of the most deprived communities in the UK. Almost one-third of Muslims of working age have no qualifications, the highest proportion for any faith group.[5] Muslim children experience high levels of the risk factors associated with child poverty (national average figures are shown in brackets): 42% live in crowded accommodation (12%); 12% live in households without central heating (6%) and over one-third (35%) are growing up in households where there are no adults in employment (17%).[6] Muslims are the most disadvantaged faith group in the British labour market; they are three times more likely to be unemployed than the majority Christian group. Of those that are employed, job prospects are poor; Bangladeshis and Pakistanis are 2.5 times more likely than the white population to be unemployed and 3 times more likely to be in low-paid jobs.[7] Muslims are over-represented in the prison system. They make up 3% of the population but 9% of the population of prisoners.[8]

The relationship between Muslim communities and 'mainstream' British society (as if there were such a thing) has been the subject of much debate and analysis in recent years. A survey conducted by several Muslim groups found that since 9/11, 80% of Muslim respondents reported being

---

[3] H. Khan, "Unite but follow me: The tragic comedy of Muslim representation", *Q News*, March 2004, pp. 24-25; H. Khan, "Portfolio: Who speaks for British Muslims", *Q News*, March 2004, p. 23; S. El-Hassan, "A Report on a Consultation with Individuals from the Muslim Community", *IQRA Trust*, 2003, p. 2.

[4] A. Yunas Samad and Kasturi Sen, *Islam in the European Union:Transnationalism, Youth and the War on Terror* , Chapter 1, Oxford: Oxford University Press, 2007.

[5] Bunglawala, Halstead, Malik and Spalek, op. cit., p. 14.

[6] Ibid.

[7] Samud & Sen, op. cit.

[8] F. Guessous, N. Hooper and U. Moorthy, *Religion in Prison 1999 and 2000, England and Wales*, Home Office, 2001, 15/01, p. 1.

subjected to Islamophobia; 68% felt they had been perceived and treated differently; and 32% reported being subjected to discrimination at UK airports.[9] Some have argued that young Muslim men suffer disproportionately; Alexander suggests that they have emerged as the new 'folk devils' of popular and media imagination,[10] and Archer notes that in public discourse Muslim men are not only conceptualised as 'dangerous individuals' with a capacity for violence and/or terrorism, but also as 'culturally dangerous' – as threatening 'the British way of life'.[11]

A succession of opinion polls have shown many Muslims are uncomfortable with life in the UK, more so than those in mainland Europe.[12] The polling organisation, Pew, created a religious-cultural negativity index based on seven characteristics (selfishness, arrogance, immorality, violence, greediness, generosity and honesty). Britain's score, based on the perception of British Muslims of Western non-Muslims with regards to these characteristics, was higher than other European Muslims, and in fact, closer to the score (opinion) of Muslims in Muslim countries. British Muslims are more inclined to see a conflict between Islam and modernity; more likely to self-identify along religious lines than national lines; and more deeply concerned about the future of Muslims in Britain. When asked, "Is there a conflict between being a devout Muslim and living in a Modern society?", almost half of British Muslims (49%) felt there was.

At the same time, there is an ongoing and concerted campaign against Islamism by a coalition of both left and right who criticise the UK government for what they call a policy of appeasement towards these groups. Martin Bright of the *New Statesman* went so far as to claim that these organisations were engaged in a "sophisticated strategy of

---

[9] Forum Against Islamophobia and Racism, Al-Khoei Foundation and the Muslim College, *Counter-Terrorism Powers: Reconciling Security and Liberty in an Open Society: Discussion Paper – A Muslim Response*,London, FAIR, 2004, p. 22, quoted in Bunglawala, Halstead, Malik and Spalek, op. cit., p.19.

[10] C. Alexander, *The Asian Gang, ethnicity, identity, masculinity,* Oxford: Berg, 2000, p. 6 quoted in Bunglawala, Halstead, Malik and Spalek, op. cit., p. 19.

[11] L. Archer, *Race, Masculinity and Schooling: Muslim boys and education,* Maidenhead: Open University Press, 2003, p. 157,quoted in Bunglawala, Halstead, Malik and Spalek, op. cit., p. 19.

[12] http://pewglobal.org/reports/display.php?ReportID=253.

implanting Islamist ideology among young Muslims in Western Europe".[13] The groups to which he and others refer are, on the whole, actually pretty mainstream, often progressive ones, such as the FOSIS (Federation of Student Islamic Societies), which is the Muslim equivalent of NUS (National Union of Students) and Leicester's Islamic Foundation which has been at the forefront of efforts to foster understanding between communities. Islamism is not inherently violent,[14] but these nuances are rarely acknowledged and casual links are made between these groups and more specific concerns about violent extremism. This makes balanced debate difficult and affects the analysis of many of the groups outlined in later sections of this paper.

2. Al-Qaeda-linked and -inspired terrorism

MI5, the British security service, has said that it believes that there are 2,000 individuals who pose a direct threat to national security and public safety, and a further 2,000 who are actively plotting but not individually known to the authorities. It is thought that the UK faces 30 known plots, and the security service is monitoring 200 networks.[15] The threat was described by MI5 chief, Jonathan Evans as "the most immediate and acute peacetime threat in the 98-year history of my service". He also said that recruits are getting younger and that international influences are now much more diverse; it is no longer just links to Pakistan.[16]

There have been more than 200 terrorist convictions in the UK since 11 September 2001; the following summarises the details of the most notable cases and is correct as of June 2008.[17]

---

[13] Martin Bright, "When Progressives Treat with Reactionaries", *Policy Exchange*, 2007.

[14] Sara Silvestri, "Europe and Political Islam: Encounters of the Twentieth and Twenty-first Centuries", in Tahir Abbas, *Islamic Political Radicalism: A European Perspective*, Edinburgh: Edinburgh University Press, 2007.

[15] Gorden Brown's statement to Parliament, 19 March 2008.

[16] http://www.guardian.co.uk/terrorism/story/0,,2205608,00.html

[17] "'Thousands' pose UK terror threat" (http://news.bbc.co.uk/1/hi/uk/7078712.stm).

7/7 Co-conspirators

On 22 March 2007, Waheed Ali (born Shipon Ullah), 26, Sadeer Saleem, 27, and Mohammed Shakil, 31, all from Beeston, Leeds, were arrested on allegations that they were co-conspirators in the London bombings of 7 July 2005, and are currently on trial at Kingston Crown Court.[18]

It is alleged that Waheed Ali and Mohammed Shakil travelled with Mohammed Sidique Khan to Pakistan and it is believed that Shakil trained with him in a terrorist training camp there.[19] All three men have admitted that they travelled to London in December 2004 with 7/7 bomber Hasib Hussain, met up with Germaine Lindsay and visited together various London locations. The prosecution argues that these were scouting trips for the eventual attacks, something the defendants deny.[20] Prosecutors also claim that Khan and Shakil met with convicted terrorist Mohammed Junaid Babar and another man at Islamabad Airport on 24 July 2003. There is allegedly evidence on Ali's computer of frequent visits to jihadi affiliated websites, and police found a piece of paper in Shakil's possession with instructions for sending money to the Taliban embassy in Pakistan, and a long letter on his computer praising the 9/11 attackers. Similar documents about 9/11 were found on Saleem's seized computer.

On 9 May 2007, Khalid Khaliq, 34, was arrested on suspicion of "commission, preparation or instigation of acts of terrorism". He pleaded guilty to possession of an al-Qaeda training manual and was sentenced at Leeds Crown Court to 16 months.[21] Khaliq was apparently a single, unemployed father of three children. He was also a volunteer and trustee at Iqra Bookshop, which served as a centre for Muslim youth: 7/7 bombers Tanweer and Khan were also trustees of the bookshop. Khaliq is featured in a photograph along with Tanweer and Khan white-water rafting in Northern Wales.

---

[18] "More time to quiz 7 July suspects", *BBC News On-line*, 23 March 2007.

[19] David Williams and Lucy Ballinger, "Stunned families of 7/7 victims see first images of suicide bombers in the moments before they brought carnage to Tube", *The Daily Mail*, 11 April 2008.

[20] Ibid.

[21] "Man jailed over al-Qaeda training manual", *Sky News On-line*, 11 March 2008.

21/7 Co-conspirators

Muktar Ibrahim (or Ibrahim Muktar Said),[22] 29, Ramzi Mohammed, 25, Hussain Osman, 28, and Yassin Omar, 26, were found guilty of this attempted attack and sentenced to life imprisonment on 11 July 2007. Manfo Asiedu, 35, believed to be Ghanian, is considered to be the fifth bomber, abandoned his bomb and went back to Ibrahim's apartment to defuse a booby-trap bomb. He was convicted of conspiring to cause explosions and sentenced to 33 years.

All four would-be bombers had come under the influence and guidance of Abu Hamza and Abdullah el-Faisal in their teens and early twenties.[23] Ibrahim had apparently 'trained for jihad' in Sudan in 2003 and was under surveillance in May 2004. He was also stopped and questioned at Heathrow on his way to Islamabad in December 2004, and the prosecution speculated that he might have attended the same training camp as Sidique Khan.[24] He had been involved in criminal gang activity for which he picked up a custodial sentence.

Yassin Omar's flat in New Southgate, North London, served as the bomb-making factory. Omar was born in Somalia, and came to London in 1990 with his sisters where he was placed under the care of the local authority. He became increasingly attracted to Islam around 2000, began wearing a robe instead of Western clothes and started espousing support for the Taliban.

The fourth would-be bomber, Ramzi Mohammed, came to the UK from Somalia via Kenya when his father was forced to fight in one of the warring militias there.[25] He was placed in the care of social services in Slough. Until 2003, Mohammed led a Western lifestyle, but he then began attending the Finsbury Park Mosque and going to Hyde Park to listen to sermons. In January 2004, he began associating with Ibrahim and Omar. Police found a suicide note to his girlfriend and two children and extremist literature in his apartment.

---

[22] This is how he is referred to in the following article: "Ten in court for 'shielding' 21/7 attackers", *Times On-line*, 11 August 2005.

[23] Sandra Laville, "21/7 bombers: ringleader slipped through police net", *The Guardian*, 10 July 2007.

[24] "Profile: Muktar Ibrahim", *BBC News*, 11 July 2007.

[25] "Profile: Ramzi Mohammed", *BBC News*, 9 July 2007.

A number of individuals have been found guilty of helping the 21/7 plotters. Adel Yahya, 25, from Ethiopia was sentenced to 6 years and 9 months for collecting information that was useful to a person preparing a terrorist attack. He met Omar at school and they attended Finsbury Park Mosque together. Yahya accompanied the other bombers on the training trip to the Lake District in 2004 and extremist literature was found in his apartment.

The following individuals were found guilty of giving assistance and protection to the bombers while they were in hiding. Muhedin Ali, 29, from Ladbroke Grove was sentenced to 7 years (Ramzi Mohammed's suicide note was found in Ali's apartment). Wahbi Mohammed, 25, from Stockwell, brother of Ramzi Mohammed, was sentenced to 17 years. Ismail Abdurahman, 25, from Lambeth was sentenced to 10 years for failing to disclose information about Said and assisting Osman in evading arrest. Siraj Yassin Addullah Ali, 33, from Enfield, was sentenced to 12 years for failing to disclose information about Ibrahim and Omar. Ali was fostered by the same family as Omar and lived in the same block of flats in Southgate. Abdul Sherif, 30, from Stockwell, brother of Hussain Osman, was sentenced to 10 years. Osman travelled to Italy with Sherif's passport.[26]

A number of other individuals have recently been found guilty of assisting Osman: his wife, Yeshiemebet Girma,[27] 31, from Stockwell was jailed for 15 years for failing to inform police of her husband's plans to launch a terrorist attack and helping him to escape to Rome; Esayas Girma, 22, from Stockwell (brother of Yeshi Girma) and Mulumebet Girma, 23, from Brighton (sister of Yeshi Girma) were both sentenced to 10 years each; and Mohammed Kabashi, 23, (boyfriend of Mulu Girma) was jailed for 9 years.

London Fertiliser Plot

The group charged with this plot had purchased over 600 kg of ammonium nitrate in order to construct a bomb and had stored it in an Access Self-Storage unit in Hanwell, West London, and surveillance revealed a number

---

[26] "The accomplices to terror", *BBC News*, 4 February 2008.

[27] "Wife 'failed to report bomber's plans'", *Channel 4 News On-line*, 27 February 2008.

of targets including the Ministry of Sound nightclub in London and Bluewater shopping centre in Kent.

Omar Khayam, the ringleader, is a British citizen born and raised in Crawley, West Sussex in a largely secular Muslim home. He attended Al-Muhajiroun meetings and travelled to Pakistan to train in a Mujahideen training camp to fight in Kashmir. After returning home to Britain, he left again for Afghanistan in 2001 and met with members of the Taliban. He was deeply affected by the war in Iraq, and after the invasion returned to Pakistan, met with al-Qaeda member Abdul Hadi, and began planning attacks in the UK.

Jawad Akbar was born in Pakistan but moved to Crawley when he was eight. He attended Brunel University where he became involved in a radical Islamist political group. Akbar travelled with Khayam to Pakistan in 2003.

Salahuddin Amin was born in London but raised in Pakistan. He attended Al-Muhajiroun meetings in Luton, where he met individuals who were attempting to set up 'jihadi support networks' between the UK and various groups abroad. Eventually Amin moved back to Pakistan, where UK officials claim he was a facilitator between the UK and extremists in Pakistan. In 2005 he was sent to Britain where he apparently gave a "full and frank" interview that figured prominently in the trial. He later retracted his story, denying any knowledge of the plot.

Waheed Mahmood met Khayam at the local mosque in Crawley, and participated in meetings held in Luton. Mahmood had a family home in Pakistan where the plotters met and decided to attack the UK. Mahmood had dismantled his hard drive and thus there was only verbal evidence against him. He was caught on tape praising the attacks on Madrid as a "beautiful job", and discussing possible attacks on Bluewater shopping centre in Kent.

Anthony Garcia (born Rahman Benouis in Algeria) claimed that seeing videos of atrocities in Kashmir was a turning point for him. He travelled to Pakistan in 2003 and attended the same training camp as Khayam. Back in the UK, Garcia was the individual who purchased the fertiliser and accompanied Khayam and Nabeel Hussain to the Access Storage Unit.

Mohammed Khawaja, of Pakistani origin, was born and raised in the suburbs of Ottawa, Canada. He attended the same training camp in

Pakistan as the other plotters and agreed to provide the detonator for the bombs. He is still awaiting trial in Canada.[28]

Mohammed Babar acted as the key witness for the prosecution, after turning against the other defendants. He is an American of Pakistani descent who travelled to Pakistan shortly after the 9/11 attacks, reportedly to take part in the jihad, and while there came into contact with the other defendants in the case. He is serving three years in an American prison – a reduced sentence given in exchange for his testimony in the UK – and will enter the Witness Protection Program once he is released.

Abu Hamza

Abu Hamza (Mustafa Kamel Mustafa) emigrated to the UK from Egypt in 1979. He came into contact with Afghan Mujahideen fighters who had come to the UK to seek medical attention, and eventually left the UK to work and fight in Afghanistan, where he suffered the loss of his hand and eye. He also served in Bosnia. When he returned to the UK he became a leading figure in the Islamist movement and began to establish himself at the Finsbury Park Mosque, where he eventually gained de facto control. He was questioned about plots, including the massacre of tourists in Luxor, Eygpt, and the alleged bomb plots in Yemen, for which his son was jailed for three years. The mosque was raided in January 2003, in connection with the so-called 'ricin plot' of 2002, after which Hamza lost control of the mosque, although he continued to preach outside it. In 2004, the US government named Hamza as a 'terrorist facilitator with global reach'. He was successfully convicted on 11 counts and sentenced to seven years in jail.[29] In February 2008, the Home Secretary approved his extradition to the US, an appeal against which he recently lost.[30]

---

[28] Ian MacLeod, "Supreme Court rejects terrorism law challenge", *National Post*, 3 April 2008.

[29] Information taken from "BBC Profile: Abu Hamza", *BBC News*, 8 February 2008. See also "Timeline: Hamza Trial", *BBC News* (http://news.bbc.co.uk/1/hi/uk/4644030.stm).

[30] David Batty, "Abu Hamza loses legal fight against extradition to US", *The Guardian*, 20 June 2008

Plot to attack the US and UK – Dhiren Barot

Dhiren Barot was the mastermind behind a number of plans to attack targets in the UK and US, for which he was sentenced to life in prison. Seven other men also received jail sentences as co-conspirators. Their plans included blowing apart a London Underground tunnel and bombings using an explosives-packed limousine and a dirty radiation device. Barot allegedly showed his plans to al-Qaeda operatives who were hiding in Pakistan, while the other seven individuals made preparations back in the UK.

Barot was born in India to a Hindu family who emigrated to Kingsbury, in northwest London shortly after he was born. Barot converted to Islam when he was 20, reportedly after a visit to Kashmir.[31] In 1995, he allegedly went to Pakistan where he attended a terrorist training camp. Police found a manual with extensive notes on various weapons, chemicals for bomb-making and bomb-making instructions. Intended targets in the US included the IMF and World Bank in Washington, D.C., the Stock Exchange and Citigroup headquarters in New York and the Prudential Building in Newark, NJ.[32]

The co-conspirators were: Mohammed Naveed Bhatti, 27, of Harrow, North London, who was sentenced to 20 years; Junada Ferozem, 31, of Blackburn, who was sentenced to 22 years; Mohamed ul-Haq, 28, of Wembley, who was sentenced to 18 years; Abdul Aziz Jalil, 24, of Luton, who was sentenced to 26 years; Omar Abdul Rehman, 23, of Bushey, Hertfordshire, sentenced to 15 years; Quaisar Shaffi, 28, of Willesdon, sentenced to 15 years; and Nadeem Tarmohammed, 29, of Wembley, who was sentenced to 20 years.[33]

Transatlantic attack

In August 2006, a number of people were arrested on suspicion of plotting to blow up transatlantic planes using explosives disguised as soft drinks.

---

[31] Sandro Contenta, "He embraced Islam, then terrorism", *Toronto Star*, 16 October 2006.

[32] "Profile of Dhiren Barot", *BBC News*, 7 November 2006.

[33] Information taken from: "Dhiren Barot's co-conspirators", *BBC News*, 15 June 2007.

Eight men are currently on trial in the UK,[34] facing charges of conspiracy to murder and prepare acts of terrorism. All deny the charges. The prosecution's evidence consists of jihadi-related literature and images found in their homes, and 'martyrdom videos' made by six of the eight defendants.[35] Those on trial are: Abdula Ahmed Ali, 27, of Walthamstow; Tanvir Hussain, 27; and Assad Ali Sarwar, 28, who have all pleaded guilty to conspiracy to cause explosions and conspiring to cause public nuisance by distributing al-Qaeda-style videos threatening suicide bomb attacks in Britain.[36] They stand alongside Umar Islam and Ibrahim Savant, 27 (who reportedly left a suicide note for his wife),[37] both of whom admit conspiring to cause a public nuisance. Alongside them are Mohammed Yasar Gulzar; Wabeed Zaman, 22, of Walthamstow and reportedly follower of Tabligh Jamaat; and Waheed Arafat Kahn, 24, of East London.[38] Khan was a student at London Metropolitan University, was president of the Islamic Society affiliated with FOSIS, and he was also reportedly a Tabligh Jamaat follower. Two others are charged with failing to disclose information, but have not yet come to trial: Cossor Ali, 25, of Walthamstow; and Mehran Hussain, of Chingford.[39]

Rashid Rauf, a British-born citizen, was thought to be the mastermind behind the attacks and was arrested by Pakistani authorities at the urging of British and American authorities in August 2006. Pakistani courts ruled that there was not enough evidence to convict him of terrorism-related charges, so the charges were reduced to forgery, although Britain and the US continued to press for his extradition. He is alleged to have escaped police custody,[40] although there are suspicions that the Pakistani authorities still have Rauf in custody but simply do not want to extradite him to Britain for reasons unknown.[41]

---

[34] Taken from: http://www.dawn.com/2008/04/05/top13.htm.
[35] See http://www.bucksfreepress.co.uk/display.var.2177305.0.0.php.
[36] See "Terror Trial: Three admit parliament bomb plot", *The Guardian*, 15 July 2008
[37] "Paradise plea by plotter", *The Sun*, 19 April 2008.
[38] See http://news.bbc.co.uk/1/hi/uk_politics/7348936.stm.
[39] "Two Terror plot suspects freed", BBC News, 24 August 2006.
[40] "Pakistan manhunt for escaped terror suspect", *The Guardian*, 17 December 2007.
[41] "The mysterious disappearance of an alleged terrorist mastermind", *The Guardian*, 28 January 2008.

London and Glasgow airport plots (29/30 June 2007)

The most recent high-profile terrorist plots occurred on 29 and 30 June 2007, when two cars loaded with explosives were parked outside a nightclub in London's West End and the next day an attempt was made to drive a truck loaded with explosives into the entrance of Glasgow airport. The two men who drove the truck into Glasgow airport – Dr. Kafeel Ahmed, 27, from Bangalore, India and Dr. Bilal Abdullah, 27, an Iraqi doctor registered to work in the UK – are thought also to have parked the 'bomb cars' in London. Dr. Ahmed suffered 90% burns and died in hospital, while Dr. Abdullah was charged with conspiracy to cause explosions and was scheduled to stand trial in October 2008 with Dr. Mohammed Asha, a doctor from Jordan of Palestinian descent who is charged with conspiracy to cause explosions.[42]

Five other individuals were arrested, including Dr. Asha's wife, but three were released shortly after without charge. A fourth individual, Dr. Mohammed Haneef, was arrested in Australia but all charges against him have been dropped. Additionally, Dr. Kafeel Ahmed's brother, Dr. Sabeel Ahmed, was arrested and charged with withholding information about the attacks. Kafeel Ahmed had emailed his brother on the morning of the attack to instruct him to withhold information from the police. Dr. Sabeel Ahmed pleaded guilty to the charge and was sentenced to 18 months in jail, a lesser sentence due to the fact that he received the email after the attacks had already occurred. It was reported in various Indian papers that the two Ahmed brothers had undergone a change after becoming members of Tabligh e-Jamaat.[43]

Lessons from UK terrorism cases

Many academics have sought to construct overarching theories about the causes and drivers of radicalisation, but these normally seem to prove only the exceptions rather than the rule. The case studies above show that few – if any – patterns are universal, and that it is difficult to draw causal links. However, these cases do highlight a number of factors that are often present, although it is impossible to know with any certainty how

---

[42] "Bomb plot: Arrests and releases", *BBC News*, 5 October 2007.

[43] See http://www.dnaindia.com/report.asp?NewsID=1109091. http://sundaytimes.lk/070708/International/i503.html.

instrumental each one is on the path to violence. Several factors illustrated in the table below stand out as important, namely 'places', 'leaders', 'relatinships', 'experiences' and 'grievances'.

Factor	Examples
Key places	• Finsbury Park Mosque (now known as North London Mosque, apparently purged of its radical elements) (21/7) • Speakers Corner, Hyde Park (21/7) • Iqra bookstore in Beeston (7/7) • Local mosques (fertiliser plot) • Trips to Pakistan (fertiliser plot; Khan reportedly met Khayam and others involved in the fertiliser plot at a training camp in Pakistan) • Tablighi Jamaat meetings/events (transatlantic attack plot, London/Glasgow airport plot) • Universities, Islamic students groups: London Metropolitan University (transatlantic attack plot, 21/7 plotters); Brunel University (fertiliser plot) • Websites (Numerous individuals in different plots had evidence of accessing jihadi websites; Al-Muhajioun – now known as Ahl ul-Sunnah Wa al-Jamma operates exclusively by invitation-only internet chat room) • Al-Muhajiroun meetings – Crawley, Luton: (fertiliser plot)
Charismatic leaders	• Abu Hamza (influenced 21/7 plotters) • Sheikh el-Faisal (influenced Germaine Lindsay of 7/7, Richard Reid and Zacarias Moussaoui) • Omar Bakri (influenced fertiliser plotters) • Dhiren Barot (influenced his co-plotters, as well as Ramzi Mohammed, 21/7)
Relationship links	Family Links (Britain and Pakistan, in particular): • Rashid Rauf's (transatlantic attack plot) wife is reportedly closely related by marriage to Maulana Masood Azhar, the founder of Jaish-e-Mohammed, an armed group that fought in Kashmir and was connected to Pakistan's intelligence service, ISI* • Waheed Mahmood (fertiliser plot) had a family house in Pakistan where the conspirators met to plan Friendships (Britain and Pakistan): • Salahuddin Amin (fertiliser plot) was born in Britain but raised in Pakistan and was the facilitator between British extremists and al-Qaeda Local friendships:

	• 7/7 plotters all grew up together in Beeston, Leeds. Khan referred to his friends in one of his videos as his daughter's 'uncles'
Experiences	Immigration and asylum systems: Yassin Omar, Ramzi Mohammed, Adel Yahya (21/7); Jawad Akbar, Anthony Garcia (fertiliser plot); Dhiren Barot (UK/US plots); Dr Kafeel Ahmed, Dr Bilal Abdullah (London and Glasgow airport); Social services: Yassin Omar, Ramzi Mohammed (21/7)
Stated/assumed grievances	British foreign policy: Mohammed Siddique Khan (7/7); Omar Khayam, Anthony Garcia (fertiliser plot); Abu Hamza

* Duncan Campbell and Randeep Ramesh, "Mysterious Disappearance of an alleged Terrorist Mastermind", *The Guardian*, 14 August 2006.

3. Radical Groups and Movements

What follows is an account of organisations and networks within the three categories of radicalisation that form the structure for this collaborative research project: non-political religious, religious and political, and non-religious political. Where there is evidence of links to violence, this is documented, although in many cases this is based on subjective judgments and fragmentary evidence. It is therefore more appropriate to view these groups as 'radical' rather than radicalised, where the latter term is assumed to infer an intention to use violence. Groups often cross the boundaries between the three categories so this should be viewed as a broad analytical tool rather than a precise typology.

3.1 Non-political religious groups

Tablighi Jamaat

Britain is the current locus of Tablighi Jamaat in the West, with the Dewsbury Central Mosque in West Yorkshire serving as its European headquarters, although the group is highly decentralised.[44] It has been claimed that terrorists have used membership of this apolitical group as cover,[45] and that it has served as a first stop to violent extremism. But although its fundamentalist ideas are appealing, its apolitical stance means

---

[44] Ibid.

[45] See http://www.dailymail.co.uk/pages/live/articles/news/news.html?in_article_id=466015&in_page_id=1770

that many move on. It has even been criticised by some Muslims for failing to condemn Israel or release comments in support of Muslims in Chechnya, Kashmir and elsewhere.[46]

Tablighi Jamaat attracts a wide range of individuals, from business and political leaders to those seeking to turn their lives around after going off the rails. Its anti-Western, isolationist and fundamental characteristics also draw young Muslims who are disillusioned with modern society. Farad Esack, a South African Islamic scholar who spent 12 years with the group in Pakistan, said of the group, that it "attracts angry people -- people who need absolutes, who can't stand the grayness of life".'[47] Convicted and suspected terrorists in the UK who have been or are suspected of being members include: Richard Reid, Kafeel and Sabeel Ahmed, Mohammed Sidique Khan, Shehzad Tanweer, and some of those involved in the transatlantic plot.

Deobandism

Deobandism advocates a return to traditional interpretations of Islam and is often associated with Tablighi Jamaat. Some have argued that it has connections to violent groups like al-Qaeda and the Taliban, but its followers claim these groups have distorted their faith.[48] Deobandism is now the dominant force in British Islam.[49] Riyadh ul Haq – reportedly in line to become the spiritual leader of Britain's Deobandi adherents – runs an Islamic Academy in Leicester and used to be imam at Birmingham Central Mosque. One of the main reservations concerns its alleged advocacy of separatism. It is claimed that Riyadh ul Haq has urged Muslims to segregate themselves from non-Muslims; he has reportedly stated that friendship with Christians and Jews makes a "mockery of Allah's religion", that football is "a cancer that has infected our youth", and that music is the "Satanic web" Jews spread to corrupt Muslim youth.[50] It

---

[46] Ibid.

[47] Ibid.

[48] Randeep Ramesh, "Indian Islamic Group attacks BBC Film for Bin Laden Link", *The Guardian*, 29 October 2007.

[49] Ibid.

[50] Andrew Norfolk, "Hardline Takeover of British Mosques", *The Times*, 7 September 2007.

has also been claimed that he has argued that Muslims ought to "shed blood" overseas in jihad, in defence of Islam.[51]

Salafism (Saudi-Wahhabism) (da'wa)

Salafism in the UK is organised under the name of Markaz Jamiat Ahl-e-Hadith and is centred at the Green Lane Masjid/Mosque in Birmingham. There are over 40 M.J.A.H branches throughout England and two based in Scotland.[52] The Green Lane Mosque was brought to national attention when a Channel 4 *Dispatches* programme claimed to uncover 'hateful' sermons delivered at the Mosque;[53] "speaker after speaker uttering hate speech against unbelievers, Jews, women and homosexuals."[54] The mosque complained that the programme had taken a handful of phrases out of context.[55] A report by the right-wing think tank, Policy Exchange, went on to claim that UK Islamic organisations were receiving significant funding from Saudi government-related groups who espouse a fundamentalist view of Islam.

Salafism has come under scrutiny because groups such as al-Qaeda and the Taliban draw their interpretation of Islam from Salafist origins. However, as Trevor Stanley notes, there are various groups of Salafis who claim to be 'true Salafist' and who consider others – such as al-Qaeda – as takfiris or 'ex-communicators'. Moreover, while they share similar beliefs about the interpretation of a pure form of Islam, they disagree over the means of changing society either through da'wa or through violence. An article in the *Studies in Conflict & Terrorism Journal* argues that there are three different types of Salafists: purists, politicos and jihadists.

---

[51] Ibid.

[52] See http://www.mjah.org/ContactUs/MJAHVenuesCircles/tabid/65/Default.aspx.

[53] *The Guardian*, reporting on the Channel 4 Dispatches programme, mentions radical imams and sermons at the Green Lane and Sparkbrook Mosques. Jamie Doward, "Revealed: preacher's messages of hate", 7 January 2007.

[54] "The Hijacking of British Islam", The Policy Exchange, London, p. 19.

[55] Ibid., quoting another source.

3.2 Religious and political groups

Hizb ut-Tahrir (Liberation Party)

Hizb ut-Tahrir was founded in 1953, in Jordanian-ruled Jerusalem by Taqiuddin al-Nabhani with the goal of uniting Muslims under one supreme Islamic state or caliphate. Officially, HT disavows violence, but defends the right to self-defence (by means of violence). The organisation's lack of clarity on this issue leaves it open to accusations of promoting violence. The group is said to be at its strongest and best organised in Britain (although membership remains low in comparison to other groups) and Croydon Mosque has been considered a base for HT events and operations. HT first became prominent in the UK in the mid-1990s with a noticeable presence on university campuses. In fact, throughout its history, there has been a keen focus on recruiting university students. HT's leader in Britain during the mid-1990s was Omar Bakri, who left the group in 1996 to form the more radical Al-Muhajiroun.

The group seemed to fade in the late 1990s, but has re-emerged in an ostensibly more respectable incarnation. Following the attacks in London on 7 July 2005, the British government sought to ban HT,[56] but was forced to back down after police and intelligence agencies reported that there was no direct and explicit connection between HT and violent extremism. HT was, however, banned from UK university campuses by the National Union of Students, although it is thought to continue to operate covertly.[57] Controversy surrounding the group continues. In a 2007 BBC *Panorama* programme, a former member argued for the organisation to be outlawed in Britain, claiming that the softer image presented by HT Britain is a ploy to enable its continued legal functioning. He also claims that Asaf Hanif and Omar Sharif, the two British citizens responsible for a terrorist attack on a bar in Tel Aviv in 2003, were members of HT in Britain, and that Bilal Abdulla was also part of HT circles with Maher in Cambridge.[58]

---

[56] "PM forced to shelve Islamist group ban", *The Independent*, 18 July 2006.

[57] Steve Bloomfield, Raymond Whitaker and Sophie Goodchild, "Islamic group in secret plan to recruit UK students", *The Independent*, 4 September 2005.

[58] "Hizb ut-Tahrir under Increasing Pressure in the UK", *Terrorism Focus*, Jamestown Foundation, Volume 4, Issue 29, 18 September 2007.

Al-Muhajiroun, The Saviour (or Saved) Sect and Al Ghurabaa

Al-Muhajiroun was founded by Sheikh Omar Bakri Mohammed in 1996, and he shared leadership with Anjem Choudary. Its version of Islam is described as neo-Kharijite, which is a sect of Islam distinct from Sunni and Shia. The group gained notoriety when it held the now infamous 'Magnificent 19' conference glorifying the 9/11 hijackers at Finsbury Park Mosque. It has been reported that three of the 9/11 hijackers were connected with the group in Germany, and former students from British universities have been discovered fighting amongst "terrorists" abroad – at one point leading the Russian government to ask Britain to ban the group when British students were found fighting in Chechnya.[59] Al-Muhajiroun disbanded in 2004 in anticipation of a ban, and split into two separate groups, The Saviour Sect and Al Ghurabaa. These two groups were banned under the British Terrorism Act of 2006, but by the time the ban had come into force these groups had already created dozens of front organisations, many of which were located in Britain.[60]

There is evidence to suggest a link to violence. Abu Izzadeen and Sulayman Keeler – both found guilty of inciting terrorism – were members of both groups.[61] Other alleged members include Abdul Saleem, 32 years old, charged with inciting terrorism, but cleared of fundraising; Ibrahim Hassan, 25 years old, charged with inciting terrorism, but cleared of fundraising; Shah Jilal Hussein, 25 years old, found guilty of funding terrorism remains missing after failing to turn up to court; Abdul Muhid, 25 years old, found guilty of funding terrorism; Hussain Rajib Khan, 29 years old, was cleared of funding terrorism, and the jury was unable to reach a verdict on a charge of inciting terrorism; and Omar Zaheer, 28 years old, for whom the jury were unable to reach a verdict on a charge of inciting terrorism.

---

[59] "Muslim student group linked to terrorist attacks", *The Guardian*, 19 September 2001.

[60] Ian Cobain and Nick Fielding, "Banned Islamists spawn front organisations: Al Ghurabaa tries to ensure survival with groups across UK", *The Guardian*, 22 July 2006.

[61] "Islamist Activist guilty of funding terror", *The Guardian*, 18, April 2008.

Ahl ul-Sunnah Wa al-Jamma (ASWJ)

Sulyaman (Simon) Keeler formed ASWJ in 2005 as the reunification of The Saved Sect and Al Ghurabaa, with Omar Bakri Mohammed, Abu Yahya, Abu Izzadeen, Abu Uzair, and Anjem Choudary all extensively involved. They have claimed it is not a jihadist group, but evidence from their invite-only Internet forum suggests otherwise. Infiltrators to the site claim that Bakri preaches under a number of aliases, and has been quoted as praising the 7/7 attackers saying they were "in paradise".[62] It has also been reported that the ASWJ website has called for British Muslims to travel to Somalia to fight against Ethiopian troops, who they claim are supported by Western countries and Israel.[63] The group claims to have 1,000 followers.

Islamic Council of Britain

This organisation was apparently formed by Abu Hamza and centred around the Finsbury Park Mosque. It was responsible for organising the infamous conference held there celebrating the 9/11 attackers. It seems it was disbanded with the arrest and conviction of Abu Hamza and the instatement of new mosque leadership (the mosque is now known as the North Central London Mosque).

Alleged Jamaat-e-Islami Affiliates

Jamaat-e-Islami is primarily an Islamist political party based in Pakistan. It was founded in 1941 by Abu al-A'la al-Mawdudi and is the oldest political party within Pakistan. Jamaat-e-Islami opposes all types of Westernisation, including democratically structured government and seeks to establish an Islamic state in Pakistan. JI also supports, and is affiliated with, the Muslim Brotherhood. There is disagreement over whether JI supports or condones violent struggle. JI itself claims to work only through non-violent means of persuasion, but US intelligence claims to have found links between JI and al-Qaeda after the arrest of Khalid Sheik Mohammed and other al-Qaeda members in the homes of JI members.[64] While Jamaat-e-Islami does not have an explicit party or group in Britain, some commentators have

---

[62] "Covert preaching of banned cleric", BBC News, 14 November 2006.

[63] "UK Website: Join Somalia Jihad", www.ynetnews.com, 28 December 2006.

[64] "Jamaat-e-Islami, Hizbul Mujahideen & Al Qaeda", South Asian Analysis Group, www.southasiananalysis.org, 29 May 2003.

claimed that a number of British Muslim organisations – including the Muslim Association of Britain, the Islamic Foundation, and the United Kingdom Islamic Mission – have close ties to Jamaat-e-Islami.[65] Ed Hussain has claimed that East London Mosque is controlled by the Bandladeshi JI and that the mosque serves as a gateway to extremism.[66]

Muslim Association of Britain

MAB was founded in 1997 and describes itself as a "mainstream grass roots organisation" which "actively seeks to dispel the misconceptions about Muslims and helps to act as a bridge to promote better understanding between the UK and the Muslim World". It has worked closely with the Stop the War Coalition and the Campaign for Nuclear Disarmament. It has been accused of links to Hamas and other such groups. Policy Exchange claims it is the closest thing in Britain to the Muslim Brotherhood and Jamaat-e-Islami and MP Louise Ellman claims that Azzam Tamimi has been an adviser to Hamas and a spokesperson for the Muslim Brotherhood. She also quotes him in a number of instances making comments in defence of suicide bombers in Palestine as martyrs: "do not call them suicide bombers, call them Shuhada [martyrs"; "they [Israelis] have guns. We have the human bombs. We love death, they love life"; "For us Muslims, martyrdom is not the end of things, but the beginning of the most wonderful of things."[67] He made the following comment to the BBC: "Sacrificing myself for Palestine is a noble cause. It is the straight way to pleasing God and I would do it if I had the opportunity." Although individual accusations have been made, there is no evidence to suggest MAB has played any role in violent extremism in or towards the UK.

3.3 *Non-religious political groups*

In recent years, there has been a substantial rise in the amount of political activism within Muslim communities in the UK. This developed in two waves: first, that sparked by the build up to the invasion of Iraq in 2003,

---

[65] Most notably the Policy Exchange report cited previously

[66] Dr. Muhammed Abdul Bari, now Secretary-General of the Muslim Council of Britain, was chairman of the East London Mosque. See report by Denis MacEoin, "The Hijacking of British Islam", Policy Exchange, London, 2007.

[67] Ibid.

and second following 7/7 when communities decided to organize themselves helped by a massive influx of government funding for 'capacity building'. This activity is, on the whole, entirely non-violent and groups include the Asian Youth Movement (which no longer exists); the Stop the War Coalition; the Respect Coalition; School Students against War (affiliated with Stop the War); the Socialist Workers Party; Globalise Resistance; Permanent Revolution (UK); and the Workers Power. Most groups are small-scale, tend to have regional bases rather than national reach, and are often allied to other issues, such as housing, foreign policy, deprivation, student politics, and so forth. Only the Stop the War Coalition is large enough to merit a detailed description, and is also important because it is linked to and spawned so many of the other movements and organisations.

Stop the War Coalition

The Stop the War Coalition is important for a number of reasons: it gained huge traction politically; it attracted a massive following, not just in the UK but in many other countries; it became a focal point for other protest; and because it brought Muslims and non-Muslims working together for a common goal. The key actors in the movement are the Socialist Workers Party and the Muslim Association of Britain (mentioned in the previous section); and its most notable members are George Galloway, Tony Benn, Tariq Ali and Salma Yaqoob.

One of the other interesting things about the Stop the War Coalition is that it managed to span the generational divide that runs deep within many Muslim communities, where older generations have often tended to stay out of formal politics. While the Coalition was led by the young, it attracted older participants, too. As Mobeen Azhar said of the Coalition's activity in Leeds, "I have grown up in a climate of disagreement and apathy in the mosque. My peers (and organisations like MPAC) will bear testament to the frustration of many in my generation with the depoliticised mentalities so unavoidably associated with many of our religious leaders. To get my parents' generation engaging, talking and organising was a very personal breakthrough for me."[68]

---

[68] R. Briggs, "A new political landscape: Who's afraid of the Respect Party? Dissent and Cohesion in Modern Britain", *Renewal*, 1 June 2007.

In most cases, these non-violent forms of political activism make a positive contribution to political and civic life in the UK and are empowering for communities which suffer high levels of deprivation (and are therefore in need of activism to change their circumstances). They might also prove to be part of the solution to violent extremism. As Salma Yaqoob says, '…the dominant character of Muslim radicalisation in Britain today points not towards terrorism or religious extremism, but in the opposite direction: towards political engagement in new, radical and progressive coalitions that seek to unite Muslim with non-Muslim in parliamentary and extra-parliamentary strategies to affect change.' She added, '…it is only by encouraging the widening of this progressive expression of Muslim radicalism that the political purchase of strategies based on either terrorism or Muslim sectarianism can be minimised.'[69]

Some have sought to present these movements as dangerous and have described their emergence as a sign of the Muslim community's desire for separatism.[70] But this is not supported by polling which shows that young Muslims are keen to engage.[71] Analysis of the 2003 Home Office Citizenship Survey suggests that political activity by Muslims positively contributes to their sense of identification with Britain. What's more, in a recent survey four-fifths (81%) of Muslims said it was important to proactively engage in British politics,[72] and in another, two-thirds of Muslim students said they did not see a conflict between loyalty to the Ummah and to the UK.[73] Set alongside Pew's data, this creates a confusing picture of the Muslim community in the UK. However, one must remember

---

[69] S. Yaqoob, "British Islamic political radicalism", in T. Abbas (ed.), *Islamic political radicalism: A European perspective,* Edinburgh: Edinburgh University Press, 2007.

[70] *When Progressives Treat with Reactionaries,* Martin Bright, Policy Exchange, London, 2007.

[71] It should be noted that many opinion polls have been conducted in recent years on these themes. However, very few can be considered reliable as they tend to draw on a very small sample that cannot be seen as representative.

[72] S Gohir, *Understanding the Other Perspective: Muslim and non-Muslim relations,* Birmingham, Muslim Voice UK, 2006.

[73] Federation of Student Islamic Societies (FOSIS), "The Voice of Muslim Students: A report into the attitudes and perceptions of Muslim students following the July 7th London attacks", FOSIS, London, 2005.

that community attitudes are never straightforward and there is not necessarily anything contradictory in a community feeling unhappy about life in the UK and also wanting to do something about it through increased political activity.

Riots in northern towns

Although not a movement or organisation, it is worth noting in this section the disturbances in Northern towns which saw violence on the streets in a number of places which was in large part explained by the socio-economic circumstances of Muslim and Asian communities set out in an earlier section. In the summer of 2001, a number of northern towns experienced violent clashes predominantly caused by racial tensions, exacerbated by orchestrated rivalries between criminal gangs. In Oldham, the riots took place over three successive nights in May and left 86 police officers injured. Violence then erupted in Burnley, resulting in clashes between hundreds of white and Asian youths and widespread damage to property and businesses. On 7 July 2001, the worst violence broke out in the Manningham area of Bradford when 1000 young men took to the streets, leaving 120 police officers injured.[74]

The causes of the riots differed in each place; in Oldham they were due to racial tensions between Asian and white communities caused by social division and poverty; in Burnley gang rivalries were blamed; and in Bradford, tensions flared when an Anti-Nazi League march led to a stand-off with National Front supporters. A number of independent reviews were commissioned for each city, along with an overarching national report authored by community cohesion expert, Ted Cantle. He pointed to the fact that many communities lived 'parallel lives' and made recommendations around a number of underlying causes, including housing, youth, regeneration, politics and education.[75]

---

[74] "Q&A: 2001 northern town riots", http://newsvote.bbc.co.uk/mpapps/print/news.bbc.co.uk/1/hi/uk/5032166.stm (accessed 21/07/2008)

[75] *Community Cohesion: A Report of the Independent Review Team*, Ted Cantle (Chairman), UK Home Office.

4. Policy Responses

The UK government's counter-terrorism policies are brought together under the CONTEST strategy. It is a 4-pronged approach which covers the so-called 'four p's': prevent, pursue, protect and prepare. The government's security budget (which covers all security, not just counter-terrorism spending) was £2.5 billion in 2007 and will rise to £3.5 billion by 2010, reflecting the growing importance of security. Increased resource to the Security Service (MI5) gives a clue as to the importance placed specifically on counter-terrorism; its staffing levels were 2000 in 2001, but by 2007 they had risen to 3,300 and will grow until they reach 4000 in the next few years. The Prime Minister also announced at the end of 2007 that the government had established dedicated regional counter-terrorism units with more than 2000 police and support staff.

There have been two significant changes to government policy in the last year or so: increased emphasis on 'prevent', and the realisation of the importance of language and communication.

Engagement work with Muslim communities began in earnest after 7/7 when the Home Office set up a formal process called the Preventing Extremism Together (PET) working groups. The process was a step in the right direction, but was widely criticized for being rushed, government-led, and involving too narrow a group of individuals,[76] but it established the principle of engagement and many lessons have been learned as a result. Since then, the government has greatly widened the range of individuals and organisations it engages and works with and has injected much needed money into creating, sustaining and developing community infrastructure that in many cases wasn't there to begin with. But decisions about engagement are always fraught, especially when so much is at stake and the complexities of community politics are difficult for outsiders to navigate. In July 2008, there was considerable controversy surrounding the second bi-annual Islam Expo, whose main organizers include individuals involved with MAB. Some accused them of being supporters of Hamas,[77]

---

[76] *Bringing it Home: Community-based approaches to counter-terrorism*, Rachel Briggs, Catherine Fieschi and Hannah Lownsbrough, Demos, London, 2006.

[77] Stop pandering to the Islamist extremists, Ed Husain, Evening Standard, 070708

which led the Communities Secretary, Hazel Blears, to ban any government involvement in the event.[78]

The Prime Minister, Gordon Brown, signaled his commitment to the prevent agenda by announcing several hundreds of millions of pounds of new funding over the next three years. This includes an additional £240 million to the Home Office between now and 2011 towards counter-terrorism policing; £400 million in the next 3 years invested through the Foreign Office, Department for International Development, and the British Council to tackle radicalisation and promote understanding overseas; and £70 million towards community projects dedicated to tackling violent extremism. In announcing this spending in a November 2007 speech to Parliament, he said:

> To deal with the challenge posed by the terrorist threat we have to do more, working with communities in our country, first, to challenge extremist propaganda and support alternative voices; secondly, to disrupt the promoters of violent extremism by strengthening our institutions and supporting individuals who may be being targeted; thirdly, to increase the capacity of communities to resist and reject violent extremism; and fourthly, to address issues of concern exploited by ideologues, where by emphasizing our shared values across communities we can both celebrate and act upon what unites us.

The second and related major change has been a marked shift in government tone and language in recognition of the fact that the government was often making matters worse. The Research Information and Communications Unit (RICU), a unit within the newly formed Office for Security and Counter-Terrorism (OSCT) in the Home Office but with cross government reach, is seeking to improve government language in a way that avoids playing into the hands of the violent extremists and wins the hearts and minds of Britain's Muslim communities. Ministers will no longer use the phrase 'war on terror'; they will talk about a 'struggle' rather than a 'battle' and will stop talking about the 'Muslim problem'.[79] While

---

[78] Hazel Blears' speech to Policy Exchange seminar can be accessed: http://www.policyexchange.org.uk/Events.aspx?id=688

[79] http://www.guardian.co.uk/terrorism/story/0,,2213958,00.html
http://www.guardian.co.uk/terrorism/story/0,,2215012,00.html

this shift in Ministerial and offical language is visible, it has yet to make significant inroads at the operational level.

The policy setting for Muslims is also influenced by a wider range of policies, such as immigration, integration, citizenship and cohesion, and in these areas the rhetoric has on the whole become harder in response to wider public concerns about security and fairness in resource allocation. In terms of policies relating to 'living together', there has been a shift from multiculturalism and the celebration of difference towards integration (for example, the Commission on Integration and Cohesion and the Green Paper on Citizenship), with the emphasis on immigrants and minority communities fitting into life in Britain, becoming active citizens, learning the language and playing a role in wider society. These specific initiatives are happening against the backdrop of an increasingly vocal debate about Britishness and identity.

Conclusions

The threat to the UK from radicalisation will remain present for a long time yet; it has been described by MI5 as the most serious danger to face the UK for the last century. As we search for solutions, it is perhaps not surprising that suspicion falls on a range of groups and individuals whose behaviour may on the surface appear dangerous or subversive. However, if alienatiion of the next generation of young Muslims is to be avoided, it will be important to engage in greater depth with these groups, understand the complexities of community politics, and come to a more nuanced understanding of the rich mosaic of political mobilisation that is now flourishing across large parts of our Muslim communities. This mobilisation will in fact, with some notable exceptions, offer part of the solution to radicalisation: it gives positive alternatives for those who feel disillusioned and voiceless, it provides vehicles for solving the deeply entrenched problems associated with deprivation suffered by many Muslims, these organisations can challenge extremist rhetoric and build community resilience, and it will eventually provide a mechanism for political integration.

7. Muslims in Spain and Islamic Religious Radicalism
Patricia Bezunartea, José Manuel López & Laura Tedesco

Introduction

Spain has historically been considered a country of emigration, but this has recently changed. The year 2000 was a turning point, as since then the immigration issue has been on the political agenda. Indeed, the administrative institutions for managing immigration were created between 2000 and 2004. Spain's immigration law was amended four times during that period and four regularisation processes were implemented. A further 600,000 immigrants underwent a regularisation process in 2005.

Immigration is the most important socio-economic change that has taken place in Spain in recent years, putting an end to Spain's demographic stagnation and energising its economy. Between the years 2001 and 2006, 50% of GDP growth was owing to the positive effect that immigration had had on per capita income.[1]

Immigration in Spain is thus a recent phenomenon. As a result, there are no clear models with which to approach this issue, nor are there well-established social structures to deal with possible conflicts or social confrontations. There is still much to be done and while this is the cause of uncertainty, it is also the source of many opportunities to improve and learn from other European experiences.

---

[1] See Cámara Madrid, *Las Relaciones entre Europa y América Latina a debate*, Cámara Oficial de Comercio e Industria de Madrid, October 2007.

This chapter starts from the assumption that the process of integration in Spain is different from that in other EU countries and that it is marked by two main characteristics. First, immigrants from Muslim countries are fewer in number than immigrants from Latin American countries. Second, the existence of domestic terrorism, through the Basque separatist group ETA, tempers the impact of tensions and conflicts from radical Islam.

Recent polls indicate that immigration and terrorism are among the main concerns of Spaniards. According to the 2007 Opinion Barometer survey conducted by the Sociological Research Centre (CIS)[2], immigration (a concern for 11.6% of the population) stands fourth behind terrorism (23.6%), unemployment (14.4%) and housing (14.1%) in terms of the problems perceived as affecting Spain most acutely. This reference to terrorism focuses more on that perpetrated by ETA than that of the Islamic terrorist cells. Of course, the 2004 Madrid attacks changed many aspects of Spaniards' perception of Islamic terrorism, making it much more real and threatening. Nevertheless, ETA's permanent campaign and the failed Basque peace processes are still much more at the forefront of people's minds.

Therefore, the tensions and conflicts having the greatest impact on Spain do not appear to focus on immigrants from Muslim countries. These groups blend together with other groups of immigrants – the majority of whom are South American – and the threat of Islamic terrorism is blurred by the ETA attacks, street violence in the Basque country, extortion of the Basque business community, court trials of ETA members, the capture of wanted terrorists and the permanent debate among the majority parties on the nation's stance against ETA.

Taking all these issues into consideration, this chapter offers an analysis of the situation of immigrants in Spain from predominately Muslim countries. A first section focuses on recent immigration into Spain from all sources to help put the situation of Muslim immigrants into perspective. The second gives a brief recent history of the Muslim community in Spain and a description of how its institutions have been formed. The third section provides a study of the tensions and conflicts

---

[2] See Centro de Investigaciones Sociológicas (CIS), Barómetros de Opinión, CIS, Madrid, 2007 (retrieved from http://www.cis.es).

revolving around the 11 March 2004 attacks, their political impact, the court trial and judgement. A final section looks briefly at the situation of the cities of Ceuta and Melilla, Spanish enclaves in Morocco. The conclusions offer some reflections on the future of the Muslim community and its potential for integration.

One of the overarching questions dealt with in this volume is how one can change the al-Qaeda narrative and undo the relationship established between Islam, al-Qaeda and international terrorism.[3] We feel that this is genuinely possible in Spain if the government is able to help the first and second generations of immigrants to integrate, especially the Moroccans as the largest group, because it is our belief that, for the time being, the Muslim community in Spain has not embraced violence but rather integration.

1. Recent immigration in Spain

As mentioned above, immigration has grown considerably over the last several years. A closer look at the figures helps to put the reality of Spain's Muslim communities into context.

Immigration in Spain is very recent and has progressed swiftly. In just a decade, the number of immigrants has skyrocketed, growing from half a million in the middle of the 1990s to over 5 million today. The largest group is from Morocco (676,405) followed by Ecuador (451,072), Colombia (326,459), Argentina (287,760), Bolivia (238,605), Peru (160,603), Brazil (140,942), Venezuela (142,709) and the Dominican Republic (113,681). There are in total 2,273,324 Latin American immigrants residing in Spain (the sum of Central and South Americans plus Mexicans) compared with approximately 800,000 from Arabic-speaking and Muslim countries (Morocco, Algeria, Senegal, Nigeria, Bangladesh, India and Pakistan).[4] These figures point to a clear difference between Spain and the other European countries analysed in this volume, where in most cases the number of Muslim immigrants is well over the 1 million mark. For example, in France, Muslim immigrants account for between 7 and 10% of the total population while in Spain that figure is barely above 1%.

---

[3] See O. Roy, *L'Islam mondialisé*, Paris: Seuil, 2002.
[4] See Instituto Nacional de Estadística (retrieved from http://www.ine.es).

Of the Muslim immigrants, the Moroccans are those who tend most to come with their families, 20% of them being under the age of 16, while those from Nigeria, Senegal, Algeria, Pakistan, Bangladesh and India are mostly men who immigrate alone in search of employment. According to the National Statistics Institute, on 1 January 2008 there were 676,405 Moroccans, 55,042 Algerians, 44,898 Senegalese and 33,692 Nigerians legally residing in Spain. There are 944,672 total immigrants from Africa. Additionally, there are 47,422 immigrants from Pakistan, 28,367 from India and 7,565 from Bangladesh. There are 281,402 total immigrants from Asian countries, the majority of whom are from China, accounting for 125,301.[5]

A study of the immigrant Muslim population was conducted in 2007 by Metroscopia, funded by the Ministries of Justice, Labour and Social Affairs and the Interior.[6] The survey was conducted during June and July 2007, involving 2,000 persons from Morocco (57% of the sample), Senegal (12%), Pakistan (11%), Algeria (5%) and Gambia, Mali, Bangladesh, Mauritania and Nigeria (all under 5%). The questions were designed to discover Muslim immigrants' perception of their integration process in Spain, their standard of living, their work and family situations, their image of Spain and their expectations. The results showed a Muslim population that is integrated into Spanish society, Westernised and tolerant. This mirrors the results of the study conducted by the PEW Research Centre of Washington D.C., which in 2005 confirmed that Spain had a Muslim community that was very well integrated.

Immigrant integration has been a concern of the Spanish government, and at the national, regional and local levels, it has begun to create an infrastructure designed to formulate and implement immigration policy. Over the last several years, at the national level the Comisión Interministerial de Extranjería [Interministerial Commission for Alien Affairs], the Foro para la Integración Social de los Inmigrantes [Forum for the Social Integration of Immigrants], the Observatorio Permanente de la Inmigración [Permanent Immigration Observatory], the Consejo Superior

---

[5] Although there are no figures grouping immigrants by religious affiliation, these numbers broken down by nationality help us to calculate the number of Muslims residing in Spain.

[6] See Metroscopia, *Musulmanes de España: Segunda Oleada del Estudio de Opinión a Población Musulmana de Origen Inmigrante*, Metroscopia, Madrid, 2007.

de Política de Inmigración [High Council for Immigration Policy] and the Fundación Pluralismo y Convivencia [Pluralism and Co-existence Foundation] have been created.

In February 2007, at the request of the Ministry of Labour and Social Affairs, the cabinet of the Spanish government approved the 2007–10 Strategic Plan for Citizenship and Integration. This plan targets both immigrants and Spanish nationals in that it holds that integration is an issue concerning all members of the community. The plan follows the directives of the European Commission and seeks more suitable management of migratory flows and integration processes. It is considered the framework plan for cooperation among all stakeholders, its principles being equality and non-discrimination, citizenship and interculturalism. The plan's main areas of action are reception, education, employment, housing, social services, health, children and youth, equality, women, participation, awareness-raising and co-development. The budget for 2007–10 is €2,005 million, 40% of which is earmarked for education, 20% for reception and 11% for employment.[7]

Muslim immigration in Spain is part of a recent immigration flow that has been diverse but largely from Latin America. As such, the challenges for immigration in Spain are not so much based on the integration of Muslim immigrants but rather on the integration of nearly 2 million Latin Americans. In this connection, the tensions and conflicts focus as much on Muslim immigrants as they do on those from Latin America. Two recent attacks against immigrant women in Barcelona and Madrid involved Ecuadorians. The Latin gangs formed by young immigrants have caused concern in some local communities owing to a few isolated cases of aggression. In Barcelona, the Latin gangs turned things around and formed an association for immigrant youth rejecting the violence of the young gang members.

Immigration was an important factor in the debates leading up to the March 2008 elections. In some of these debates, it was argued that immigrants are inundating the free health services offered in Spain. The most provocative references in this connection were directed at Latin

---

[7] For further information, see the website of the Ministry of Labour and Social Affairs (http://www.mtas.es/migraciones/Integracion/Planestrategico/Docs/160207pecitextocompleto.pdf).

Americans who, given their numbers, are the most visible.[8] The nearly simultaneous arrival of immigrants of different nationalities minimises the impact of Muslim immigrants, differentiating Spain from the rest of the cases studied in this volume.

2. Recent history of Islam in Spain

To understand the social reality of Muslims in contemporary Spain, it is necessary to begin in the middle of the 1950s, when General Franco's regime began to close the cultural gap with countries of the Near East. Cultural exchanges were encouraged, including the arrival of students at Spanish universities. These initial contacts resulted in the influx of hundreds of students at the end of the 1960s and the beginning of the 1970s from countries such as Lebanon, Syria, Palestine, Jordan and Egypt. In 1971, some of these students formed the Muslim Association of Spain (Spanish abbreviation AME). Some of them were influenced by Islamic currents rooted in their home countries that have had a degree of influence on the Muslim community in Europe such as the Muslim Brothers or *At-tala'i* (known as *Atalayas* in Spanish), which evolved into associations in the main Spanish cities, especially in Granada and Madrid. The AME acted for some time as a federation of Spain's 17 regions[9] and has maintained its legal personality. Prior to the formation of the AME, a small Muslim community called the 'Muslim Community of Melilla' had arisen in the city of Melilla in 1968. No other organisation was formed in Spain until after the establishment of democracy and the ratification of the 1978 Constitution and the new Religious Freedom Act of 1980.

This initial, minority Islamic movement changed after 1990 with the appearance of immigrants from the Maghreb and the rising number of mixed families, mostly Spanish-Moroccan, within the Islamic community. Owing to the settlement process during this period of economic immigration from countries where the majority of the population is Muslim (many from Morocco), Islam has become increasingly visible in Spain in the

---

[8] See newspapers of February and March 2008 such as *El País, El Mundo, ABC* or *La Vanguardia. El Mundo* published declarations from a People's Party politician who complains about the number of immigrants, referring especially to those from Latin America (*El Mundo*, 7 February 2008).

[9] Spain is divided into 17 autonomous communities.

form of personal symbols (e.g. the headscarf and *chilaba*) and community structures (prayer houses, mosques and *halal* butcher shops).

Hence, the Muslim community's arrival and settlement process in Spain has taken place in two major stages. The first started with the creation of the first Muslim religious organisation at the beginning of the 1970s and went on to the signing of the Cooperation Agreements between Spain and the Spanish Islamic Commission (CIE) in 1992, which had been created to represent all Muslims in dealings with the government. The second stage began with the immigration of citizens from countries where the majority of the population is Muslim and it continues up to today. The turning point, however, was not the approval of the Cooperation Agreement between Spain and the CIE but rather the growing wave of immigration. Both of these events (the increase in immigration and the signing of the Agreement) took place around the same time in 1991–92.

During the first stage, the Spanish Muslim community was very small and had two main components, a scholarly group of immigrants/students from Muslim countries and the first native-born Spaniards who converted to Islam during these two decades.

The aim of the scholarly group, formed mainly of young, single or recently married men with a high level of education and from a middle or upper social class, was to complete their studies, collect their diplomas and return to their country of origin rather than settle down and form families in Spain. Given that their stay was temporary, most did not feel the need to group together into an organised community in order to protect their rights and places of worship. From a socio-economic perspective, being university students and economically well-off, in contrast to the majority of today's Muslim immigrants, facilitated their integration. As for religious practices, the majority of this group was Sunni but there was also a minority Shiite component, mostly from Lebanon and Iraq. Many made their way to Spain as refugees fleeing from their countries for political reasons or because of armed conflicts plaguing the Middle East: the Palestinian conflict, the civil war in Lebanon and the war between Iraq and Iran.

Regarding the Spanish who converted to Islam, two generations can be identified: the generation of those who converted in the 1970s and 1980s, almost all of whom are Sunnis (although there is also a Shiite minority), and the generation of converts from the 1990s. The former were mostly university students who yearned for cultural exposure and identified with Islam in the public sphere, and almost all of whom were associated with

Sufism. The latter features men and especially women who married immigrants from predominately Muslim countries and who converted to Islam either before or after marriage.

The majority of the converts who embraced Islam were originally Catholics who did not identify with the Catholic religion and felt attracted by Islam as an alternative for religious, political and social reasons. These reasons include the fact that Islam is a religion without clergy, in other words it has no ecclesiastical hierarchy. There was also a degree of idealisation of the Arab and Muslim world within the sphere of art and culture, which in some cases had to do with a certain exotic flavour related to the hippie movement, but was mostly the path taken by some groups that participated in the May 1968 movements.

Finally, new groups of Muslim immigrants began arriving in Spain around 1990. These were primarily economic immigrants. Currently, the largest group of Muslim immigrants comes from Morocco, with Algeria a distant second source, mostly along the eastern Mediterranean coast. These two countries are followed in number by immigrants from Senegal, Nigeria, Ghana, Pakistan and Bangladesh. Muslims from other European and Asian countries account for the lowest percentage: Kosovars, Albanians, Bosnians, Tatars, Chechens and Azerbaijanis. Generally speaking, there are more men than women immigrants from countries that are predominately Muslim, although in the case of Morocco the percentage of women is gradually nearing that of men. For the rest of the countries, the percentage of men is much higher.

While the second stage of immigration is more significant from a quantitative standpoint, it was during the first that the Muslims organised themselves. At the end of the 1980s, the government offered minority faiths (Jewish, Protestant and Muslim) the possibility of signing Cooperation Agreements with the condition of appointing a single representative for each. The Muslims had already formed two federations, the Federación Española de Entidades Religiosas Islámicas [Spanish Federation of Islamic Religious Groups, FEERI] and the Unión de Comunidades Islámicas de España [Union of Islamic Communities in Spain, UCIDE]. The Federation was the first of the two organisations. Because of internal differences, a splinter group later formed the UCIDE. Faced with the requirement of having a single representative, the two federations formed the above-mentioned CIE, although the two federations do not have a close relationship. This is why the two federations have maintained their legal identities within the CIE. There are, therefore, two secretary generals, one for each federation, as well as two representatives of each of the federations (four in total). The two federations operate independently of one another and the CIE only meets when it has to communicate with the national government. Hence, coordination within the CIE is anything but seamless.

In terms of the number of communities, as of 31 March 2008, 559 Muslim communities were registered in the Ministry of Justice's registry of religious organisations: 315 from UCIDE, 57 from FEERI and 187 that were not affiliated with either of the two federations. Registration of religious communities in Spain is not compulsory and thus there are unregistered Muslim communities. The total number of communities (both registered and non-registered) is estimated at 700.

The main catalyst behind this process was the creation of the Fundación Pluralismo y Convivencia by the Spanish government. The aim of the foundation is the funding of cultural, educational and social action projects of minority faiths that have signed a Cooperation Agreement with the government, i.e. Muslims, Jews and Protestants. More important than the very limited economic support earmarked for projects, the foundation has secured the recognition of these communities as social actors and this has sparked their own further calls for recognition. They are now on the political agenda and hence more open and no longer relegated to the private sphere. This openness has been evident at both state and local levels where they have begun to interact with city councils and other social organisations. The other important element in this recognition process has been the publication of the first school textbook on the Islamic religion entitled *Descubrir Islam* [Discover Islam]. The Muslims have been given the opportunity to teach religion in public schools in accordance with the Cooperation Agreements signed in 1992, but this has been done without any printed material and in Arabic. The publication of this book in Spanish by a Catholic publishing house has contributed to the mainstreaming process.

This important movement has also had an impact on the reorganisation of the federations within the CIE and the emergence of new initiatives and community groups, which will eventually lead the CIE to rethink its structure to adapt to the political organisation of Spain (and its 17 autonomous communities). Now there are at least four new, federal-type initiatives that are grouping communities together and seeking to form part of the CIE.

Regarding different groups within Islam, there is a movement attempting to join like-thinking groups together in the CIE restructuring process. This is more evident in those regions where there are a large number of communities (Madrid, Catalonia and Murcia) but is much less significant in other places where there is only one mosque per municipality (or even per district) attracting all of the Muslims of the area regardless of their branch of Islam. There are, therefore, many 'neutral' mosques where attempts to establish a particular branch of Islam are not meeting with success.

Finally, the proximity of Morocco to Spain has had an effect on the kind of person immigrating to Spain and the influence this country attempts to hold over this group. Yet, this factor may be more significant when attempting to classify communities rather than currents or branches of Islam.

3. The 11 March 2004 attacks

The terrorist attacks of 11 March 2004 are crucial to understanding the process that Islam has undergone in Spain. It is even possible to speak of a new stage in the Muslim reality in Spain resulting from the attacks. After more than four years since those events, however, it remains clear that objectively there is hardly any connection between the Islam of the religious communities in Spain and the Islam of the attacks – two worlds whose paths have not crossed, and are still not crossing now. This specific idea must be at the centre of any political proposal for action.

According to the 28 September 2005 decision of the Criminal Chamber of the National High Court delivered by Magistrate Juan del Olmo regarding the 11 March attacks, Islamic activities carried out in Spain prior to 2002 can be broken down into three stages:

1) initial organisation, which began at the start of the 1990s;
2) expansion and interconnection with other networks of the jihad and the recruiting of new members from among the immigrant community; and
3) a third stage after the 9/11 attacks on New York and Washington, D.C., with growing hostility towards Spanish interests.

During all of this time, jihad members had been using Spain to escape from the persecution they were subject to in their countries of origin. They soon took advantage of their refuge to devise propaganda activities, recruit new members and send them to training camps, collect funds and transfer them to terrorist cells in other countries, falsify documents, purchase material and seek support for their fight against governments considered unfriendly in predominately Muslim countries. Their functions were mostly logistical, consisting of support for 'combat' cells. It has even been proven that Spain was used during the preparation of the 9/11 attacks.[10]

The first attack of this sort in Spain occurred on 12 April 1985 at a restaurant in the vicinity of what was then the American base at Torrejon de Ardoz (Madrid). Eighteen people were killed and a further hundred were injured in this attack, and although the target was clearly the US military personnel who frequented this establishment, all of those killed were Spanish nationals. The ensuing investigation was unable to determine who was responsible for the attack.

Still, the establishment of Islamic terrorist cells and networks in Spain is more recent. The first arrests were made in 1997, indicating that the first contacts and establishment of residence in Spain took place at the beginning of the 1990s. Fifteen Algerians linked to the GIA (Armed Islamic Group) were arrested in Valencia and Barcelona. This was a support cell, typical of the role played by these groups in Spain with varying importance over time.

As early as 2003, some experts[11] were already suggesting a series of preventive measures as part of a strategy to thwart Islamic terrorism, which remain valid in 2008:

- *Assume that terrorists can carry out attacks in Spain* and that their consequences could be extremely serious, as was borne out by the 11 March 2004 attacks.
- *Involve the Islamic communities settled in Spain in the prevention and fight against Islamic terrorism.* At that time, it was already believed that Islamic communities were not a security problem per se and that they should be sheltered from terrorist penetration, because they could potentially contribute to terrorist objectives.

---

[10] See J. Jordán, "Las redes de terrorismo islamista en España. Balance y perspectivas de futuro", ARI No. 119-2003, Real Instituto Elcano, Madrid, 13 October 2003 (retrieved from www.realinstitutoelcano.org).

[11] Ibid.

- *Foster the integration of immigrants from predominately Muslim countries.* The importance of the socio-economic and cultural integration of immigrants and especially their descendents as an effective preventive measure to head off the emergence of radicalism had been highlighted prior to the 11 March attacks.[12]

Among the reasons Madrid was chosen as the site for a new major attack is the prior existence of radical Islamic networks organised in Spain for the provision of logistical support and the alignment and active participation of the Spanish government in the decisions leading up to the occupation of Iraq, with Spain being the 'weakest' member of that strategic alliance (formed basically by the US and the UK). The reasons also include the far greater political priority and effort placed on the fight against domestic terrorism (ETA), thus drawing attention away from this new threat.

On 11 March 2004, Spain suffered the greatest terrorist attacks in its history, an event that has marked the subsequent years of Spain's political and social life. That morning, ten explosions on four commuter trains took place between 06:45 and 07:40. In the event, 191 persons lost their lives and 2,057 were injured.

The first official versions claimed that the Basque separatist terrorist group ETA was responsible for the attacks, but during the course of the day, it became increasingly clear that the attacks had been perpetrated by radical Islamic groups. The proximity of the date of the attacks to the general elections (scheduled for 14 March) led to insistence on the part of the government (People's Party, PP) that ETA was responsible. The PP was accused by different media of manipulating information, for example by sending a note to Spanish embassies abroad urging them to blame ETA and its efforts to force through a UN resolution condemning ETA for the attack. The general media confusion caused a political and social rift that set the tone for the whole of the legislative period that followed, and which remained apparent in 2008.

On 12 March, nearly 11 million people marched through the streets of Spain condemning the attacks. On 14 March, the PP-led government lost the general elections. An endless round of political debates ensued, which

---

[12] Subsequent events point to the partial failure of these policies throughout the European Union.

mostly claimed that the perpetrators of the attacks had won given that they had managed to alter the results of the elections. Although it is true that the polls prior to 11 March indicated that the PP would win the election by an absolute majority, the reasons for the Socialist Party's (PSOE) victory are complex. In the aftermath of the attack, the Spanish electorate decided to punish the ruling PP party. Spain's participation in the war in Iraq was repudiated by nearly 90% of the population. The Spanish people viewed the 11 March attacks as a consequence of Spain's participation in the invasion. The PP government's manipulation of information in the initial hours following the attacks, doing everything in its power to link them to Basque terrorism, was what triggered the population to take a stand against the government. These events prompted a much higher-than-expected voter turnout and that is what led to the PSOE's victory in the elections. In his electoral campaign, José Luis Rodríguez Zapatero had announced that if elected, he would bring Spanish troops home unless the UN took charge of the situation in Iraq. This measure was one of the first he implemented after he won the elections. The Madrid attacks and the search for those responsible monopolised the political arena for quite some time.

On 3 April 2004, as a result of a police siege, eight members of the Islamic cell responsible for the attacks blew themselves up in Leganes (a neighbourhood in Madrid). An assistant police inspector belonging to the National Police Corp's Special Operations Group also lost his life in that explosion.

For its part, the Spanish parliament called for the creation of an investigation commission (enquiry) charged with analysing the political consequences of the attacks and with tabling proposals to address similar situations in the future. The report was approved with the votes of all members of parliament with the exception of the PP. In addition to recommendations and proposals, the report censured the media manipulation and the actions taken by the government at the time of the attacks and proposed five overarching principles on which the fight against international terrorism should be based:

- solidarity with the victims of terrorism;
- unity among all democratic political forces;
- cooperation at different levels, i.e. international and European, collaboration among the national, regional and local governments and coordination among the state police and security forces and intelligence services;

- international initiatives to eradicate the underlying causes conducive to or aiding the criminal actions of terrorists; and
- protection of civil liberties and citizens' rights.[13]

Court proceedings and the judgement concerning the 11 March attacks[14]

After several years of investigation and numerous arrests, the legal order that brought the investigative stage of the terrorist attacks to a close put 29 individuals on trial (9 of whom were Spanish nationals). This same court decision affirmed that the attacks had been inspired but not executed by al-Qaeda and identified the Islamic Moroccan Combatant Group, the most representative group of the jihad Salafist movement in Spain, as being responsible for the attacks.

The judgement convicted those directly responsible for the attacks but failed to find sufficient evidence to convict those accused of being the intellectual planners. Of the 29 accused, 7 were acquitted by the judgement and another was exonerated during the trial. The participation of ETA was also ruled out. Among those accountable for the massacre (aside from those convicted and those who died in Leganes), 4 remain at large and 7 genetic profiles have yet to be identified. Appendix A reports those who were convicted.

The trial of the leaders of the attacks concluded with the certainty that al-Qaeda inspired the attacks but did not order or organise them. The group that carried out the attacks was formed by young immigrants, some of whom were childhood friends from Tetuán (Morocco), who had ended up taking part in a network selling hashish. The genesis of this group was around phone centres and not mosques. In fact, one of the group's most violent members was expelled from Madrid's main mosque because of his violent opinions. It was the community itself that had expelled him.

These Islamic terrorist groups are composed of very young persons whose community of reference is not visible but rather virtual and who see themselves as 'heroes'. They do not have direct contact with al-Qaeda leaders but nonetheless form part of a virtual space that nourishes them

---

[13] See the opinion containing the conclusions of the investigation debated at Spain's Cortes Generales at the 22 June 2005 session.

[14] The judgement was delivered by Section Two of the National High Court's criminal chamber on the 11 March 2004 attacks.

with ideology. Within this space is a jihad composed of cells that individually decide on their objectives. It was within this framework that the 11 March attacks were perpetrated.

Today, it is the communities themselves that have the greatest vested interest in preventing violent movements within their ranks and swiftly expelling those who upset the community. A close look at the arrests made through anti-terrorist operations in the last three years that have targeted Islamic violence in Spain shows that only one focused on a mosque-based group. All of the arrests, with the exception of those made in January 2008 in Barcelona at a mosque frequented mostly by Pakistanis, were of persons who recruited at the community level (appendix B).

4. The situation in Ceuta and Melilla

An analysis of the situation in Spain requires special mention of Ceuta and Melilla, which, owing to their geo-strategic location, play a major role concerning the Arab–Muslim world in Spain. Approximately 50% of the population of these two autonomous cities professes the Muslim religion, which makes them an ideal observatory to study potential conflicts and the possibility of the co-existence and cohesion of a multi-faith society.

A close look at the local press indicates that these issues appear much more frequently than in other regional or national media. The basic problems of inter-religious relations are much more evident and the political discourse of Spain's major parties makes exceptions when referring to the populations of Ceuta and Melilla.

Political discourse opposed to Muslim women wearing the *hijab*, claiming that this poses a threat to Spain's alleged national 'Christian essence' (some right-wing and extreme right-wing groups), or a threat to the separation of church and state (some left-wing parties), is toned down in references to Ceuta and Melilla. Women's right to wear the Islamic veil freely is defended because 'they are Spanish', or comment is simply withheld.

Owing to their geographical and geo-strategic position, these two cities are also key to some of the most important issues on the political agenda in Spain. These two small enclaves are consistently at the heart of matters such as immigration, foreign relations with the Moroccan government and Islamic religious radicalism. The issue of radicalism and terrorism is crucial not only because these cities have been or could be terrorist targets as temporary homes to potential jihadists or operation centres for radical Moroccan groups, but also – over and above the pride felt for the harmonious mix of cultures – there is a growing concern about the tension between Catholics and Muslims caused by fear of terrorism.

Yet, of the 32 persons arrested up to August 2008 for their alleged ties with Islamic terrorism, only 2 were arrested in Melilla and that was the fruit of police cooperation with Morocco, where they had been wanted by the judicial authorities.

Conclusions

When addressing the issue of Islam it is fair to say that we have two very different groups operating in two very different contexts but which are perceived by Spanish society as a single group, and this could have negative consequences if an active policy is not implemented.

First, we have a group that includes the vast majority of Spanish Muslims, whose numbers in 2008 reached 800,000. This group is composed of immigrants practicing their faith who are from predominately Muslim countries and who have permanently settled in Spain. The second generation (their descendents) is becoming Spanish citizens, and is in the process of finding their place in society. In other words, even if they are not yet all Spanish citizens they are destined to be in the near future.

Not all are Muslims. According to recent studies[15] nearly 20% of the immigrants from predominately Muslim countries consider themselves 'non-believers'. It is therefore erroneous to confuse 'Moroccan' with 'Muslim' or 'Muslim' with 'immigrant'. The second generation is caught up in the same processes as the rest of the Spanish youth. A strong secularisation process is giving rise to a fall in the number of believers.

Before the 11 March attacks, what the public saw were 'immigrants' rather than 'Muslims'. After that date, the religious factor was used to refer to this group of immigrants. In other words, the collective mindset viewed this as more of a 'cultural' than a 'religious' phenomenon.

Second, there are the international terrorist groups operating in Spain. These groups are ideologically aligned with al-Qaeda, especially the Algerian Salafist Group for Preaching and Combat and more recently the

---

[15] See Metroscopia (2007), op. cit.

Moroccan al-Qaeda in the Islamic Maghreb. While there are other factions[16] motivated through Islamic websites, these groups do not have strategic interests in Spain[17] but rather use Spanish territory as a base for fundraising and the recruitment of persons willing to fight in Iraq and Afghanistan. Their operations revolve around phone centres but they have no roots or relationships with the religious communities. Nearly all authors agree that these groups have no real intention of 'recovering the ancient al-Andalus', the latter only forming part of a narrative to attract young persons willing to fight for an intangible cause. Their real objective is to radicalise their societies of origin by attacking Western societies as a tactical ploy.

Although what we have here are two different worlds, we must also be aware that under certain circumstances they may intersect and therefore feed off one another. Such a situation would be more liable to arise if a deep sense of belonging is not developed among young Spanish Muslims and a generation of socially maladjusted youth emerges. Here we run the risk that if a person does not have a clear identity associated with the society in which s/he lives and is compatible with the latter, this identity may be sought in 'virtual Islam'. [18] This situation is especially prevalent in a context of economic crisis linked to economic cycles and processes involving the dismantling of the welfare state. To keep situations such as these from emerging, sufficiently specific, active policies must be implemented so that society is capable of clearly distinguishing between these two phenomena. Spain could be at a crucial crossroads in the prevention of radicalism of second- and third-generation immigrants by

---

[16] See J. Jordán, "El terrorismo yihadista en España", *JihadMonitor.org*, 2005 (retrieved from http://www.Jihad.monitor.org) and also Jordán (2003), op. cit.

[17] See J. Halliday, "Tendencias internacionales: seguridad y conflictos" in M. Mesa and M. Gonzalez (eds), *Poder y Democracia. Los retos del multiculturalismo*, Barcelona: Icaria Editorial, 2008 and J. Avilés, "Una amenaza compartida: la Yihad Global en Europa y el Magreb", ARI No. 15/2005, Real Instituto Elcano, Madrid, 2005 (retrieved from http://www.realinstitutoelcan.org).

[18] See M. Sageman, *Understanding Terror Networks*, Philadelphia: University of Pennsylvania Press, 2004 and also M. Sageman, "La nueva generación de terroristas", *Foreign Policy* (Edición española), April–May 2008.

promoting their integration and drawing a clear distinction between their identity and that of Islamic terrorists.[19]

We identify two differentiated lines of political action based on the situation described. One involves police intervention at both national and international levels fighting against terrorist networks. The other focuses on integration processes and generating a sense of belonging with an irrefutable national and even European component. The latter action is the most complex but requires the greatest attention in Spain.

These politico-religious radical groups operate outside the network of mosques and places of worship in Spain and largely have logistical functions of recruiting individuals willing to fight in Iraq or fundraising. The political objectives of these groups are in Iraq or Afghanistan, and the use of Spain as a base for their terrorist actions is a strategic decision (a means but not an end in itself); still, owing to the seriousness of the acts perpetrated, this is extraordinarily serious all the same.

We have also observed growing unease on the part of Spanish society stemming from co-existence with different cultural or religious groups, including immigrants from Latin America and Muslim countries. Despite the high opinion held by immigrants from predominately Muslim countries of Spain, of Spanish society and of opportunities gained and freedoms enjoyed, these groups are not highly regarded by Spanish society. Nevertheless, social conflict and rejection on the part of society has more to do with the very rapid growth of immigration in Spain than with issues relating exclusively to the religious factor. Not only is Spain's immigration model not exhausted but it is also safe to say that it is still under construction, thus providing an opportunity to make co-existence and social cohesion a constructive and enriching reality for all.

Hence, Spain could create a different narrative, moving away from radical Islam towards integration and an identity rooted in a different starting point, since the Muslim immigrants are part of a larger and diverse group of immigrants and the threat from ETA seems to be more real than that from radical Islam.

---

[19] See F. Fukuyama, "Identity, Inmigration and Democracy", *Journal of Democracy*, Vol. 17, No. 2, 2006.

Appendix A. Individuals convicted in the judgement on the 11 March 2004 attacks

José Emilio Suárez Trashorras, Spanish

Essential collaborator; sold explosives used in the attacks that he stole from the mine where he worked; contacted by Jamal Ahmidan through Rafá Zouier to supply the explosives subsequently used in the attacks.

Jamal Zougam, Moroccan

Member of the terrorist cell that perpetrated the attacks; directly responsible for planting the explosives; owner of the mobile telephone shop and phone centre that supplied the telephones used as detonators.

Othman El Gnaoui, Moroccan

Member of the terrorist cell that perpetrated the attacks; responsible for handling and falsifying documents; delivered his ID documentation to Jamal Ahmidan knowing that they would be falsified.

Hassan El Haski, Moroccan

Member and leader of an armed terrorist organisation; leader of the Moroccan Islamic Combatant Group wanted by the Belgian authorities; arrested on 17 December 2004.

Basel Ghalyoun, Syrian

Member of an armed terrorist group; had numerous contacts with Mohamed Larbi Ben Sellam; recruited and indoctrinated future terrorists and provided support and assistance to seasoned terrorists; closely linked to the leaders of the cell that committed suicide in Leganes.

Fouad El Morabit Anghar, Moroccan

Member of an armed terrorist group; recruited and indoctrinated future terrorists and provided support and assistance to seasoned terrorists; closely linked to the leaders of the cell that committed suicide in Leganes and with Rabei Osman El Sayed Ahmed (convicted in Italy in 2006 for forming part of a terrorist organisation).

Mouhannad Almallah Dabas, Syrian

Member of an armed terrorist group; recruited and indoctrinated future terrorists and provided support and assistance to seasoned terrorists; in charge of one of the premises where the activities were carried out; closely linked to the leaders of the cell that committed suicide in Leganes.

Appendix A. cont'd

Sael El Harrak, Moroccan

Member of an armed terrorist group; member of the cell that committed suicide in Leganes; had close personal and telephone contacts with the other members of the group.

Mohamed Bouharrat, Moroccan

Member of an armed terrorist group; a recruiter who compiled information on possible targets for violent attacks, which he then delivered to the cell.

Youssef Beljadt, Moroccan

Member of an armed terrorist group; a member of one of the groups of the al-Qaeda network and a proselytiser who was involved in fundraising activities to finance international jihad activities. He lived in Brussels where he undertook his operations and housed radicals and jihadists. He was in Spain from the middle of February until 3 March 2004, and was arrested in Brussels on 1 February 2005.

Mohamed Larbi Ben Sellam, Moroccan

Member of an armed terrorist group; his mission was to indoctrinate, recruit and support individuals in the formation of a jihad; had close relations with Jamal Ahmidan, Mohamed Oulad Akcha and Said Berraj.

Rachid Aglif, Moroccan

Member of an armed terrorist group and keeper of explosives; in charge of buying and handling explosives; had contact with Jamal Zougam.

Abdelmajid Bouchar, Moroccan

Member of an armed terrorist group and keeper of explosives; in the Leganes flat with the suicide terrorists, but had left to take out the rubbish when the police raid took place and consequently escaped.

Hamid Ahmidan, Moroccan

Member of an armed terrorist group and drugs trafficker; drugs, cash and false documentation bearing the name of Jamal Ahmidan were found in his home; personal effects belonging to the user of the stolen van used to transport the terrorists responsible for the attacks were found in his car.

Rafá Zouhier, Moroccan

Trafficker and supplier of explosives in collaboration with a terrorist organisation; police confidant; the contact person between José Emilio Suárez Trashorras and Jamal Ahmidan for the sale of explosives.

Appendix A. cont'd

Agdelilah El Fadoual El Akil, Moroccan

Collaborator with an armed organisation and a friend of Jamal Ahmidan's; in Holland in the 1990s, he and Ahmidan contacted Imad Eddin Brakat Yarkas, the person responsible for recruiting jihad terrorists at that time; he shipped a car used to transport the explosives to Ceuta.

Nasreddine Bousbaa, Algerian

Falsifier of official documents; forged two passports and driving licenses that he then gave to Jamal Ahmidan; these were delivered before 6 March 2004 to the Lavapies neighbourhood of Madrid.

Mahmoud Sleiman Aouin, Lebanese

Falsifier of official documents; carrying false documentation when arrested.

Raúl González Peláez, Spanish

Supplier of explosives; collaborated in the organisation of the transport of explosives.

Antonio Iván Reis Palicio, Spanish

Transporter of explosives; transported explosives from Asturias to Madrid on 9 January 2004 for a fee of €300.

Sergio Álvarez Sánchez, Spanish

Transporter of explosives; transported a 40kg bag of explosives from Asturias to Madrid on 5 January 2004 for a fee of €600; these were delivered to Jamal Ahmidan and used in the attacks.

Gabriel Montoya Vidal, Spanish

Transporter of explosives; convicted by Juvenile Court given that he was a minor at the time the crime was committed; transported explosives from Asturias to Madrid at the end of January or beginning of February.

Source: Derived from the judgement delivered by Section Two of the National High Court's criminal chamber on the 11 March 2004 attacks.

Appendix B. Arrests of alleged Islamic terrorist cells in Spain, during the period 2005–08 – Dates, places (numbers arrested) and description

January 2005, Bilbao (1)
  One Algerian individual in relation to the 11 March court case

February 2005, Leganés, Madrid and Melilla (6)
  Individuals related to the 11 March court case

March 2005, Fuenlabrada (1)
  Individuals related to the 11 March court case

April 2005, Madrid (14); Operation 'Saeta'
  Individuals related to the 11 March court case

May 2005, Madrid and Granada (3)
  Individuals related to the 11 March court case; arms traffickers and those involved in financing their business

July 2005, Barcelona, Madrid, Valencia and Cadiz (18); Operation 'Tigris'
  Individuals from the Iraqi branch of al-Qaeda involved in fundraising activities

July 2005, Madrid (5); Operation 'Sello'
  Individuals related to the 11 March court case

November 2005, Alicante (8), Granada (2) and Murcia (1)
  Algerian members of the Salafist Group for Preaching and Combat who stole cars and other property, printed counterfeit cards and were involved in drug trafficking to finance their activities in Algeria

December 2005, Malaga (7)
  Algerian members of the Salafist Group for Preaching and Combat who harboured Algerian terrorists on their way to Iraq

December 2005, Malaga (9), Lleida (3), Seville (1) and Palma (1)
  Individuals who recruited others to send to Iraq

January 2006, Vilanova i la Geltrú (16), Madrid (3) and Lasarte (1)
  Individuals who frequented phone centres with the aim of recruiting others to carry out terrorist attacks in Iraq

December 2006, Ceuta (11)
  Individuals who formed part of a Moroccan Salafist cell under surveillance by the police of that country

Appendix B. cont'd

June 2007, Barcelona (2)

Individuals who formed part of a group known as Al-Qaeda in the Islamic Maghreb, composed of Moroccans recruiting followers for operations in North Africa

January 2008, Barcelona (14)

Arrest at a mosque of Pakistanis who met in one of the mosques in the El Raval neighbourhood; material intended for the manufacture of explosives was confiscated

February 2008, Vitoria (3)

Arrest of persons at a phone centre, who had a police record for petty crime

April 2008, Melilla (2)

Arrest of individuals wanted by the Moroccan police force for alleged involvement in Islamic terrorism networks and arms trafficking; one of those arrested was linked to the 'Maghreb Mujahideen Movement' and to the Casablanca attacks of 16 May 2003. The other was linked to a terrorist network dismantled by the Moroccan authorities in February 2008.

June 2008, Barcelona, Castellón and Pamplona (8)

Eight Algerians were arrested, accused of indoctrination and economic and logistical support of terrorists forming part of the al-Qaeda structure in the Islamic Maghreb (AQMI). Most of those arrested belonged to the Salafist Group for Preaching and Combat.

July 2008, Huelva and Guipúzcoa (4)

Algerian Salafist group accused of funding al-Qaeda activities in the Maghreb by falsifying documents and brand-name clothing. Those arrested were allegedly linked to an investigation conducted in the UK in 2001.

August 2008, Alicante (1)

One person was arrested in Alicante in relation to the June 2008 arrests, having escaped to Algeria on that occasion. He was accused of recruiting mujahideen and sending funds to the Maghreb to finance the AQMI.

October 2008, Burgos (6)

Algerian group accused of fundraising for terrorists imprisoned for the Casablanca attacks and of recruiting and indoctrinating mujahideen through the Internet; according to those leading the investigation, the cell was based in Spain but formed part of a more complex structure operating internationally. Its leader had a record for petty crime.

Source: Data based on press clippings from Spanish newspapers.

8. Radicalisation of Russia's Muslim Community
Aleksei Malashenko & Akhmet Yarlykapov

The phenomenon of 'Islamic radicalism' is an extremely significant one for Russia because of at least two circumstances: a) there are about 20 million Muslims living in Russia (including 3.5 to 4 million migrant Muslims), and b) in the 15 years since the collapse of the USSR, Russia has been shaken by ethno-political conflicts with an apparent confessional component.

Islamic radicalism has become an integral feature of the internal situation in Russian society, exerting an influence on the country's public policy. It includes two closely intertwined components – a purely religious and a political one. To ensure a correct assessment of radicalism, however, it is advisable not to combine these two trends into one. In addition, as noted further on, religious radicals may be loyal to the authorities in respect of specific issues.

Not infrequently, information about Islamic radicals' activities is inaccurate. Its source is law enforcement bodies, which for various reasons present it in a distorted form, and therefore this type of information needs to be verified.[1] Information coming from their opponents, who aim at presenting themselves solely as fighters for social justice and for purity of

---

[1] This tendency is explained by the fact that religious radicalism (and extremism) in Russia is used as a political tool of the ruling establishment. In certain periods, the role of extremism was exaggerated, so that the authorities had a sufficient pretext for a general tightening of the screws, curtailing the freedom of the press, etc. Since approximately 2003, however, the ruling circles have been trying in every way to demonstrate their successes in the struggle against radicals, and therefore restricting information about their activities.

religion, also needs verification. Nor are the mass media always objective in covering issues relating to Islamic radicalism either.

Russia's Muslim community is not uniform. Singled out in it may be two socio-cultural realms, the Northern Caucasian and the Tatar-Bashkir (for simplicity we call it Tatar), which, as a consequence of increased migrations, have recently been in active contact with each other alongside the direct participation of a third force – Central Asian Muslims. Without touching upon the differences between them, we note one characteristic: in the Northern Caucasus, radical tendencies and sentiments are stronger than in the rest of Russia. This characteristic sometimes makes it necessary separately to describe processes and situations related to Islamic radicalism.

1. The spread of radicalism

The eastern and central parts of the Northern Caucasus – Dagestan, Chechnya and Ingushetia, and also the adjoining districts of the Stavropol territory with its substantial Muslim population – are the most radicalised regions. While it is true that radical elements in Chechnya are being squeezed out of the republic, they are settling down in the neighbouring territories. As a result, Dagestan's Islamic *jamaats* [Muslim communities] are growing stronger, indicative of which is the increasing activity of the republic's law enforcement bodies, which are compelled regularly to carry out special operations against militants. Radical sentiments are quite widespread in Kabarda, Balkaria and Karachai, although the situation there is somewhat quieter than in Dagestan, Chechnya and Ingushetia. The level of Islamic radicalism is lowest in the Republic of Adygeya and the Krasnodar territory in which it is located, among other things because ethno-nationalism has not yet been superseded there by religious radicalism. Nevertheless, Islamic radicals have been stepping up their activity in the Republic of Adygeya.

In the rest of Russia, there is less activity by radicals and it is not structured. Their small groups are scattered across the Volga area, the southern Urals and southern Siberia. Manifestations of radicalism have been noted in Tatarstan (Naberezhniye Chelny, Almetyevsk, Nizhnekamsk and Kukmor), in Bashkiria (Agidel, Baimak, Oktyabrsky, Sibai and Ufa), in Mordovia (Belozerye), in the Samara region (Togliatti), and in the Kurgan, Orenburg, Penza, Perm, Ulyanovsk, Chelyabinsk and Tyumen regions. Radicals have also been detected in Moscow, although no activities on a permanent basis have been observed there on their part. Small, unconnected groups of radicals exist even in cities remote from Islamic hotbeds such as in Kaliningrad on the Baltic Sea and Vladivostok on the Pacific. If you were to mark 'areas of Islamic radicalism' on the map of Russia, the resulting picture would be quite impressive.

Opposition forces advocating radical Islamic ideology are called fundamentalists and Islamists; the term 'Wahhabites' has become particularly widespread in Russia. It would be more correct to call them Salafists, since their ideology goes back to the 8th–9th centuries AD, when those who urged believers to adhere to the norms of religious and everyday life followed by the 'righteous ancestors' (*as-Salaf as-Salihun*) called themselves Salafists. Today's radicals act as preservers of that tradition, referring to the medieval ideologists of Salafism; adjusted for time, they may be regarded as neo-Salafists.

On the other hand, there exist various schools of thought within the framework of Islamic radicalism. In particular there are differences between Salafists proper and Hizb ut-Tahrir al Islamiyya (HTI – the Islamic Liberation Party),[2] which has come to Russia from Central Asia. The main goal of HTI is a political one – the establishment in the territory of Central Asia (and its subsequent expansion) of an Islamic state, the caliphate, whereas the Salafists are focused on a gradual (re-)Islamisation of society and the establishment of sharia. In addition, the ideology of Salafism places emphasis not only and not so much on struggle against the regime as on its transformation from within. The Salafists, acting very diplomatically, are gradually penetrating administrative bodies, avoiding making outspoken statements that contradict the official precepts. But they remain radicals, even though their radicalism is of a more subtle character.

In Russia, the authorities turn out to be somewhat disoriented, for in confronting Islamic opposition groups, whose members they call 'bandits', they are in fact fighting against one of the movements in Islam that enjoys wide popularity and claims to possess the 'final truth' in both religion and the socio-political sphere.

---

[2] Hizb ut-Tahrir, founded in 1953 in East Jerusalem, has managed to retain its influence in Central Asia, above all in Uzbekistan.

2. Radical movement participants and their activities

In the Northern Caucasus, the basic cell of radicalism is the *jamaat*. The Arabic word *jama'ah* means 'society' or 'community'. *Jamaats* are an elementary, grass root form of organisation of Muslim society. It is an association of Muslims performing congregational prayer; ideally, a *jamaat* is a group of Muslims attending the same mosque. The spiritual leader of a *jamaat* is an imam – the prayer leader in a mosque who delivers a sermon on Fridays, a person who plays a great role in the life of the community because of his authority and knowledge. Underlying an imam's authority is the fact that as a rule, he is elected by the entire community from among the worthiest Muslims on a whole number of criteria: he should not only have the best knowledge of the Koran, the Sunna and the cult, but also be a model of morality and a fulfilment of the precepts of the Muslim religion. Normally, a *jamaat* and an imam are closely bound to each other with a hundred cords; they meet together not only on Fridays for a communal prayer but also on many other varied occasions. Naturally, it is very difficult for the imams of large *jamaats* to maintain strong ties with their congregations, particularly so in major cities.

In Russia, the very notion of a *'jamaat'* implicitly suggests the definition of 'radical'. Every time the word *'jamaat'* is mentioned in the Russian scholarly press or mass media, it implies precisely a collective of radically-minded Muslims, which more often than not corresponds to the actual state of affairs.

Characterised by the young age of their participants, these may be called 'youth *jamaats'*. Organisationally, they took shape in the late 1980s and early 1990s. What contributed to their separation into distinct bodies was the sharply oppositional attitude of a substantial share of the young persons who formed their backbone. They were in opposition, on the one hand, towards the official Islamic bodies – the Muslim religious boards – and on the other towards so-called 'traditional Islam', whose proponents are mainly members of the older generation advocating the observance of all the popular traditions. In the opinion of youth leaders, these popular traditions are often contrary to Islam. In Dagestan, Chechnya and Ingushetia, Muslim youth leaders have often spoken out against the local form of Sufism, which they consider full of 'pagan remnants'. (Most often, funeral and commemorative rituals have acted as irritants.)

Initially, local youth *jamaats* were headed by young imams. In most cases, they were self-taught. The level of knowledge possessed by these leaders and other mullahs was approximately the same, and polemics were conducted in a rather half-hearted fashion, only occasionally reaching fierce proportions. The leaders of youth *jamaats* made use of that time for strengthening themselves organisationally. Perfecting their ideology was the task of the next generation of leaders, who entered the scene in the early 1990s. At that time, young men who had obtained an education abroad, mostly in the countries of the Middle East, began to return home. They gradually became urban and rural leaders and united *jamaats* into a kind of network of associations of Islamic youth.

The 'breeding ground' of youth *jamaats* is the Republic of Dagestan, where these associations (circles) began to be formed among the disciples of local Sufi sheikhs as far back as the 1970s. It is precisely these circles that the Soviet security services dubbed 'Wahhabite' for the first time (following the example of the sheikhs, who had lost control over their disciples). At the time, however, the State Security Committee (KGB) quite soon got a handle on them.

Wahhabism in Dagestan reached its heyday in the 1990s. It was then that the Wahhabite communities in Kizilyurt, Karamakhi, Chabanmakhi, Gubden and other Dagestani populated areas began to gain in strength. Despite the bitter opposition of the Sufis, they succeeded in establishing their rule in a number of districts. In particular, Wahhabites managed to establish an independent territory in the so-called 'Kadar zone', which included three villages in the Buinaksk District of Dagestan–Karamakhi, Chabanmakhi and Kadar. Even though up to half the residents of the enclave did not support the Wahhabites' ideology or practice, the latter were able to keep their rule and their power for three years (1997–99).

During that period, the secular authorities were in fact non-existent in the enclave. And yet the enclave had all the attributes of a self-governing territory: it had a *shura* [council] – a body of government of an 'Islamic territory', its own militia (police) and even its own court of sharia law (*Mahkama Shariyya*). Throughout the three years of its actual independence, the extremist *jamaat* flourished thanks to its members' entrepreneurial activities, and the surrounding mountains were a convenient place for the training of future mujahideen. In the enclave itself, especially in the villages of Karamakhi and Chabanmakhi, extremists entrenched themselves in quite a professional manner militarily, which proved true in the course of a military operation against them conducted in 1999. Notwithstanding several nooses drawn around them, practically all of the extremists' leaders managed to leave the fighting zone and get across into Chechnya. It is from that time that extremists in Dagestan began step-by-step searches for possibilities to preserve their movement. Gradually they adopted the network principle, which thereafter formed the basis of their activity.

In the mid-2000s, after the end of the war in Chechnya and the suppression of a number of major Wahhabite centres in Dagestan, the Kabardino-Balkarian Jamaat became the best-known and best-organised network association. Other networks of youth *jamaats* known to exist today are those in Dagestan, Chechnya, Karachaevo-Cherkessia and the Stavropol territory. Today, youth *jamaats* are being formed before our eyes in the Republic of Adygeya.

Back in the 1990s and early 2000s, these networks were already connected to one another and exchanged information about themselves and their activities. Their leaders were personally well acquainted with one another and were thoroughly familiar with the state of affairs in the neighbouring *jamaats*. Nevertheless, *jamaats* have always preserved broad internal autonomy.

Ideologically, youth *jamaats* are unstable. Their members represent highly varied views, spanning the ideological spectrum from extremism to moderate radicalism. The activities and form of organisation of youth *jamaats* have been patterned after the forms and experience of Muslim organisations in the Middle East, which are distinguished by the unity of ranks, internal mutual assistance and charity.

In the Caucasus, youth *jamaats* turned out to be quite an easy catch for destructive forces, including separatists, which gradually infiltrated the youth setting, exerting an ever-greater effect on it. As a result, in the 1990s a substantial proportion of youth *jamaats* turned into a base of the separatist movement, whose ethnic character (war for the liberation of Chechnya) was replaced by a religious one – the proclamation of a Northern Caucasian emirate as a first step towards building a worldwide Islamic state.

The second half of the 1990s saw a slow but steady change in the qualitative composition of the leadership of the radical Islamic movement in the Caucasus. Its first semi-literate leaders, who at best had received a local education in the late Soviet and early post-Soviet years, were replaced by young imams, who had obtained a fundamental Islamic education abroad, mainly in the Middle East. A few examples of such leaders are Musa Mukozhev, Anzor Astemirov (the Kabardino-Balkarian Jamaat) and

Kurman Ismailov (the *jamaat* of Russia' famous health resort of Mineralniye Vody) among others.

Anzor Astemirov, calling himself Amir Sayfullah [Sword of Allah], a descendant of a family of Kabardin princes, was born in 1976. In the early 1990s, the Muslim religious board of the Kabardino-Balkarian Republic sent him to study at Imam Muhammad bin Saud University in Saudi Arabia to obtain a theological education. Having graduated from the university, he returned home, where he preached at one of the mosques in Nalchik, the capital of Kabardino-Balkaria.

In 1993, with the active participation of Astemirov and his associates, the Islamic Centre of Kabardino-Balkaria (ICKB) was founded. Soon a Kabardino-Balkarian Jamaat emerged on the basis of the ICKB, and then later became the most serious force in opposition to the official Muslim religious board of the Kabardino-Balkarian Republic. Anzor Astemirov was a close friend and deputy to Artur (Musa) Mukozhev, the amir [head] of the *jamaat*. The numerical strength of the *jamaat* kept growing and reached, according to its leaders, 10,000 persons (in all, there are about 650,000 so-called 'ethnic Muslims' living in the republic).

In 1999–2001, Anzor Astemirov was more than once suspected of committing wrongful acts. Attempts were mainly made to charge him with participation in preparations for terrorist acts; however, the law enforcement authorities failed to prove his guilt. The persecution of the Kabardino-Balkarian Jamaat members increased, and Anzor Astemirov drifted towards more radical positions.

On 14 December 2004, there was an attack on the Department of the Federal Drug Control Service of the Russian Federation for the Kabardino-Balkarian Republic in Nalchik. The law enforcement authorities accused Anzor Astemirov and Ilyas Gorchkhanov, a resident of Ingushetia (leader of the 'Taliban Jamaat'), of mounting the attack.

On 13 October 2005, more than 200 militants attacked all the buildings in Nalchik associated with the security forces of the Kabardino-Balkarian Republic. In the two days of fighting, 80 militants, 33 law enforcement officers and 12 civilians were killed in the city. Subsequently, about 70 persons who (in the opinion of the security services) had been involved in the raid were arrested and more than 20 others were put on the wanted list.

On 17 October 2005, in a statement posted on the Chechen-separatist website KavkazCentre.com, Chechen warlord Shamil Basayev claimed that the attack on Nalchik was carried out by combatants of the Kabardino-Balkarian segment of the 'Caucasian Front' under the command of Amir Sayfullah – that is, Anzor Astemirov. In a video recording attached to the statement, the latter was shown beside Basayev during a sitting of the *majlis* [council] of Kabardino-Balkarian mujahideen in a forest outside Nalchik on the eve of the 13 October events. The law enforcement agencies of the Russian Federation put Astemirov on the wanted list.

On an ever-greater scale, young intellectuals are joining the Islamist movement. One example is the Dagestani Abuzagir Mantayev, who defended his candidate's degree in Political Science on the topic of Wahhabism in Moscow and then turned up in the ranks of the extremists. Mantayev was killed together with other extremists by security forces in Makhachkala on 9 October 2005. Another example is Makhach (better known as Yasin) Rasulov, born in 1975. This graduate of Dagestan State University worked for some time as a religious columnist for the newspaper *Novoye delo* and anchored a religious show on Dagestani television. Over the course of a year, he secretly cooperated with extremists and even earned the title 'Amir of Makhachkala', having participated in several audacious attacks on Dagestani police officers. On 10 April 2006, the authorities announced that he had been killed in the course of a special operation in Makhachkala.

Since the late 1990s, a major restructuring of the separatist underground has been taking place in the Northern Caucasus. This restructuring includes the distribution of forces across the widest possible territory and the creation of a network structure, in which the nodes are formally autonomous yet closely communicate with each other to coordinate their actions using communication agents and electronic means of telecommunication. In setting up this network, use is also made of 'influence agents', particularly disgruntled local residents and especially those who have been abused by the local law enforcement agencies.

The organisational structure of the separatist communities – *jamaats* – does not coincide with that of traditional Muslim communities in the region, which are also called *jamaats*. The traditional *jamaats* incorporate the population of a single village or one or several city districts grouped around a mosque. That is, the traditional *jamaats* are organised according to a territorial principle, whereas the separatist *jamaats* are extra-territorial and dispersed. One *jamaat* may encompass many small groups, united into one or several networks. Such is the case, for example, with the Dagestani *jamaats* 'Shariat' and 'Dzhennet'. They were created on the basis of loyalty to the ideology and practice of the separatist movement. Organisationally, these *jamaats* do not represent any kind of united association. Their structure includes de facto autonomous groups, made up of a small number of members who frequently are not acquainted with the members of the other cells. It is particularly difficult to unravel such a network since finding one cell usually does not lead to uncovering others. While making it difficult to manage such a network, this kind of organisation helps the entire network to survive confrontations with the security forces.

The *jamaats* are international in composition; usually their members are from the different ethnic groups of the Northern Caucasus, but there are also representatives of other countries, including Tajikistan, Uzbekistan, Pakistan and the countries of the Middle East. Official Russian statements typically describe them as mercenaries, yet many of them have come to the region for ideological reasons, as participants in a 'world jihad against *kafirs* [non-Muslims], Jews and Crusaders'. Those who have extensive battlefield experience work as instructors. Foreigners, however, do not always become instructors: sometimes they are just rank-and-file fighters, which particularly applies to those coming from Central Asia. Through the foreigners, the groups often establish ties with donors from Islamic countries. Delivery of financial aid to the separatists is frequently criminalised: for example, through these channels counterfeit hard currency is laundered. Other types of fundraising are also employed such as donations from various supporters and ransoms collected from the relatives of hostages.

Sometimes the separatists form special units – 'battalions' organised along ethnic lines. Thus have come into existence the 'Nogai', the 'Karachai' and other ethnic battalions. In reality, no such battalions exist as permanent military units. Armed forays and terrorist acts ascribed to one ethnic battalion or another are carried out by the members of separatist *jamaats* of the corresponding nationality (even though the *jamaat* itself is international). In particular, the Nogai battalion typically includes members of the Shelkovskoi Jamaat, which is based in the Shelkovskoi District of Chechnya and the Neftekumsky District of the Stavropol territory. The Shelkovskoi Jamaat has become notorious for large-scale actions against the federal troops, including the recent clashes in the village of Tukui-Mekteb of the Neftekumsky District. Its activities receive wide attention because raids often take place beyond the borders of the Northern Caucasian republics, angering the federal government. And yet the Shelkovskoi Jamaat is not the largest network structure of the separatist forces.

With respect to the rest of the Muslim space in Russia, the concept of *jamaat* is practically never used. What is found in its place is simply a small community or even just a circle composed of a few persons or two to three dozen.

The communities exist in towns or they are formed around mosques. The latter is less and less frequently the case, since an overwhelming majority of mosques are controlled by Muslim religious boards loyal to the authorities and are constantly monitored by the security services. In 1999, Islamist communities were formed in Kumkor (200 persons), Vyatskiye Polyany (in the Kirov region – 100–150 persons), and Neftekamsk (in the Perm region – up to 50 persons). In the Republic of Tatarstan, in an abandoned village located in the Ogryz District, 30 Islamists attempted to reproduce the experience of the Dagestan village of Karamakhi and formed a so-called 'Islamic territory'. Quite soon, however, the community was dispersed by the local administration and law enforcement bodies.

A mosque may also turn out to be a centre of religious radicalism. Similarly, a madrasah or Islamic institute functioning at a mosque may turn out to be such a centre. It should be noted that the title of institute rarely corresponds to the level of education provided by an Islamic educational institution positioning itself in this way. An overwhelming majority of Russia's Islamic institutes may be ranked with certain reservations as secondary educational institutions.

In the Northern Caucasus, where the *jamaat* is the organisational basis, the mosque may be regarded rather as its adjunct, whereas in the Tatar-Bashkir area a mosque and an Islamic educational institution act as an independent or even the main centre of attraction.

In nearly each region with a sizable Muslim community, there is one or sometimes several radically-oriented mosques (with a madrasah or institute it runs). They include, for example, the White (Gilyan) Mosque in the Astrakhan region, the so-called 'Historical Mosque' in the Samara region, the Rahman and al-Bukhari mosques in the territory of the Ural Federal District, the mosque at the Imam Fakhretdinov Institute in Almetyevsk (Bashkortostan) and the mosques in Nizhnekamsk (Tatarstan). In Moscow, the authorities have brought charges of supporting radicals against the Historical Mosque and the recently built mosque on Poklonnaya Hill.

A stressful situation developed around a mosque and madrasah in the city of Buguruslan in the Orenburg region (bordering on Kazakhstan). According to the law enforcement agencies, the training of militants was conducted at that madrasah: six men who took part in terrorist acts in Moscow (the seizure of hostages at the theatre on Dubrovka street) and Beslan (the hostage-taking and murder of schoolchildren) had been trained at that madrasah.[3]

In 1999–2002, the most prominent hotbed of Islamism was the Yodyz Mosque and madrasah in Naberezhniye Chelny, where 'Arabian Islam' was taught and where, according to the security services, militants were also trained. Later on, some of them were detained on suspicion of connections with al-Qaeda.

In addition to *jamaats*, mosques and Islamic educational institutions, several radical Islamic organisations have been active in Russia. At one time, the most prominent of them was the Islamic Revival Party established in Astrakhan in 1990, which gave an impetus to the politisation of Islam back in Soviet times. It had a branch in Dagestan, which adopted the name of the 'Islamic Party of Dagestan'. Despite the relatively hard phraseology of its leaders, the Islamic Revival Party can hardly be fully identified with Islamic radicalism. It may be described as a moderately radical organisation. Ahmed Qadi Akhtayev, the leader of the party, was rather in favour of dialogue with both Islamic traditionalists and the secular authorities. Yet after his death in 1998, radical and even extremist sentiments grew stronger in the Islamic Revival Party; it was true, however, that by that time the party was close to disintegration and soon it ceased to exist.

In Tatarstan, the Iman Youth Islamic Cultural Centre, formed in 1990, characteristic of which were separatist sentiments, adhered to radical positions. (In 1991, the Iman Centre even applied to the Organisation of the Islamic Conference (OIC) with a request to accept Tatarstan as a member.) That same year, the radical nationalist party Ittifaq was founded in the republic, with the Islamic component very prominent in its ideology. The

---

[3] See "Uspekh zavisit ot kazhdogo" [Success Depends on Everyone], an interview with Kharun Karchayev, Head of the Department of the Federal Security Service of Russia for the Orenburg region, *Pervaya Redaktsiya*, Orenburg, 8-14 March 2008, p. 3.

programme of Ittifaq stated that the party "fights for purity of religion, for faithfulness to the precepts of the Koran".[4]

On the whole, in contrast to the Northern Caucasian *jamaats*, radical groups in the rest of Muslim Russia do not pose any serious threat to stability. They are supported by an insignificant number of Muslims. On the other hand, it should not be ignored that 15 years ago there were no such groups in Russia except in Tatarstan and three or four Russian cities. Therefore, while recognising their insignificance in the overall religious and political palette, one cannot but notice the presence, even if slowly growing, of Islamic radicalism in the Russian Federation.

3. The absence of charismatic Muslim leadership

In Muslim Russia today there are no charismatic figures whose influence would encompass the entire Islamic community. For example, Talgat Tadzhutdin, Chairman of the Central Religious Board of Muslims of Russia, claims the status of an all-Russia Muslim authority, yet even in the Republic of Bashkortostan where his residence is located, he has been recognised as a spiritual leader by only 18.5% of Muslims.[5] Ravil Gainutdin, Chairman of the Council of Muftis of Russia, Chief Imam of the Moscow Cathedral Mosque, enjoys countrywide popularity in Russia, but he also lacks strong influence. It should be noted that neither Tadzhutdin nor Gainutdin can be classed among the radicals.

Perhaps Mukaddas Bibarsov, Chairman of the Muslim Religious Board for the Volga area, who, despite his general loyalty to the authorities, sometimes ventures risky statements and acts, has some elements of regional-level influence.

Certain features of charismatic leadership, albeit 'inert', are displayed by Nafigulla Ashirov, Chairman of the Religious Board of Muslims of Asian Russia. While not directly participating in the activities of radical organisations, Ashirov has won renown for his numerous statements in support of Hamas, the Taliban and even al-Qaeda, as well as his criticisms of the Russian Orthodox Church, his call to remove the cross from the coat

---

[4] See *Altyn Urda*, No. 6, Kazan, 1993.

[5] See A.B. Yunusova, *Islam v Bashkortostane* [Islam in Bashkortostan], Ufa, 1999, p. 301.

of arms of the Russian Federation, etc. He occupies an intermediate position between 'classical' radicalism and the clergy loyal to the authorities. Still, it is true that in the last few years his popularity has waned.

In the mid-1990s, Geydar Dzhemal, one of the founders of the Islamic Revival Party, who later on became chairman of the 'Islamic Committee of Russia', claimed the role of a charismatic figure in Russia's Muslim community. He failed to reach this goal, however. Coming from the Soviet and subsequently post-Soviet intellectual underground, he was perceived as an Islamic ideologist mainly by Russian non-Muslims, scaring them with his radicalism and even with his formidable appearance, and he actually turned into a sophisticated showman.

Finally, we mention Tatar poet Fauziya Bairamova, an ideologist of local nationalism, who is also not averse to Islamic rhetoric. Even so, her appeal is limited to the narrow circle of admirers of her literary talent.

The authority and popularity of the radicals proper do not go beyond the boundaries of their milieu. The political conditions for the emergence of charismatic figures existed in the Northern Caucasus. It was there that politicians and ideologists with leadership ambitions emerged in the 1990s. They included the above-mentioned Ahmed Qadi Akhtayev, Sheikh Bagauddin (Bagauddin Kebedov), a leading ideologist of the Salafists in the 1990s, and Nadirshah Khachilayev, head of the Union of Muslims of Russia (killed in 1999). But none of them ever succeeded in becoming a full-fledged popular leader.

Perhaps Shamil Basayev, one of the leaders of Chechen separatism (killed by the federal security services in 2004), approached closest to it; however, his charisma was mainly of a political nature, while Islam served above all as an instrument for preserving his political prestige.

It seems highly unlikely that charismatic figures will emerge in Russia's Muslim community in the near future. First, there are no appropriate political conditions for this; second, the security services, ready at any time to isolate an exceptional personality, are keeping a close watch on Muslims; third, a majority of Russia's Muslims are not very susceptible to radical ideas and slogans tinged with a revolutionist hue. Today, only one Muslim politician, Ramzan Kadyrov, the young president of Chechnya, boasts charisma. There is a growing Islamic motivation in Ramzan's politics, but he cannot be classed with Islamic radicals and therefore his portrait is not a subject of our analysis.

4. Texts propagating the ideas of radicalism and their impact

Texts propagating the ideas of radicalism in Muslim Russia – not only in the Caucasus but also in other regions – are quite varied. In the Northern Caucasus, they have a broader audience; in the 2000s, however, materials of this kind have become relatively widespread in Tatarstan, the southern Urals, western Siberia and the Volga area. In the 1990s, at a number of bookstores in Russia one could buy fundamentalist literature – Russian translations of works by Ibn Taimi and Ibn Abd al-Wahhab, the founders and ideologists of fundamentalism, Hassan al-Banna, the first head of the Muslim Brotherhood organisation, and Sayyid and Muhammad Qutb. Works by contemporary Islamic radicals, such as Abd as-Salam Farag, Ayman az-Zawahiri, Abbud az-Zumr and natives of Russia Magomed Tagayev (*The Army of the Imam*) and Nadir Khachilayev (*Our Road to Gazavat*), are being published.

The most traditional forms of presenting the material are leaflets, brochures and sermons. In the early 1990s, publications of texts in religious newspapers and magazines played a crucial role. Their impact can hardly be overestimated; for example, a whole generation of young Islamic radicals in the region has been brought up reading the Dagestani newspaper *Al-Qaf*. In the Urals, western Siberia and the Volga area, Islamic radicals read *al-Wa'i*, a printed organ of HTI.

Sermons were video-recorded, and their dissemination was one of the leading methods of propagandising radical ideas among the peoples of the Caucasus in the 1990s. By the late 1990s and early 2000s, video began to be ousted by the Internet, which today has become one of the main resources for spreading radical views and an efficient lever for influencing young Muslims in Russia.

In addition, mention should be made of lectures delivered by ideologists of radicalism at educational institutions and militant training camps that operated in the Caucasus throughout the 1990s. Sometimes texts of the lectures were disseminated in other regions of Russia as well, including Moscow. Records of the lectures that have come down to us are amazing for the scale of ideological brainwashing of young students, who were offered a systematic, integral view of the world through a radical interpretation. This approach was clearly presented and substantiated with quotations from the Koran and the Sunna, along with examples from history and the present-day world political situation.⁶

Still another method of propagandising radical ideas was the use of possibilities offered by seemingly innocuous Arabic language textbooks. Sheikh Bagauddin, a major, radical ideologist of the Caucasus, widely used the principles of the Wahhabite doctrine in an Arabic language textbook that he had written. In his textbook for the first year of study, a great deal of interesting thoughts are to be found in texts for translation into Arabic, such as the following: "We are fighting with gyaurs (i.e. infidels), and gyaurs are constantly fighting with us. Today they are possessors of power and possessors of numerous weapons, but we are possessors of iman [faith], that is why we will definitely win, for we have Allah and they have Satan."⁷ Here are a few more characteristic quotations from the textbook: "I have understood the lesson well. We must be soldiers of Islam. We must learn at schools and at institutes and at universities. And we must defend our religion and our homeland. We must defend our Muslim brothers. Long live our state, a state of Islam!"⁸ Next, "This article has been written about spreading Islam among the peoples of the world, especially among young people. Why among young people? Because they [young people] are quick in understanding everything, and as for old people, they never understand."⁹ And, finally, "Big and small states all over the world should unite and create a Great Islamic Power."¹⁰

By way of an illustration of Sheikh Bagauddin's methods, we draw from records made by one of his 'students', which can be unequivocally described by the title, the Wahhabite Student's Summary Notes.¹¹

---

⁶ Similar texts are familiar to the authors from materials obtained in Central Asia.

⁷ See B. Muhammad, *Uchebnik arabskogo yazyka. Perviy god obuchenya* [Arabic Language Textbook, for the First Year of Study], Moscow: Santlanda Publishing House, 1992, pp. 173-174.

⁸ Ibid., p. 97.

⁹ Ibid., p. 124.

¹⁰ Ibid., p. 161.

¹¹ Here and further below, the text cited (with minor punctuation corrections) is from lecture summary notes kept in one of the author's personal archives. Some of these summary notes have been published; however, since their unpublished parts will often be cited, reference is made to the author's personal archives.

The basis of the Wahhabite doctrine is the requirement for comprehensive implementation of the principle of *tawhid* [monotheism]. This requirement proceeds from a literal understanding of this principle with very strict limitations. The Wahhabite Student's Summary Notes read, "Most Muslims, who very often repeat, 'There is no god but Allah,' know no sincerity or meaning or do this out of tradition or custom. Most of their deeds are emulation or following the example, and they best correspond to the Word of Supreme Allah in His Koran: 'We follow what we found our fathers upon.'" In other words, it is recognised here that most Muslims are not sincere believers and their Islam is mainly 'inherited', and they regard themselves as Muslims by force of habit.

The ideology of the Caucasus Wahhabites is based on recognition of only the Koran and the authentic – as they emphasise – Sunna as the source of the doctrine. The Wahhabite Student's Summary Notes add that "Muslims must wholeheartedly embrace the teaching of Islam embodied in the Holy Koran – the Word of Allah, and the Sunna – sayings of the Prophet Muhammad". Hence, there is the Wahhabites' call for cleansing Islam of 'impermissible innovations' (*bid'ah*) with which, in their opinion, Islam has become fouled in the Northern Caucasus. They come out sharply against many of the local Muslims' customs and rituals such as the cycle of commemorative rites including Koran reading for the deceased, the ritual for redeeming the sins of the deceased (*deur*), distribution of alms at the graveyard and the celebration of *Mawlid* (the birthday of the Prophet Muhammad). Moreover, the Wahhabites are particularly irreconcilable towards local Sufism and the related cult of saints. The Wahhabites regard the veneration of sheikhs, *zikrs* [religious remembrances], pilgrimages to the graves of holy sheikhs (*ziyarat*) and many other things from the practices of the followers of local *tarikats* [Islamic religious orders] as an indication of their most profound and conscious fallacy, polytheism (*shirk*) and disbelief (*kufr*). Not only are the followers of *tarikats* accused of disbelief: the Wahhabites also declare as infidels all the Muslims who do not share their point of view. There is only one way out for them: they must repent and "embrace Islam once again": "A Muslim who has committed at least one of these [deeds] must renew his Islam by doing *Tawba* [repentance], and embracing Islam once again, since all the above is the abandonment of Islam or the gravest sin."[12]

The ideologists of Wahhabism allot one of the leading places to jihad, understood as an armed struggle for the faith. The Wahhabite Student's Summary Notes state that "Islam is a religion of jihad and life. Islam prescribes to every Muslim to spare neither his property nor his energies for the sake of the victory of Islam."[13] In other words, the Wahhabites regard the conducting of jihad as an obligation of every Muslim. For example, in 1999, in declaring the "revival of the Islamic state of Dagestan", the 'Islamic Shura of Dagestan' expressly pointed out that "jihad in Dagestan is farz'ain [i.e. personal religious obligation] for every Muslim".[14] They believe that today jihad invariably takes the form of an armed struggle against the enemies of Islam. In one of the leaflets disseminated in Dagestan by the so-called 'Badr Islamic Call Centre', jihad (again, naturally understood as an armed struggle) is named under number four among the ten pillars of an Islamic *jamaat*. Sheikh Bagauddin pursued this idea consistently and methodically: he called for conducting an armed struggle against "infidels" not only in his sermons and writings but also in such literature, seemingly remote from ideological disputes, as Arabic language textbooks.

Another accusation advanced by the Wahhabites against the rest of Muslims is an accusation of departure from monotheism (*shirk*). In the Wahhabites' opinion, they are becoming *mushriks*, i.e. polytheists, or *kafirs*, i.e. infidels. This applies in the first place to the Northern Caucasian followers of Sufism and near-Sufi cults. Here is what we find in the Wahhabite Student's Summary Notes:

> Mushriks venerating their sheikhs or their graves utter the testimony La-ilaha-illallah [there is no god but Allah] with their tongues and contradict its meaning with their deeds. They utter the testimony and then deify someone else besides Allah, turning their worship to him, be it love, praise, fear of him, hope, recumbence,

---

[12] Derived from the author's (A.Ya.) personal archives, the Wahhabite Student's Summary Notes.

[13] Ibid.

[14] See R.G. Gadzhiyev, *Vakhkhabitskii factor v kavkazskoi geopolitike* [The Wahhabite Factor in Caucasian Geopolitics], Grozny, 2004, p. 262.

prayer, and its other varieties, for all of these are worship, but Allah, the Exalted and Mighty, is the only one who deserves to be worshipped.[15]

This last statement, which is quite correct from the point of view of any Muslim believer, is treated out of proportion by the Wahhabites. Basing themselves on this postulate, the Wahhabites flatly refuse to recognise any religious authority whatsoever and emphatically express defiance against the traditions of respecting elders, widespread in the Northern Caucasus (which they interpret as veneration of feeble old men). In a Wahhabite community, an emphasised equality of all of its members reigns supreme. No one, not even the amir is given any special deference. Interestingly, it is precisely their lack of deference to elders that opponents of the Wahhabites from among ordinary Muslims have often mentioned as the Wahhabites' negative trait.

Naturally, the ideology of a Great Islamic Power or of the caliphate has always had (and still has) limited popularity in Russia. In the late 1990s, it spread in the Northern Caucasus, when Shamil Basayev spoke of a "Dagestani-Chechen Caliphate", which was subsequently to incorporate the rest of the Northern Caucasus. Incidentally, most of the Dagestanis and the peoples of the Northern Caucasus in general held a cautious, negative attitude towards the idea of a caliphate, viewing it above all as an embodiment of the ambitions of the Chechen separatist leadership.

At approximately that time, there appeared leaflets and other texts mentioning a 'Volga Caliphate', which was to incorporate the Ulyanovsk, Saratov, Samara, Volgograd and Astrakhan regions, and also Tatarstan and Bashkortostan. Interestingly, the leaflets were anonymous (or signed by fictitious names, which gave rise to talk that they were a provocation of the security services). None of the Islamic authorities of any significance admitted to being their author.

At the same time, the talk about the possibility of creating a caliphate in the territory of the Russian Federation attests to the existence among Muslims of radical sentiments, which of course reflect certain utopias but which, on the other hand, stay on in the mind, awakening in it feelings of religious solidarity with radicals in the rest of the world – in the Middle

---

[15] Derived from the author's (A.Ya.) personal archives, The Wahhabite Student's Summary Notes.

East, Iraq, Afghanistan and Europe. This also promotes the emergence of hope for a future Islamisation of Russia.

It should be noted that the Russian authorities are keeping a close watch on religious literature, imposing a strict censorship on publications that, in their opinion, preach religious intolerance. Books by Ibn Abd al-Wahhab and a number of other classics of Islamic radicalism have been banned in Russia. In 2008, still another list of banned literature was drawn up. It was stressed that the banned books that are already in libraries (mainly at Islamic educational institutions and mosques) are subject to destruction.

This censorship sparked strong protests, including public ones, on the part of the Muslim community. Curiously, certain Russian liberals sided with this view, believing that in this case works by Vladimir Lenin (the founder of the Soviet state, who openly preached hatred among various groups of society and hatred for religion) should also be destroyed.

5. A 'portrait' of adherents of radicalism and converts

Recently, the qualitative composition of radically-minded Muslims as a group has changed substantially. Now they are by no means poor, uneducated, jobless persons having a low social status. Today, the young and the intelligentsia are perhaps the main sources for replenishing the ranks of radically-minded Muslims. The young respond very keenly to the problems of a society thoroughly penetrated with corruption, clannishness and economic problems. The intelligentsia also respond to the problems of society, for they are by definition prone to reflecting on the subject.

Contributing to the broad spread of radicalism is also the de facto absence of civil society and actual public discussion, alongside a growth in nationalism – both Russian nationalism and the nationalism of ethnic minorities. In the Northern Caucasus as well as among natives of that region living in the centre of Russia, negative emotions are nourished by a feeling of their 'second-ratedness' compared with the non-Muslim majority.

Today's Muslim radical is, as a rule, a young man engaged in some business such as trade or the transit of goods. He is an active, energetic and sociable individual. The last trait is of particular significance, for the ability to establish contact with another person and convince him of one's rightfulness constitutes half the success of propaganda. It is hard to single out any specific group that is most prone to radical propaganda. It is designed for everyone, including drunkards, drug addicts and 'life wasters', as well as intellectuals who are indifferent to Islam.

It should be added that many, if not a majority, of Muslim radicals avoid public expression of their views. In this respect, they may be likened to Soviet dissidents, who expressed their true convictions, in the phrase of the day, 'while sitting in the kitchen'. This line of conduct is widespread, in particular among students. The short period of existence of post-Soviet Russia does not make it possible draw a conclusion about the stability of Islam's impact on the minds of the young. World experience tells us that as an individual grows older, s/he becomes more pragmatic and backs away from radical attitudes. And yet the same experience attests to the possibility of a permanent reproduction of radicalism in the youth milieu. Somehow or other, a stable niche of Islamic radicalism has been formed among the young, which is expanding, albeit slowly. Contributing to the above-mentioned causes is the growing level of Islamophobia in society. Therefore, Islamic radicalism is to a certain extent a reaction to the negative view of Islam.

Finally, a growing number of neophytes of Slavic origin are to be found among Islamic radicals. It is known that in the late 1980s, the conversion of Slavs (Russians and Ukrainians) to Islam had to do with the shock that Soviet servicemen went through in Afghanistan. Psychologists explained their conversion to the enemy's religion by a feeling of guilt before the people against whom they had been fighting and by the recognition of the strength of Islam. Later on, the conversion of some individuals to Islam was their response to and a kind of resentment against the attitude towards them by Russian society and the state. It was also because of their disenchantment with 'their own' Orthodox faith. It may be said that the change of religion was, in a sense, a result of a crisis of Russian (on a broader scale, Slavic) identity, which began back in the days of perestroika.[16]

Today, for some the conversion to Islam (the number of neophytes runs into hundreds and probably already thousands) is a continuation of

---

[16] In 1995, Vladimir Khotinenko, the noted Russian film director, made the film *The Muslim*, telling the story of a Russian soldier who had embraced Islam. The Council of Muftis of Russia awarded the film director a special Golden Minbar prize.

their search for identity, an attempt to find a radical, even extreme, form of self-expression, for Islam is perceived as a religion of resolute action. Anti-Americanism, which is widespread in Russian society, also leads one to embrace Islam. Islamic radicals of Slavic origin have been noticed in the Rostov, Samara and Saratov regions, in the Stavropol territory, in the Urals and in Tyumen. Russian Muslim Viktor Senchenko participated in the attack on Nalchik on the militants' side.[17] Another Russian Muslim, Vyacheslav Panin, distributed HTI leaflets.[18] Certainly, the role of Slavic Islamists should not be overestimated; however, Muslim ideologists and propagandists consider their presence valuable, for it offers proof of the supranational nature of Islam and neophytes' readiness to take a direct part in jihad, as well as still another confirmation of the point that the Islamisation of Russia has gotten underway.

6.   Methods of violence or manifestations of tension

Violence inevitably follows from the ideology of radicalism. In the Caucasus, practical violence substantiated by religious ideology may be divided into two types with respect to its object: violence in relation to non-Muslims, including that against the state and its structures, and violence in relation to Muslims. A list of the numerous major terrorist acts in Russia from 1994 to 2006 is given in appendix A.

Radicals represent the modern secular state to be devoid of divine blessing and therefore deserving destruction. It should be replaced with a state founded on 'divine' laws, which will be built by an appropriate society. From this follows, first, participation by 'true Muslims' in militant *jamaats* and the conduct of military actions against power structures – the army, the security services, the militia, etc. Second, acts of terrorism are called for to spread panic among peaceful populations and to stir anti-Russian sentiments in its midst. Quite often, acts of terrorism are directed against carriers of Russian cultural influence – Russians and Russian-speaking people, as well as teachers, public servants, etc.

---

[17] See R.F. Pateyev, *Islam v Rostovskoi oblasti* [Islam in the Rostov Region], Moscow: Logos, 2008, pp. 38-39.

[18] See V.V. Semyonov, *Islam v Saratovskoi oblasti* [Islam in the Saratov Region], Moscow: Logos, 2007, p. 70.

The concept of charging fellow Muslims with unbelief (*takfir*) gives the radicals grounds to state that many Muslim politicians have actually renounced Islam. Hence, there is the active use of violence against ethnic Muslims serving in state power structures – and not against them alone. Militia officers who are members of the local ethnic groups in Dagestan, Chechnya, Ingushetia and the eastern districts of the Stavropol territory are among the terrorists' main targets. Islamists believe that the family members of militia officers and other representatives of the authorities may be killed because they voluntarily stay with apostates and therefore support their position. A true Muslim must disown such relatives. Those who accidentally die in acts of terrorism will become *shahids* [martyrs] and go directly to paradise.

With the exception of the Northern Caucasus, calls to violence on the part of Islamic radicals in the other regions practically have not been noticed. Quite the contrary, even HTI followers stress in every way possible that they do not view confrontation with the authorities as their main objective, laying the key emphasis on propaganda. An interesting fact is that, in detaining HTI members in the territory of Russia, none of them could be charged with violent methods of struggle. The detention, however, was done not without grounds by the authorities of the Central Asian states of Uzbekistan and Kazakhstan, to which the detainees were extradited.

In the mid-1990s, the question began to be debated among some of the young Tatars, especially those who had been in contact with the Chechen separatists, about possible direct support of the separatist fighting in Chechnya and about rendering it assistance with concrete actions in the rest of the territory of the Russian Federation. Yet, things never came to practical action: only a few Tatars took part in the first Chechen war on the separatists' side. (No accurate data on the subject are available.)

In 1995, one of the authors of this chapter had a chance to talk in Kazan with a radically-minded member of the All-Tatar Public Centre, who literally said the following: "We, the Tatars, are weaker in character than the Chechens and we have no mountains or we would have also shown to Moscow" [*sic*]. It should be noted that shortly before the meeting, the author's collocutor had spent 15 days in custody on a charge of organising an unauthorised rally. We repeat once again, however, that even in that period, which was quite tense for Moscow, calls for violence voiced by Tatar and Bashkir radicals were not supported by practical actions.

It is quite clear that today calls for violence are even less likely to find any substantial support among the Tatars or among Muslim migrants from Central Asia who come to Russia to earn money and not at all to participate in jihad. Quite the contrary, Muslim migrants themselves are under constant pressure not only by the Russian militia but also by Russian nationalists. (It is known that in the last two years attacks on and even killings of immigrants from Central Asia have become a kind of routine, and their number has grown so much that the federal authorities have been compelled to pay attention to this.)

7. Response of the state and society to Islamic radicalism

The response of the state to the activities of Islamic radicals is by far not always adequate and quite often may provoke conflicts between the authorities and the Muslim community at large.

At both the federal and local levels, the state takes a very rigid position in respect of 'Islamic dissidents'. In the Northern Caucasus, they are outlawed and an unceasing warfare is carried on against them. The authorities, however, are ignoring the fact that nearly the entire Muslim community in the region is, in varied form and degree, drawn into this warfare. A substantial share of it sides or at least sympathises with radicals and is embittered by extremely rigorous and not always justified measures against them and especially against their relatives on the part of the militia and other power structures.

In particular, an exceptionally repressive policy has led to radicalisation of the Kabardino-Balkarian *jamaat*. From the middle of 2004, militarised extremist cells began to step up their activities in the Northern Caucasus, including in the Kabardino-Balkarian Republic. The acme of the destructive activity of the local Wahhabite Yarmuk Jamaat was the previously mentioned attack on the Department of the Federal Drug Control Service in Nalchik in December 2004. The federal and republican power bodies scored a success when they liquidated the leading nucleus of the *jamaat* with its amir, Muslim Atayev, in the course of a special operation in Nalchik at the end of January 2005. This move, however, turned out to be a Pyrrhic victory. It was quite clear that the *jamaat* itself was not eliminated. As a result, the situation became even more exacerbated: Kabardino-Balkaria turned into still another explosive territory and its Islamic youth structures began de facto actively to cooperate with the Chechen radicals.

The Muslim religious boards have turned into bureaucratic structures having no control over the religious situation at the local level and enjoying no authority among believers. Moreover, they may stir conflicts within Muslim communities with their incompetent actions. It is not to be ruled out that the authorities will be compelled to switch from unqualified support of the Muslim religious boards, which are failing to cope with their tasks to engage in dialogue with and even to draw to their side informal Islamic structures, having legitimised them. These latter structures are communities of 'new Muslims', which, while not being Wahhabites, refuse to recognise the authority of the religious boards. In addition, such communities have levers of influence for radicalising young persons whom the authorities could use in their own interests. Naturally, the state will not undertake a compromise with extremist groups, yet at the same time it should clearly determine whom it regards as extremists and who, their radicalism notwithstanding, have not yet overstepped this boundary. What presents an additional complexity for the state is the non-uniformity of youth communities in the Northern Caucasus – which, because of lack of registration, find themselves outside the legal framework, thus fostering the preservation and growth of radicals' and extremists' influence on them.

Although the state policy in respect of Islamic radicalism remains mainly repressive, some of the public officials speak up from time to time for the need for a more balanced approach to the opponents and sometimes even admit errors (although very rarely) committed by the authorities. In this connection one may note the views of Yevgeny Primakov, former Minister of Foreign Affairs and Prime Minister of Russia, who does not consider Islamic fundamentalism an indubitable evil, and also ex-premier Sergei Stepashin, who said during his visit to the Dagestani territory controlled by radicals in August 1998 that the inhabitants of that enclave were quite "nice" people and "by no means Wahhabites".[19]

Arsen Kanokov, who became president of Kabardino-Balkaria in 2005, publicly admitted that ill-considered actions by the local Ministry of Internal Affairs, which systematically refused dialogue with young Muslims, had been one of the causes of the Nalchik tragedy.

---

[19] It is true, however, that certain experts believe that Stepashin, who was the minister of internal affairs of Russia at the time, made a grave mistake when he assessed local radicals in this way.

It is also known that in the Astrakhan region (Southern Federal District) the local administration took a relatively reserved attitude towards local radicals and their head, Ayub Astrakhansky, which was instrumental in avoiding an exacerbation of the situation. Still, such examples remain exceptions.

The relatively brief history of the existence in the Northern Caucasus of Islamic radicalism has shown that its emergence was brought about by a profound crisis that had swept the region and its society. To neutralise protest sentiments, the federal authorities are attempting partially to replace the elites in the republics and show resolve to combat total corruption and the inefficiency of the local economies. The replacement of the republics' leaders in Dagestan, Adygeya and Kabardino-Balkaria, demonstrative actions against corrupt officials, and the implementation of economic projects, including those for the development of tourism, are well received by the local population. Given the scale of the problems the region is facing, however, cosmetic measures alone (such as those taken in the past years) are clearly insufficient. The Northern Caucasus needs systemic reform, which the Kremlin is having a hard time deciding to conduct. No less important is the shaping of a common national identity: this is impeded by the growth in Russia of anti-Caucasus sentiments, which is understandably very painfully perceived by Muslim youth. The integration of the Muslims of the Northern Caucasus into civil society is moving forward with insufficient decisiveness and speed, and is thus fraught with serious consequences.

In the Muslim Volga area, the Urals and Siberia, the situation is more tranquil. Terrorist acts that took place in the second half of the 1990s and early 2000s were linked to events in the Northern Caucasus. The authorities systematically carry out 'preventive' measures, keeping a close watch on radicals' activities and detaining Muslims who, from their point of view, pose the most danger. Every year, court trials of members of radical groups are held in Russia. The main conclusions drawn after the trials are that religious radicals' activities are directed from abroad.

In addition, one cannot fail to notice that struggle against extremism serves the Russian authorities as a pretext for tightening the screws, for imposing even more harsh control on the mass media and for persecution of the opposition. Quite often, measures taken by the authorities are absolutely unrelated to the struggle against extremism. Thus, for example, after the terrorist act in Beslan the direct elections of governors were abolished – allegedly to promote security. Sometimes the authorities deliberately exaggerate the factor of extremism and the struggle against it. Certain cities and even regions of Russia are nearly declared hotbeds of Wahhabism.[20] Yet even in 1999, when the aggravation of the situation in the Northern Caucasus reached its height, it was quite clear that Wahhabism was by no means the main problem for Tatarstan or for the Muslim Volga area in general.[21]

8. Influence of the international situation and current world events

Radicalisation of the Muslim community in Russia has mainly internal causes, and therefore it may be positively stated that world events have a secondary, even though marked, influence on this process. Nevertheless, radically-minded Islamic ideologists are making wide use of the world situation in their reasoning and propaganda.

Of much significance is the playing on anti-Western feelings. The Wahhabite Student's Summary Notes read, "If one takes a look at the history of the West's relations with the Muslim peoples, one may find that the Europeans' souls were so much filled with spite and animosity that these things have driven them to the brink of insanity. Spite, animosity and fear is what they feel towards Islam."[22] The Summary Notes also describe in detail problems that are painful for Muslims and which they tie in with the politics of the West. Zionism and Israel's politics are one of the most irritating factors. The Summary Notes mention Eritrea, Bangladesh, Pakistan and Lebanon, whose difficulties are regarded as consequences of the Western forces' inimical activities. The Summary Notes end with an eloquent appeal: "We Muslims are slaves of All-Mighty and Great Allah. We must break our fetters and restore our strength and our power! And deliver the world from the tyranny of the Western kafirs!"[23]

---

[20] See V.M. Viktorin, *Islam v Astrakhanskom regione* [Islam in the Astrakhan Region], Moscow: Logos, 2008, p. 61.

[21] See R. Mukhametshin, *Islam v obshchestvennoi i politicheskoi zhizni tatar I Tatarstana v XX veke* [Islam in the Public and Political life of the Tatars and Tatarstan in the 20th Century], Kazan: United Humanitarian Publishing House, 2005, p. 150.

[22] Ibid.

[23] Ibid.

The above example reflects broader sentiments widespread among Russia's Muslim community. Muslims' overall and in a sense, formal loyalty does not imply their total solidarity with Moscow's stand on Islam and the Islamic world. On the one hand, Russia's Muslims support Moscow's official policy on the Middle East and its stand on Iran and Afghanistan. From 2004, a parliamentary association named "Russia and the Islamic World: Strategic Dialogue" has been functioning at Russia's State Duma (parliament). According to State Duma Deputy Shamil Sultanov, its aims are as follows:

> Providing legislative support for the development of Russia's relations with Muslim countries and international Islamic organisations, above all the Organisation of the Islamic Conference (OIC)...putting forward initiatives for participation in integration processes in the Islamic world; ...creating conditions for constructive dialogue between the political and economic elites of Russia and the Islamic world, [etc.][24]

Veniamin Popov, former special envoy of the Russian Ministry of Foreign Affairs, has repeated more than once that "Russia can and must come out in favour of maintaining Christian-Muslim dialogue". Islam, according to Popov, is the only religion that has established its own interstate structure – the Organisation of the Islamic Conference.[25]

Conducive to the establishment of special relations with Islamic countries is the admission of Russia as an observer – a country with a Muslim minority – in the OIC. (The OIC, established in 1969, has today 57 countries as members, including two European and two Latin American countries, and also six member countries of the Commonwealth of Independent States.) There were sporadic contacts with the OIC back in the Soviet times. In particular, the OIC was instrumental in liberating prisoners of war from Afghanistan. In 1994 and 1997, the organisation's secretaries general visited Russia.

Islamic radicals are – publicly or unofficially – in agreement with the intensity of Russia's policy in the Muslim area. Visits by Hamas delegations

---

[24] Derived from "Rossia i Islam" [Russia and Islam], an interview with Russia's State Duma Deputy Sh. Sultanov, *Literaturnaya Gazeta*, 13-19 October 2004.

[25] See "Islamskii mir i vneshnyaya politika Rossii" [The Islamic World and Russia's Foreign Policy], *Mezhdunarodnaya Zhizn*, No. 5, 2005, pp. 77-79.

to Moscow, which began in March 2006, and active support of Iranian President Mahmoud Ahmadinejad are regarded by the radicals (and by the rest of Muslims) as evidence that Moscow seeks to play an intermediary role in relations between the Muslim world and the West, which are anything but simple. Sometimes Moscow's position de facto comes out on the side of the anti-Western segment of the Muslim community, thus encouraging Islamic radicals and convincing them of their rightfulness.

It should be noted that Moscow's contacts with Hamas are regarded with approval by the moderate part of Russia's Muslim community as well. For example, in 2006 Jafar Bikmayev, Mufti of the Rostov region, said during his meeting with Sergei Lavrov, Minister of Foreign Affairs of the Russian Federation that "if there is hope for alleviation of that organisation's position, meetings should be held with it".[26]

At the same time, there is awareness in the Russian establishment that 'external' Islamic radicalism is an ally of internal radicalism, which has developed as a response to the complexities that have arisen in Russia's public and political life. The barrier between 'domestic' and 'foreign' radicalism is, in a sense, conventional and the ties among Russia's Muslims – whether in the Northern Caucasus or to a lesser degree, in the Volga area and the southern Urals – are regular and versatile. On the territory of the Russian Federation, a whole variety of charity organisations with an ideological and political bias, such as the International Islamic Relief Organisation, Jamiat Ihia Al-Turath Al-Islamiya [Revival of Islamic Heritage Society], Al-Harameyn [The Two Holy Places], El-Hairiya [Charity], the Benevolence International Foundation, 'Qatar' and also such groups as Hizb ut-Tahrir, al-Qaeda and the Muslim Brothers, have been and are active even though today on a reduced scale.

What could Islamists' practical – tangible, so to say – goals be in Russia?

Certainly, today only through a flight of fancy can one imagine the creation of a caliphate in the territories of the eastern Caucasus. It is also hard to imagine the formation under radical slogans of an all-Russia Muslim separatist movement. Yet, the spreading of Islamist sentiments among believers, principally among young believers, and the infiltration of

---

[26] See the Regnum News Agency website (http://www.regnum.ru/news/598661.html).

Islamist preachers into mosques have turned out to be quite practicable. The lack of centralised structures at the Islamic radicals' disposal and the passivity of the followers of Islamism do not signify its disappearance. Rather, it is biding its time. Islamist ideology easily gets through state borders. A symbiosis is taking place between internal and external Islamic radicalism.

9. A new trend

In the last few years, a new, previously unknown trend has been noted in Russia – namely, the radicalisation of traditional Islam, whose major figures have always been conformist-minded towards the state and have sharply criticised their opponents, the Salafists. This trend may be conventionally described as 'neo-traditionalist'. It is present in Russia on a nationwide scale; however, it is in the Northern Caucasus that this trend is seen most clearly.

In Dagestan, the radicalisation of traditional Islam is directly related to the activity of the Sufi Nakshbandiya, Kadiriya and Shaziliya *tarikats*. The spiritual guides of the Nakshbandiya *tarikat*, who have open support from the authorities, enjoy the greatest influence, just as they always have. Today, it is from sheikhs and their loyal *murids* [disciples] – many of whom hold responsible posts in local administration – that the impetus towards shariatisation of society originates. Dagestani sheikhs, under slogans of struggle against Wahhabism, have created, not without assistance from the authorities, their own system of education operating under their patronage.

Formally, the Sufis, just as before, come out flatly against Wahhabites; at the same time, they are ready to side with them concerning certain general Muslim issues such as support of the Palestinians and criticism of the US policy in the Middle East, in Iran and in Afghanistan. Moreover, in 2000 there were cases in which followers of traditional Islam became members of Wahhabite *jamaats*, while preserving the specific features of their understanding of Islam.

Traditionalists and Wahhabites are united by a call for shariatisation of society, which both regard as quite a feasible goal. Furthermore, present-day Sufi communities in Dagestan, led by sheikhs, are establishing a sharia governance framework in their midst without the preliminary consent of the authorities. Practically all litigations in their midst are decided by a sheikh and persons assigned by him – naturally, on the basis of sharia law and not on Russian secular laws. The expansion of sharia law to cover the criminal and state administrative spheres is just a matter of time, for the creeping spread of influence through a network of *murids* is a time-tested and reliable tactic known since the Middle Ages.

The position taken by the clergy in areas of compact residence of Muslims, for example, in Tatarstan, combines "loyalty" to the state with a call to "adhere to the idea of the expediency of gradual Islamisation of Tatar society" and allows for "combining [s]haria law with secular laws".[27] One gets the impression that some of the spiritual leaders see the present stage as transitional to a situation in which the influence of Islam on society will increase immeasurably. Under this logic, concessions to the state appear temporary and forced, for, as Valiulla Yakubov, Deputy Mufti of Tatarstan, believes, "so far, you cannot come to power on the basis of a religious idea".[28] This statement coincides with the opinion of popular Dagestani politician Surakat Asiyatilov, former chairman of the Islamic Party of Dagestan, who, while admitting that "today one should not harp on the issue of establishing an Islamic republic in Dagestan", dreams of the day when "Islamic order will be established in his country and he will be tried by a sharia court and not by the double-headed eagle".[29] The idea of a gradual yet inevitable Islamisation is evolving into a final concept. It certainly cannot be regarded as a guide to action, yet it is gradually sticking in the minds of Muslims, prompting them to more vigorous action on the religious path, intensifying their conviction and asserting the primacy of their religious identity.

It should be noted that today neo-traditionalism looks increasingly impressive in the religious domain proper. The niche of Islamic modernisation in Russia is amorphous and unpersuasive. As Dagestani Islam scholar and sociologist Enver Kisriyev believes, the number of Muslims of "modernist" and traditional type "may be approximately

---

[27] See R.M. Mukhametshin, "Bogoslovsko-pravovoi aspekt islamskogo vozrozhdeniya v postsovetskom Tatarstane" [The Theological and Legal Aspect of Islamic Revival in Post-Soviet Tatarstan], *Islam i Pravo v Rossii*, No. 2, Moscow, 2004, p. 93.

[28] See *Iman*, No. 5, March 1998.

[29] See S.Kh. Asiyatilov, *Islam spasyot budushcheye Dagestana* [Islam Will Save the Future of Dagestan], Makhachkala, 1999, pp. 77, 27.

estimated as being in equilibrium",[30] with modernists prevailing in towns and conservators in the countryside. One should think that there is no contradiction in this, since modernism is determined by the urban way of life and by the character of labour activity, in the course of which direct religious consciousness is little demanded. It should be noted, however, that when things concern the topic of Islam, the very same modernists quite often take a protective stand. In other words, people try to make up for their urbanite manner of conduct with affective adherence to Islam.

It is worthy of note that, for example, in Tatarstan (and not only there) neo-traditionalist positions are strong especially among the well-educated segment of the urban population.

Conclusions

Islamic radicalism in Russia will not disappear; it will remain a factor of the political and religious life of its Muslim community and of relations between Muslims and the rest of the country's citizens.

It may grow stronger under the influence of the internal situation, acting as a form of protest ideology. The radicals' activity also depends, among other things, on the international situation – especially on relations between the Muslim world and the West.

Considering the fragility of stability in the Northern Caucasus, this region in particular is most likely to become a field of activity for Islamic radicals.

Competition between Islamic radicals (Salafists and Wahhabites) and traditionalists – both Muslim orders and followers of Hanafism and Shafiism (in the Caucasus) will continue. This process is a particular case of general competition between universalist and regional, ethnic Islam.

On the other hand, in the Northern Caucasus there have appeared indications of a 'truce' and even rapprochement on a number of issues between universalist radicals and traditionalists. This concerns, in the first place, the need for a shariatisation of Islamic society and a unity of views on relations between Islam and the West.

---

[30] See E.F. Kisriyev, *Islam i vlast v Dagestane* [Islam and Power in Dagestan], Moscow: United Humanitarian Publishing House, 2004, p. 77.

The state and society are faced with the need to work out a more flexible and selective approach towards Islamic radicalism, singling out in it a relatively moderate and an extremist wing and combining contacts with the former with suppression of the latter.

Today, a repetition of terrorist acts similar to those that took place in the late 1990s and the first half of the 2000s is hardly possible in Russia. Even if terrorist acts were to be committed, they would most probably be limited to the Northern Caucasus and would be a response to the antiterrorist struggle being waged by the power structures.

The question of links between Russia's Muslim radicals with their kindred spirits in Europe remains open. Most likely, however, these links will be gradually developing, the more so as a number of instances of mutual contacts between Russian and European Islamist network structures have already been taking place.

Appendix A. Major terrorist acts in Russia from 1994 to 2006

Date	Event
28.07.1994	Capture of the Pyatigorsk–Stavropol–Krasnogvardeisk coach – 5 killed
29.07.1994	Mineralnye Vody, hijacking of a helicopter at the airport – 4 killed, 15 wounded
14.06.1995	Budennovsk, Stavropol region, hostage-taking in a hospital (more than 1,600 persons, including children and pregnant women) – 166 killed, more than 400 wounded; a terrorist gang was headed by Shamil Basaev
09.01.1996	Kizlyar, Dagestan, assault and capture of 3,000 hostages, kept in a hospital – 78 killed, hundreds wounded; Salman Raduev headed about 500 terrorists
28.06.1996	Nalchik, explosion of a bus at a bus terminal – 8 killed, 23 wounded
04.09.1998	Makhachkala, explosion on Parkhomenko street – 18 killed, 160 wounded
19.03.1999	Vladikavkaz, explosion in the central market – 62 killed, 118 wounded
04.09.1999	Buinaksk, Dagestan, explosion in an apartment building – 61 killed, 130 wounded

Date	Event
08.09.1999	Moscow, explosion in an apartment building on Guryanova street – 94 killed, 164 wounded
13.09.1999	Moscow, explosion in an apartment building on Kashirskoe street – 124 killed, 9 wounded
16.09.1999	Volgodonsk, Rostov region, explosion near an apartment building – 18 killed, 130 wounded; this series of September explosions is considered one case by intelligence services, masterminded by Arab mercenaries Khattab and Abu Umar; most of the executors were later killed in Chechnya
24.03.2001	Explosions of cars in Mineralnye Vody, Essentuki and Cherkessk – 21 killed, 140 wounded
09.05.2002	Kaspiisk, Dagestan, a terrorist act on the Victory Day celebrations – 42 killed, over 100 wounded
23.10.2002	Moscow, hostage-taking at the theatre on Dubrovka street – 129 killed; 41 militants, headed by Movsar Baraev, nephew of terrorist Arbi Baraev, killed by federal forces in Chechnya
05.07.2003	Moscow, explosion at a rock festival in Tushino – 16 killed, 69 wounded; carried out by two female suicide-bombers, Zalikhan Elikhadgieva, a 20-year old from a Chechen village, and Zarema Mugikhoeva, who was arrested five days later in Moscow. They had been trained by Khamzat Tazabaev, who was close to Shamil Basaev and who was killed during the special operation in Ingushetia.
03.09.2003	Stavropol region, explosion on a Kislovodsk-Mineralnye Vody train – 5 killed, about 40 wounded
05.12.2003	Stavropol region, explosion on a Kislovodsk-Mineralnye Vody train – 47 killed, 180 wounded; blamed on members of the 'Nogai battalion'
05.12.2003	Stavropol region, explosion on a Kislovodsk-Mineralnye Vody train – 47 killed, 180 wounded; blamed on members of the 'Nogai battalion'
06.02.2004	Moscow, explosion on the metro between the Avtozavodskaya and Paveletskaya stations – 40 killed, 134 wounded; attributed to an Arab from Chechnya, Abu al-Valid, the successor of the eliminated Khattab
09.05.2004	Grozny, the explosion at Dinamo stadium – 6 killed, over 40 wounded; Shamil Basaev claimed responsibility

Date	Event
22.06.2004	Several terrorist attacks on buildings of the Ingush interior ministry and the 137th frontier detachment in Nazran, Karabulak and Sleptsovskaya – 100 killed
24.08.2004	Bomb attacks on two airline flights, Moscow–Volgograd and Moscow–Sochi – 89 killed; carried out by female suicide-bombers
31.08.2004	Moscow, explosion outside the Rizhskaya metro station – 11 killed, 41 wounded; Shamil Basaev claimed responsibility, the 'Karachai battalion' were accused
01.09.2004	Beslan, North Ossetia, the school hostage siege (over 1,200 children and adults) – 330 killed, several hundreds wounded; Shamil Basaev claimed responsibility, declaring that the attack was carried out by 12 Chechen men and 2 Chechen women, 9 Ingush men, 3 Russian men, 2 Arab men and 2 Ossetian men, 1 Tatar, 1 Kabardinian and 1 from the Zabaikal region
1st half of 2005	Dagestan, over 60 terrorist attacks; responsibility was attributed to the 'Jenet' and 'Sharia' Dagestan *jamaats*
13.10.2005	Attack on Nalchik – 33 law enforcement officers and 12 civil servants were killed; a large majority of the over 100 wounded were secret service officers; 80 militants were killed and 27 captured; responsibility claimed by the Kabardino-Balkaria Jamaat
09.02.2006	Battle in the village of Tukui-Mekteb (Stavropol region) – 4 law enforcement officers were killed; 12 militants of the 'Nogai battalion' (which is part of the Chechnya Shelkov *jamaat*) were killed

Source: Authors' compilation.

About the Authors

Samir Amghar is a PhD candidate in Sociology at Ecole des Hautes Etudes en Sciences Sociales in Paris and a consultant for the Swiss Ministry of the Defence.

Edwin Bakker is head of the Clingendael Security and Conflict Programme of the Netherlands Institute of International Relations 'Clingendael', The Hague.

Patricia Bezunartea is the Director of Research, Development and Communications at the Fundación Pluralismo y Convivencia [Pluralism and Co-existence Foundation], Madrid.

Jonathan Birdwell is a Researcher at Demos, a London-based think-tank focused on power and politics, specialising in radicalisation and Islam in Britain and Canada.

Rachel Briggs is Senior Research Fellow in the National Security and Resilience Department at the Royal United Services Institute (RUSI); Senior Associate at the Institute for Community Cohesion and a Senior Honorary Research Associate at University College London (UCL). She is also part-time Director of Hostage UK, a charity chaired by Terry Waite which provides support to the families of hostages.

Michael Emerson is Senior Research Fellow and Head of the EU Foreign, Security and Neighbourhood Policies research programme at the Centre for European Policy Studies, Brussels.

Theodoros Koutroubas is an invited lecturer at the Catholic University of Louvain (UCL) in Louvain-la-Neuve, Belgium. His interests include the relations between the State and organised religion, cultural and religious minority politics in Europe and the Middle East and participative democracy.

José Manuel López is a Director of the Fundación Pluralismo y Convivencia [Pluralism and Co-existence Foundation], Madrid.

Aleksei Malashenko is a Scholar-in-Residence at the Carnegie Moscow Center, where he co-chairs the Religion, Society and Security Programme, and a Professor at the State University – Higher School of Economics, Moscow.

Olivier Roy is Research Director at the French National Center for Scientific Research (CNRS) and a lecturer at both the School for Advanced Studies in the Social Sciences (EHESS) and the Institut d'Etudes Politiques de Paris (IEP).

Laura Tedesco is an Associate Researcher at the Fundación para las Relaciones Internacionales y el Diálogo Exterior (FRIDE), Madrid and a Visiting Professor at the Universidad Autónoma de Madrid [Autonomous University of Madrid].

Tinka Veldhuis is researcher at the Department of Sociology of the University of Groningen and the Interuniversity Center for Social Science Theory and Methodology (ICS).

Ward Vloeberghs has a background in Arabic and Islamic Studies and is currently working as a teaching assistant and PhD candidate (Political Science) at the University of Louvain (UCL, Belgium).

Akhmet Yarlykapov is a Senior Research Fellow at the Institute of Ethnology and Anthropology, Russian Academy of Sciences, Moscow.

Zeynep Yanasmayan is PhD candidate at the Social Science faculty of Leuven University, researching the Turkish minorities in Europe.